AMERICAN POVERTY IN A NEW ERA OF REFORM

AMERICAN POVERTY IN A NEW ERA OF REFORM

HARRELL R. RODGERS, JR.

M.E.Sharpe
Armonk, New York
London, England

Copyright © 2000 by M.E. Sharpe, Inc.

Library of Congress Cataloging-in-Publication Data

Rogers, Harrell R.
　　American poverty in a new era of reform / by Harrell R. Rodgers, Jr.
　　　p.　cm.
　　Includes bibliographical references and index.
　　ISBN 0-7656-0625-9 (cloth : alk. paper)—ISBN 0-7656-0626-7 (pbk. : alk paper)
　　　1. Poverty—United States. 2. Poor—United States. 3. Public welfare—United States. I.
Title.

HC110.P6R638 2000
362.5′0973—dc21　　　　　　　　　　　　　　　　　　　　　　99-086079
　CIP

Printed in the United States of America

The paper used in this publication meets the minimum requirements of
American National Standard for Information Sciences
Permanence of Paper for Printed Library Materials,
ANSI Z 39.48-1984.

BM (c)　10　9　8　7　6　5　4　3　2
BM (p)　10　9　8　7　6　5　4　3　2

Contents

List of Tables and Figures

Tables

Figures

Acknowledgments

It is a genuine pleasure to give thanks to everyone who has played an important role in helping bring a new book to completion. As always, I received a great deal of assistance from some very talented and generous people, and to each of them I am truly grateful. I have been fortunate to have a considerable number of graduate students who find social welfare policy interesting and important. A number of my graduate students helped me research specific topics and evaluate a couple of hundred recent research projects. Without their help I could have never plowed through the thousands of pages of research that have been published on the impact of the new welfare reform act. Alissa Johnson, Jenny Hill, Michael Hickey, Joyce Poan, and William Barns were particularly important.

My friend Jean Lewis, statistical assistant at the Bureau of the Census, continues to be an invaluable source of information and tireless in tracking down unpublished census data and much-needed reports. I am very grateful for her willingness to take time out of her own hectic schedule to help me time and again. Gordon Fisher, program analyst with the U.S. Department of Health and Human Services, is another wonderful friend who helped me more than I can truly acknowledge. Gordon literally knows more about the nation's struggle to define poverty and identify the poor than anyone else. He is also an excellent poverty scholar. Our discussions and his critiques of my work have helped me to better understand both topics and have saved me from some serious mistakes. I am grateful for his help and patience. Gordon also introduced me to one of his colleagues, Elizabeth Lower-Basch, who turned out to be simply invaluable. Elizabeth evaluates state implementation of the new welfare reform act. Her hands-on experience has given her insights that can be found in no published source. Elizabeth critiqued the chapters on the passage of the Personal Responsibility and Work Opportunity Reconciliation Act of 1996, its early implementation at the state level, and my evaluation of this bill. She gave me dozens of extremely valuable insights and saved me from a number of mistakes. I very much appreciate all of her hard work and help. Those chapters are considerably better as a result of her talent and generosity.

As usual, the crew at M.E. Sharpe was wonderful. Patricia Kolb, executive editor, is always encouraging and supportive. Her assistant, Elizabeth T. Granda, knows how to keep all the trains running. Susan Rescigno, production editor, handled the editing, artwork, and printing with the skill of a consummate pro. To each my continuing thanks and admiration.

It is traditional that authors absolve those who have assisted them of the mistakes and sins of their work. In the case of this book, that disclaimer must be real. The government officials who have helped me sometimes disagree with my interpretation of events and facts. They gave me a great deal of information and help; they are in no way responsible for how I have used those facts and insights.

To my four-year-old son, Michael, I give thanks for his daily reminders that life is full of wonder, mystery, joy, and hope. Thanks pal.

Harrell Rodgers
Houston, 2000

AMERICAN POVERTY IN A NEW ERA OF REFORM

1

Introduction

Poverty may well be America's most serious and costly social problem. Each year millions of Americans live in poverty, and hundreds of billions of public and private dollars are spent annually on efforts to assist the poor. Poverty is also causally interwoven with other costly social problems such as crime, drug and alcohol abuse, homelessness, out-of-wedlock births, poor educational achievement, and domestic violence. Cumulatively these problems account for a huge percentage of all governmental and charitable expenditures.

The number of poor Americans is enormous. Each year since the mid-1960s the federal government has attempted to identify those Americans living in poverty. In the latest available figures, the federal government estimated that over 35 million Americans were poor in 1997, some 13.3 percent of the population (Table 2.1; Figure 3.1). To put this number in perspective, the collective poverty population in 1997 was larger than the total population of California, almost twice the size of the population of Texas, and several million larger than the entire population of Canada.

The cost of services to the poor is staggering. Considering only the major welfare programs (e.g., Temporary Assistance to Needy Families, Food Stamps, Medicaid, Supplemental Security Income), expenditures at the state and federal levels substantially exceed $300 billion a year (Table 5.1). Of course, poverty is expensive not just in outlays and social costs. People idled by poverty reduce the overall productivity of the workforce, lower tax revenues, and reduce the nation's ability to compete in the global economy. Poverty, in all its manifestations, reduces the viability of the whole nation.

Poverty also weighs on the national conscience because the poor are primarily the most vulnerable members of the American population—single-parent households, children, the least well educated, the aged, and the handicapped. Black and Hispanic Americans suffer particularly high rates of poverty. Children, regardless of race or ethnicity, are especially vulnerable. In the 1990s over 14 million children a year have lived in poverty, about one in five American children (Table 3.1). Each year children compose about 40 percent of the total poverty population.

Given the size, cost, and consequences of poverty, America has a substantial stake in preventing this condition and in helping as many of the poor as possible to become self-reliant, secure, and economically productive. Major government efforts to assist the poor grew out of the New Deal legislation of the 1930s, and these programs have evolved and grown substantially over time. As welfare programs and expenditures have grown, skepticism about the cost and effectiveness of these programs has become increasingly widespread both within the government and outside of the government. Despite the fact that only about one-third of all the poor receive any type of cash assistance (Table 5.5), program costs have soared. Much of the increase in costs is attributed to the growth of health care programs for the poor. Taking inflation into consideration, expenditures for welfare programs increased by 400 percent between 1935 and 1996 (Table 5.1). During this same period, the American population grew by only 32 percent (Table 5.1). Despite major increases in expenditures, poverty rates increased during the 1980s and most of the 1990s. In the last two decades, over 90 percent of those families receiving cash assistance lived in poverty (Figure 2.1; Table 5.6). Despite their expense, America's major welfare programs were not actually designed to reduce poverty. Because of their design, only rarely did America's complicated and increasingly expensive programs help the poor to go off welfare and become self-reliant and economically secure.

As skepticism about the design, expense, and effectiveness of American welfare programs increased, Presidents Nixon, Ford, and Carter recommended major welfare reforms to Congress. None of these reforms were passed. Presidents Reagan and Bush also recommended reforms. An important but inadequately-funded reform plan was passed in 1988, but fundamental reform was not adopted until President Clinton's first term in office. In 1996 a bipartisan coalition in Congress passed the Personal Responsibility and Work Opportunity Reconciliation Act (PRWORA). After having vetoed the first two versions of this bill, President Clinton signed the reform plan in August 1996. The new legislation, PRWORA, represents the most comprehensive reform of a major public policy in recent American history.

PRWORA is not an incremental change in welfare policy. PRWORA completely changes the philosophy of welfare policy. The focus of welfare policy under PRWORA has shifted from cash assistance to helping recipients or potential recipients become viable members of the workforce. The administration of the new reform approach was turned over to the states, and they are given considerable discretion in designing and implementing policies to help the poor become employed. To make the transition to employment feasible, the states are given grant dollars to be used to provide recipients with such critical support services as transitional child care, health care, transportation assistance, even job preparation loans, education, and training.

Additionally, PRWORA is designed to reduce future generations of poor in the following ways: (a) PRWORA funds programs to reduce out-of-wedlock births, particularly among teens. (b) It requires both parents to accept the responsibility of financially supporting their children. Over 50 changes to existing laws were made to improve the chances of identifying the parents of children and to force all absent parents to pay required child support. (c) It provides states with funds that can be used to significantly improve the quality of child care, after-school programs, and other supervised, structured activities for millions of children from poor and low-income families.

The new welfare policy is complex because states are given license to be innovative in the design and implementation of PRWORA. By 1998 all the states had written and implemented new welfare plans. These plans vary considerably in comprehensiveness and imagination, and they are being implemented with varying degrees of energy, creativeness, and enthusiasm. The result is that the pace of welfare reform differs a great deal among the states. However, by 1999 there was considerable evidence on the impact of implementing this new law. Much of this book focuses on the evolution of welfare policy, the passage and implementation of PRWORA, assessing its impact, and identifying its strengths and weaknesses.

Organization of the Book

In Chapter 2 we analyze how the federal government defines poverty and identifies the poor. After examining the government's official poverty rates between 1959 and 1997, we review the factors that have caused these rates to increase in recent years, despite major increases in expenditures. Next, we evaluate the government's measure of poverty, an evaluation that reveals serious shortcomings. We then use alternative methods to correct the most obvious deficiencies of the official measure and produce a more valid, but still flawed, poverty count. In the final analysis, the data show that regardless of the method used, America has a very large poverty population.

When we contrast the American approach of measuring poverty with the approaches used by other nations, we not only see important differences in how nations relate to poverty, but also the underlying goals of the American measure. Developing nations attempt to identify their poorest citizens primarily to prevent starvation and acute need. By contrast, the major nations of western Europe and Scandinavia are primarily concerned with maintaining the standards of living that are required for their citizens to be healthy, educated, and productive. Surprisingly, America's goals are much closer to those of third world nations than the goals of other advanced nations.

Chapter 3 examines the demographics of American poverty. The central question: Who are the poor? This chapter documents the high rate of poverty among racial and ethnic minorities, children, single-parent families, and the poorly educated. This chapter also investigates one of the major patterns identified by our analysis of the demographics of poverty—the growth of single-parent families. Why are single-parent families growing so rapidly? And why are these families so vulnerable to poverty? The answers to these questions provide insight into both the causes of poverty among so many single-parent families and the problems that must be ameliorated to reduce the poverty rate among these families.

Chapter 4 analyzes the major theories of poverty. Understanding why people are poor provides valuable insight into how poverty can be alleviated. There are many theories of poverty; by analyzing and critiquing the most widely accepted, we can gain an understanding of the causes and the possible cures for American poverty.

Chapter 5 provides an overview of the American welfare system. This chapter describes the evolving size, complexity, cost, and impact of our major welfare programs. It explains the limited ability of the welfare system to really help the poor in spite of its increasing size and costs and why major reforms were passed in 1996 as a result.

Chapter 6 examines contemporary efforts to reform the American welfare system, cumulating in the passage of the Personal Responsibility and Work Opportunity Reconciliation Act of 1996 (PRWORA). The provisions of this new act are analyzed in some detail.

Chapter 7 examines the states' efforts to design welfare programs to implement the PRWORA. To provide insight into the 1996 reform act and the discretion that states have in implementing it, the reform plan of one of the states that has led the reform movement is analyzed in some depth. Wisconsin was an early leader in welfare reform. Analyzing Wisconsin's well-designed plan, along with early evidence on its impact, provides insight into the discretion states have in designing and implementing reform, along with many of the complexities and challenges of reform. This chapter also analyzes reform by examining how the states are choosing to implement major provisions of the 1996 act.

Chapter 8 examines the early evidence on the impact of the 1996 welfare reform bill, including the significant declines that have taken place in welfare rolls and how those who have left the rolls are faring. The chapter concludes by discussing how well the major provisions of PRWORA are working thus far. Considerable evidence on the implementation of the new law and its impact on the poor is provided, as well as the problems that still need to be resolved if the poor are to escape poverty through employment.

The last chapter of the book evaluates the strengths and weaknesses of PRWORA, focusing on the policy changes that are required to achieve the major goals of the legislation. This chapter also answers two final questions: First, how can welfare reform be continued and even improved if the American economy slumps and the unemployment rate rises? Second, if welfare reform can be made to work, resulting in fewer Americans living in poverty, how should American social policy evolve?

2

How Many Americans Are Poor?

Now do we know when someone is poor or what percentage of a nation's population lives in poverty? Is someone poor only when they are close to starvation, or unable to afford shelter and other basic necessities? Or should we think of poverty as a state in which people cannot afford to live moderately close to the average standards of their society, do not have the resources to develop their potential, and cannot correct their problems? These are not easy questions, and they include some value judgments about the responsibilities that nations feel toward the development and support of their citizens. An extremely poor nation might consider the prevention of starvation as its primary and only realistic goal. A wealthier nation might be more concerned with identifying people who live so far below median levels in society that they cannot develop their abilities and become productive, contributing members of society. When poverty is conceptualized in this fashion, it is called relative poverty: people are poor in relation to average standards in a society. The alternative approach is absolute poverty: a state of acute economic distress.

Basically, then, poverty measures are either relative or absolute. A number of research commissions, including the European Commission and the Organization for Economic Co-operation and Development

(OECD), have developed relative poverty standards by which they periodically estimate the extent of poverty within the highly-developed economies of western Europe and the Scandinavian nations (Foster, 1993; Hagenaars and Zaidi, 1994; Smeeding et al., 1993; Smeeding, 1992a; Smeeding, Rainwater, and O'Higgins, 1990). These measures are based on the theoretical work of two notable scholars, Sen (1992) and Townsend (1979). Nations such as France, Germany, Belgium, Austria, Norway, Sweden, and Finland use these relative measures to estimate poverty. Sen (1992) has also used this methodology to estimate poverty in a wide range of other nations.

The relative poverty measures used by the European Commission, the OECD, and the nations of western Europe and Scandinavia are designed to identify individuals and families living in households with income below half of the national median for households of similar size. If the median income for the average household of four is $40,000, for example, any four-person household with an annual income below $20,000 would be considered poor. A relative standard is designed to identify the level at which individuals and households have adequate resources to develop their potential, be contributing members of society, and enjoy the blessings of their nation.

On the other hand, the World Bank, which is interested in defining poverty in developing nations, uses an absolute standard that measures a defense against starvation. In its 1990 decennial report an absolute poverty standard of annual income of $370 per person was used. Applying this extremely modest income standard to the world's population, the World Bank estimated that more than a billion people (about 20 percent) lived in abject poverty in 1985 (The World Bank, 1990).

As opposed to the relative standards employed by the European Commission and the OECD and most of the nations of western Europe, the United States government annually estimates poverty using an absolute standard. The absolute standard employed sets a specific dollar amount that a family of a particular size and composition must have to avoid poverty. The dollar levels set by this absolute standard are not related to the median income of similar American families. The dollar levels, in fact, are far below half the median income of similar families. Unlike a relative standard, in other words, an absolute standard is not concerned with how many families are living far below society's median standards. An absolute standard is concerned only with a dollar amount that has been determined to move a person or family out of a state of poverty. The American measure, somewhat surprisingly, is more like the methodologies used by developing nations—and by the World Bank—than the approach employed by the other advanced economies of the world.

The U.S. Bureau of the Census yearly reports data on the number of Americans living below fixed poverty thresholds (Fisher, 1998, 1997, 1992; Orshansky, 1988, 1965). The data are drawn from interviews conducted each March with approximately 60,000 households nationwide. The Census Bureau data focus on the before-tax cash income of families and households, excluding noncash benefits such as food stamps and medical services. The poverty thresholds are based on the estimated food budget needs of various types of families, differing by composition and sometimes the age of family members. The estimated food budget cost is multiplied by three to obtain a poverty threshold for various sizes and types of families. The poverty threshold for a family of four is the figure usually reported in the press.

As an example, the poverty threshold for a family of four in 1997 is illustrated below, assuming, for purposes of illustration, that the budget could be conceptualized for food, housing, and essentials.

Poverty Threshold/Family of Four, 1997: $16,036

Food Budget (one-third): $5,345
    $102.79 a week
    $14.68 a day
    $4.89 a meal
    $1.22 per person per meal
Shelter Budget (one-third): $5,345
    $445.42 per month
Essentials Budget (one-third): $5,345—Utilities, Clothing,
    Furniture, Transportation
    $445.42 per month
    $111.35 per month per person

Table 2.1 provides an overview of the poverty thresholds for 1997. Notice that the thresholds vary by the size of the family, the number of related children under 18 years of age, and are adjusted for age when the householder is sixty-five yeas or older. Single people younger than sixty-five with no children would be judged to be poor

Table 2.1

Federal Poverty Thresholds, 1997

Size of family	Weighted average thresholds	Related children under 18 years								
		None	One	Two	Three	Four	Five	Six	Seven	Eight
One person	8,183									
Under 65 years	8,350	8,350								
65 years and over	7,698	7,698								
Two people	10,473									
Under 65	10,805	10,748	11,063							
65 years and over	9,712	9,701	11,021							
Three people	12,802	12,554	12,919	12,931						
Four people	16,400	16,555	16,825	16,276	16,333					
Five people	19,380	19,964	20,255	19,634	19,154	18,861				
Six people	21,886	22,962	23,053	22,578	22,123	21,446	21,045			
Seven people	24,802	26,421	26,586	26,017	25,621	24,882	24,021	23,076		
Eight people	27,593	29,550	29,811	29,274	28,804	28,137	27,290	26,409	26,185	
Nine people or more	32,566	35,546	35,719	35,244	33,289	32,474	32,272	31,029		

Source: Poverty in the United States, 1998. Poverty In the United States, 1997. *Current Population Reports*, Series P60-201, Table A-2.

if their income fell one dollar below $8,163, or $680.25 a month. Since an absolute standard is being used, these same people would be said to have escaped poverty if their income rose as much as one dollar above the poverty threshold. At the opposite extreme, a family of nine or more would be judged to be poor if their income fell one dollar below $30,333. As noted above, the thresholds are not related to median income levels for the various types of families, and thus they do not reflect changes in living standards (Fisher, 1999; Orshansky, 1965). In 1997, for example, the median income for households with four persons was $53,165 (Bureau of the Census, 1998a, 7). The poverty threshold of $16,036 for four persons represents only 30 percent of the median. If it were set at half the median, the poverty threshold for a family of four would have been $26,583, an increase of almost 60 percent.

Applying the absolute dollar thresholds, the Census Bureau concluded that 35.6 million Americans, or 13.3 percent of the population, lived in poverty in 1997. Figure 2.1 provides an overview of the annual poverty count since 1959. Note that Figure 2.1 shows both the number of Americans identified as poor each year since 1959, and the annual percentage of the population living in poverty. Since the population grows each year, the percentage rate is a more accurate reflection of progress against poverty. Examining the annual percentage rates since 1959 shows both progress and reversals in reducing poverty since the late 1950s. The poverty rate dropped from the 22 percent range in the early 1960s to below 12 percent during several years in the 1970s, but then rose again to exceed 13 percent, even rising above 14 and 15 percent in some years since the early 1980s.

The official government measure, therefore, shows a high level of continuing poverty in America, with rather disappointing results in reducing the number of poor since the 1980s. The high poverty counts are somewhat surprising given the modest level of the income thresholds (Mogull, 1991).

While the threshold levels are generally considered to be extremely low, there are many other major problems. Many critics argue, in fact, that the methodology employed by the government is so flawed that it does not come close to really identifying the number of poor Americans. While critics point to a rather large number of problems with the measure, eight major flaws are often cited.

Figure 2.1 The American Poverty Population, 1959–1997

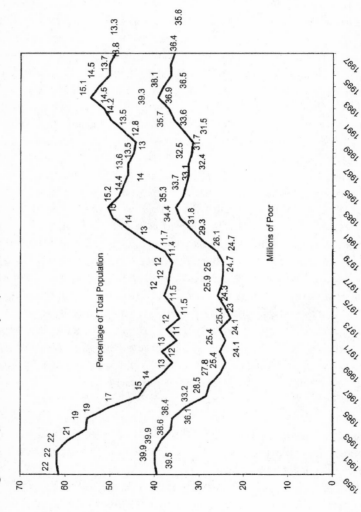

Source: Poverty in the United States, 1997. *Current Population Reports*, Series P60–201, Table A.

Flaws in Official Measure of Poverty

Lack of Regional Cost Adjustments

The poverty thresholds for various family sizes and types are uniform across the nation, although there are significant variations in regional costs of living, including expenses such as housing and food. Is it logical, for example, to use exactly the same threshold for a family of four with two children when one family lives in New York City and the other in rural Mississippi? Recent studies reveal the flaws in this approach. Two very different states, Idaho and New Hampshire, for example, have conducted bipartisan studies to determine the absolute minimum income required by families to pay for food, rent, and other necessities. The Idaho study concluded that the official measure needed to be raised by 17 percent (Skoro and Johnson, 1991). The New Hampshire study found the official measure too low by 29 percent (Bailis and Burbridge, 1991).

Failure to Include Taxes and the Value of In Kind Benefits

Because the current measure defines family resources as gross money income, it does not include the value of government programs, such as food stamps, subsidized housing, or school meal programs. These government programs significantly improve the disposable income of millions of families and, hence, their poverty status, but these are not reflected in the government measure. On the other hand, taxes such as Social Security reduce disposable income, but are not included in the calculations either.

Employed Versus Unemployed Families

There are costs associated with employment, especially because of the increased labor force participation of mothers. Since more mothers work and since more parents are single, there are more working families who must pay child care now than when the poverty thresholds were designed. But, the current measure does not distinguish between the needs of families in which the parents do or do not work outside the home.

Variations in Health Care Costs

The health care costs of families vary considerably. Some may enjoy good health and have no costs; others may require expensive care. Of those who need care, some may suffer significant out-of-pocket expenses, while others may have excellent private coverage or be covered by government programs. The current measure does not take health care costs into consideration.

Family Size Adjustment

There are many problems with the family size adjustments, including the fact that family sizes have been declining, and more families are headed by a single parent. Yet, the thresholds have not been adjusted since their original formulation.

The Food Budget Base

As the figures above show, the food budget base that forms the core of the thresholds is anything but generous. A family of four is allowed less than $5.00 per meal. While it might not be impossible to buy adequate food on this budget, it would be a continuing challenge and probably cannot be done in many high-cost cities. The original author of the poverty thresholds, Mollie Orshansky, formulated two versions, one based on the economy food plan and another based on a less stringent low-cost food plan. The government chose to adopt the version based on the economy food plan, acknowledged by the Department of Agriculture as for "temporary or emergency use when funds are low" (Fisher, 1999, 26).

Additionally, there is reason to doubt the logic of basing the thresholds only on the food base and inflationary changes in that base. Why should food costs be considered one-third of the income required by a family? As Ruggles (1990) has concluded, neither changes in living nor consumption standards are reflected in such a restrictive approach. Historically, poverty standards in the United States and other advanced nations have risen over time to reflect changes in standards of living (Fisher, 1999). This is known as the income elasticity of the poverty line. As Gordon Fisher (1999, 28) notes, ". . . there is extensive historical evidence that poverty lines and subsistence budgets tend to rise in real terms as the income of the general population rises." However, in 1969 the Interagency Poverty Level Review Committee decided against making measurement adjustments to reflect changes in the general standard of living. In 1970, Orshansky (Fisher, 1999, 28) wrote that the 1969 decision "tend(ed) to freeze the poverty line despite changes in buying habits and changes in acceptable living standards." There is considerable evidence that if changing living standards were taken into consideration, most approaches for designing thresholds would produce significantly higher income standards than the current measure (Citro and Michael, 1995).

In a 1965 article, Orshansky (1965) implicitly presented the poverty thresholds as a measure of income inadequacy, not of income adequacy. "If it is not possible to state unequivocally how much is enough, it should be possible to assert with confidence how much, on average, is too little." As Fisher (1999, 27) notes: "To the best of my knowledge, there is no analysis-based federal policy document that has presented the poverty thresholds as representing the total amount of money required for minimum basic necessities for a family, or has presented them as being enough for a family to live on."

The Missing Poor

There is widespread agreement that the Census Bureau undercounts the poor, primarily because many low-income people live with others or move too frequently to be counted. Additionally, the homeless and those individuals residing in mental hospitals, nursing homes, jails and prisons are not counted. Estimates of the number of people left out of the count vary considerably, but conservatively number several million.

The Severity of Poverty

The official standard makes no distinction between those individuals or families that fall a few dollars below the poverty threshold for their family size and those with incomes far below the standard. Most of the families and individuals who are counted as poor have incomes considerably below the poverty threshold for their family size. In 1997, for example, the difference in dollars between the average poor family's income and their poverty threshold averaged $6,602. The average income deficit for poor families headed by a female householder was even higher at $6,959. For unrelated individuals the average income deficit was $3,985 (Bureau of the Census, 1998a, xii).

In 1997 41.0 percent of all persons counted as poor had incomes below half the poverty threshold for their family size. Among persons in families with a female householder with no spouse present, 48.8 percent had incomes below 50 percent of their poverty threshold (Bureau of the Census, 1998, Table 2). Families with incomes below half the poverty threshold tend to be among the chronically poor, often little impacted by improvements in the economy. Yet, the official measure does not select out those families suffering the most severe economic crisis.

Why Is the Standard So Flawed?

Why would the federal government use such an obviously flawed methodology to estimate yearly poverty rates? The answer is somewhat complex. When the official measure was first formulated in the mid-1960s and backdated to 1959, Orshansky expected revisions to be made over time (Orshansky, 1965, 1988; Fisher, 1999; Haveman, 1987). Orshansky (1988) believed that the thresholds required amendment and updating to reflect changing standards of living. However, the Bureau of the Budget did not want to alter the standard because they understood that to do so would raise the poverty count and impact program eligibility. The original thresholds did not include government benefits such as food stamps and Medicaid services because these programs were in the early stages of development and did not serve very many people. Orshansky did not include taxes and work expenses because the measure was meant to be a starting point for the development of more refined methodologies.

But as often happens in the political arena, stalemates between conservative and liberal critics of the measure have resulted in the 1960s standard remaining the official methodology for estimating yearly poverty rates, warts and all. In recent years the Census Bureau has published some additional data on the impact that various taxes and in kind programs would have on the official estimates, along with some alternative definitions of poverty. These data are insightful and they provide a better understanding of poverty in America. How-

Table 2.2

The Marginal Effect of Taxes and Transfers on Poverty Estimates, 1997

Impact of ten changes	# of Poor (000)	% Rate
Results of official definition in 1996	35,574	13.3
Official less payroll taxes plus capital gains	37,747	14.1
Official less federal and state income taxes plus net capital gain and EITC	31,877	11.9
Official less nonmeans-tested cash transfers	54,437	20.3
Official less means-tested cash transfers	38,240	14.2
Official plus means-tested nonmedical transfers	31,856	11.9
Official plus food stamps	33,998	12.7
Official plus rent subsidies	34,333	12.8
Official plus regular-price school lunch	35,571	13.2
Official plus all nonmedical, noncash transfers	31,853	11.9
Official less taxes plus EITC and all noncash transfers	29,975	11.2

Source: Bureau of the Census, 1998. Poverty in the United States, 1997. *Current Population Reports,* Series P60-201, Table F.

ever, as we will detail below, they do not correct for all the flaws discussed above.

Table 2.2 shows the marginal changes in the official poverty count for 1997 that would have resulted from the inclusion of certain taxes and noncash transfers in the calculation of individual and family incomes. The table shows the impact of ten specific changes. Some of the changes would have increased the poverty count; others would have lowered it. For example, the first change shown on the table would adjust incomes by subtracting any payroll taxes paid while adding the value of any capital gains received. The result would raise the poverty rate to 14.1 percent. Including the value of food stamps in the estimate of income would lower the poverty rate from 13.3 percent to 12.7 percent. Adding the value of rent subsidies would reduce the poverty count from 13.3 percent to 12.7 percent. Including the value of school lunches would reduce the poverty count to a minor extent. In summary, what the table shows is that if the calculation of income were changed to reflect taxes and the value of many expensive government programs such as food stamps, the poverty count would change considerably. The impact of individual programs is not large, but what would be the cumulative impact on the poverty count if all

Table 2.3

Alternative Definitions of Poverty, 1997

Selected income definitions	Number below poverty (000)	Poverty rate (%)
Current measure	35,574	13.3
Without government cash transfers	56,390	21.0
No government cash transfers but adding capital gains and employee health benefits	54,573	20.3
No government cash transfers, capital gains and employee health benefits, less Social Security and federal income taxes	57,520	21.4
No government cash transfers, capital gains, employee health benefits, EITC, less Social Security and federal income taxes	53,601	20.0
No government cash transfers, capital gains, employee health benefits, EITC, less Social Security, federal income and state taxes	54,036	20.1
Nonmeans tested cash transfers, capital gains, employee health benefits, EITC, less Social Security, federal income and state taxes	35,849	13.4
Nonmeans tested cash transfers, capital gains, employee health benefits, EITC, regular-priced school lunches, Medicaid, less Social Security, federal income and state taxes	34,748	12.9
All government cash transfers, all government means-tested noncash transfers, capital gains, employee health benefits, EITC, regular-price school lunches, Medicare, Medicaid, less Social Security, federal income and state taxes	26,940	10.0

Source: Bureau of the Census, 1998. Poverty In the United States: 1977. *Current Population Reports,* Series P60-201, Table E.

these changes were taken into consideration? Table 2.3 answers this question.

Table 2.3 shows the changes that would take place if the official poverty measure were altered to include or exclude a combination of tax costs, program benefits such as food stamps, cash assistance, and capital gains. What would happen if there were no government cash transfer programs, such as AFDC and Social Security, but taxes and employee health benefits were taken into consideration? The analysis shows that these changes would greatly increase the poverty count, raising the poverty rate above 20 percent. On the other hand, what would happen if the Census Bureau counted all cash transfers, all in kind benefits, plus the impact of taxes paid, and added the value of employer-provided health benefits? The most inclusive measure shows that all these changes would reduce the poverty rate in 1997 from 13.3 to 10 percent, a nontrivial impact.

Should the Poverty Standard Be Changed?

Should the government change the official poverty methodology to include taxes, in kind benefits, and employer-provided benefits? Most critics would answer this question in the affirmative. But does this mean the actual poverty rate in 1997 was 10 percent rather than 13.3 percent? Probably not. The reason is that the changes shown in Table 2.3 correct for only some of the major problems with the official count. None of the changes alter the food budget or its multiple in calculating the poverty thresholds. Additionally, there are no adjustments for regional variations in cost of living, and family work costs are not calculated. And, of course, it is still an absolute poverty standard.

In 1995 a research group appointed by the National Research Council recommended that a new poverty standard be based on the actual consumption patterns of families of various sizes (Citro and Michael, 1995). The committee recommended that the median expenditures of families for food, clothing, shelter, utilities, and other needs compose the base for an improved standard. Once median expenditures were determined, some percentage of those expenditures could be calculated (e.g., 78–83 percent) and then cumulated. A modest multiplier (e.g., 1.15–1.25) could be used to allow for other needs. The committee concluded that this approach would better reflect actual consumption and spending patterns of families, yielding a much more realistic measure of poverty. Using this methodology would increase poverty thresholds for various family sizes from 14 to 33 percent (Citro and Michael, 1995; Burtless, Corbett, and Primus, 1998). Thus far, government agencies have not agreed on how to change the measurement of poverty, but the 1995 study provides insight into the type of improved measure that may be adopted in the future.

Summary and Conclusions

In the final analysis, then, the current measure of poverty is extremely flawed. Table 2.3 shows some of the alterations that could be made in the current measure by making it more sophisticated, but even the most inclusive of these changes would still not correct all the major problems with the current measure. Does this mean that we do not really know how many Americans are poor? Basically the answer is yes. The current government measure is so terribly flawed that we really have only a very crude and inaccurate understanding of how many Americans live in poverty.

But does this mean that poverty is not a serious problem in America? Not at all. In fact, a sophisticated measure of poverty would probably increase the poverty count, perhaps considerably. Notice that in Table 2.3 the most sophisticated alteration in the current measure reduces the poverty count, but shows some 27 million Americans (10 percent) living in poverty. In other words, poverty is a very serious problem in America even taking in kind benefits, capital gains, and taxes into consideration. If the alteration were expanded to correct for the other major flaws in the current measure, the count would increase. Adding regional cost-of-living variations, using a more generous food budget or a different multiple, and including work costs would all move the poverty count up. Thus, a more sophisticated measure would probably increase the poverty count, rather than lower it. This would certainly be true if the United States government dropped the absolute standard approach in favor of the type of relative standards used in the other western industrial nations.

Does the fact that the United States uses an absolute measure of poverty rather than a relative one mean that the American poor are more like the poor of the developing world rather than those individuals who are poor in other developed nations? The answer to this question is clearly no. As a group, the American poor are generally not homeless, and they are not on the verge of starvation. Most poor families, in fact, report that they have enough to eat. Yet, one in six poor households report that they sometimes have food shortages, while one in seven (over 2 million) report suffering hunger during the past six months (U.S. Department of Agriculture, 1995). A Tufts University (1995) study found that poor children often have inconsistent food supplies (Cook and Martin, 1995), while a second study found that children who live in poverty long-term are 2.7 times as likely to suffer from stunted growth (Korenman and Miller, 1997).

Some 40 percent of all poor households own their home. Among poor elderly heads the home ownership rate is about 60 percent, while it is about 29 percent for other poor households. These homes, of course, were purchased long before these household heads became poor, and most of the homes are in very bad repair (U.S. Department of Housing and Urban Development, 1995). Seventy percent of all poor households own a car; 27 percent own two or more. Without cars poor household heads generally cannot work, or even shop or transport children and family members to school or doctors. There is no reliable data on the quality of most of these cars, but if they are worth more than a few thousand dollars, they disqualify the household from receiving welfare benefits. Last, some 97 percent of all poor households report owning a color television (Council of Economic Advisors, 1995). For a poor family, a television is probably their least expensive entertainment option.

Given the information above, should we assume that poverty is not really a very serious problem? That would be a serious mistake. First, the evidence suggests that life for the American poor is difficult. Over half (55.1 percent) of all poor households report (Federman, et al. 1996): loss of utilities in the past year; food shortages over the last four months; poor quality housing, including plumbing, electricity, and rodent problems; crowded housing; lack of access to a telephone, refrigerator, or stove; eviction in the past year.

Second, the evidence is clear that children who grow up in poverty, especially early and long-term poverty, suffer terrible disadvantages. In Chapter 3 we will show that extreme poverty (living at less than 50 percent of the poverty level) among children is a problem that has grown considerable over the last twenty years. Children who grow up in poverty are twice as likely to drop out of school and one and a half times as likely to be unemployed. Poor teenagers girls are four times as likely to be unwed mothers (Gottschalk, McLanahan, and Sandefur, 1994, 102), and all poor children are at greater risk of drug and alcohol abuse, mental illness, suicide, and criminality. The data are also clear that early childhood poverty has a highly detrimental impact on the cognitive development of children (Duncan and Brooks-Gunn, 1998; Brown and Pollitt, 1996, Shore, 1997). Not surprisingly, there is a clear link between poverty and lack of educational success.

Some critics (Rector, 1998) argue that poverty does not cause low educational achievement; rather, the problem is the values of the parents. But studies show that when the income of the family increases, so does the achievement level of children in the family (Sherman, 1997; Venti, 1984). Two major studies also show that when families move in and out of poverty, the educational achievements of the children vary with the prosperity of the family. During improved economic periods, the children do better in school (Duncan, et al., 1999; Sandefur and Wells, 1997). There is a clear link, then, between the income of families and the chances that their children will obtain the education they need, not just to escape poverty and many other social problems, but also to be really productive, competitive members of American society.

Poverty, therefore, does matter. It is a problem worth careful identification and vigorous remediation. In Chapter 3, we will take a more in-depth look at who are the American poor.

3

The American Poverty Population

Despite massive expenditures by federal and state governments over the last forty years, American poverty has remained stubbornly high. As Figure 2.1 shows, the rate of poverty declined significantly during the 1970s, a decade marked by a healthy economy and rising expenditures for welfare programs. Unfortunately, the trend in poverty reduction did not continue. By the early 1980s the rate of poverty was increasing. Poverty declined somewhat in the latter part of the 1980s, but then increased quite dramatically between 1992 and 1995. In 1997 the poverty rate declined slightly, but was still higher than during any year in the 1970s.

To shed light on poverty and recent changes in the poverty rate, this chapter will focus on four major topics: (1) an analysis of the composition of the poverty population; (2) an examination of why progress in reducing poverty stagnated; (3) an in-depth investigation of poverty among American children, the largest single group of poor Americans; and (4) an examination of the rapid growth and extreme economic vulnerability of single-mother families.

Who Are the Poor?

As noted in Chapter 2, the poverty population is very large. In 1997 almost 36 million Americans were counted among the poor. The poverty population is not only large; it is also quite diverse. The poverty population consists of both the young and the old, families with one or sometimes even both parents in the workforce, families with no employed adults, single mothers and their children, street people, residents of rural areas; along with people who live in impoverished areas of inner cities. As we will detail in Chapter 4, the poverty population is both heterogeneous and complex. Only antipoverty policies sophisticated enough to meet the very different needs of the diverse groups that compose the poverty population have the prospect of being successful.

Race

Table 3.1 provides a statistical portrait of the poor since 1960. The table shows the poverty rates for various demographic groups, and what percentage of all poor Americans these rates reflect. Both figures are important because population groups vary considerably in terms of their poverty rate and their proportion of the total population. A small population group might have a high poverty rate, but constitute a rather modest percentage of the total poverty population. White non-Hispanic Americans represent the opposite side of this issue. White non-Hispanic Americans* were about 73 percent of the population in 1997 and had a relatively low rate of poverty. However, because of the size of this population (about 195 million), even a low rate of poverty involves numbers that translate into a very large percentage of all poor Americans. In 1997, for example, the poverty rate for non-Hispanic white Americans was 8.6 percent, but this was 46.4 percent of all poor Americans.

The black population is relatively small but has a high poverty rate. In 1997 the black population was about 34 million and constituted

---

*The classification Hispanic is often misunderstood. Hispanic denotes ethnicity, not race. The Census Bureau forms ask respondents to self-identify themselves into categories such as White, Black, Hispanic, Asian, or Pacific Islanders. If a respondent chooses Hispanic, they are then asked if they are White, Black, Asian, or Pacific Islander. Most Hispanics identify themselves as White, but a significant number choose Black. A small number identify themselves as Asian or Pacific Islanders. In this chapter White non-Hispanics are often separately analyzed because their economic level as a group is on average considerably higher than that of Hispanics who identify themselves as White.

Table 3.1

The Poverty Population, 1960–1997

	Percentage poor				Percentage of the poor			
	1960	1970	1980	1997	1960	1970	1980	1997
All persons	22.2	12.6	13.0	13.3				
Race								
White	17.8	9.9	10.2	11.0	71.0	68.5	67.3	68.6
White NH*	NA	NA	NA	8.6	NA	NA	NA	46.4
Black	55.9	33.5	32.5	26.5	29.0	30.0	29.3	25.6
Asian/PI	NA	NA	17.2	14.0	NA	NA	2.4	4.1
Hispanic	NA	24.3	25.7	27.1	NA	8.5	11.9	23.3
Family structure								
In families	20.7	10.9	11.5	11.6	87.6	80.0	77.2	73.7
Unrelated individuals	45.2	32.9	22.9	20.8	12.4	20.0	21.3	24.4
FH-NHP**	48.9	38.1	36.7	35.1	18.2	29.5	34.6	37.9
Age								
Children under 18	26.5	14.9	17.9	19.9	43.4	40.3	38.0	39.7
65 and older	35.2	24.5	15.7	10.5	14.1	18.5	13.2	9.5
Residence								
Metropolitan	15.3	10.2	11.9	12.6	43.9	52.4	61.6	77.0
Outside met	33.2	17.0	15.4	15.9	56.1	47.6	38.4	23.0
Type of family								
Married couple			5.2					
White			4.8					
Black			8.0					
Hispanic			17.4					
FH NHP			31.6					
White			27.7					
Black			39.8					
Hispanic			47.6					

Source: Poverty in the United States, 1998. *Current Population Reports,* Series P60–201, Table A and Table 2.
  *Non-Hispanic. Hispanic is an ethnicity. Hispanics may be of any race.
  **Female Householder, no husband present.

about 13 percent of the population. The poverty rate for black Americans has declined since the 1960s but is still very high. In 1997, over 26 percent of all black Americans lived in poverty, and this was 25.6 percent of all poor Americans. The poverty rate for the Asian/Pacific Island population was fairly high at 14 percent, but since this group constitutes only about 3.8 percent of the population (about 10 million), they were only 4.1 percent of the poor (Bureau of the Census, 1998e).

The Hispanic population, an ethnic group that may be of any race, is about 11 percent of the population (some 29 million), and they have suffered a rising rate of poverty since the 1970s. In 1997 over 27 percent of all Hispanic Americans lived in poverty, and they comprised a little over 23 percent of all the poor.

Age

Age is a relevant factor in poverty, being a particularly serious problem for the youngest Americans. Children endure a higher rate of poverty than any other age group. This problem has become worse since the 1970s. In 1997, the poverty rate for American children was 19.9 percent, and children comprised about 40 percent of all poor Americans. The poverty rate for Americans sixty-five years and older has declined significantly since the 1960s, falling from 35.2 percent in 1960 to 10.5 percent in 1997. Still, aged Americans are 9.5 percent of the poor, and when combined with poor children, the youngest and oldest Americans are about half of all the poor.

Residence

While we think of poverty as an urban problem, the rate of poverty is actually higher outside metropolitan areas. In 1997 the poverty rate was almost 16 percent outside metropolitan areas, compared to about 12.6 percent in metropolitan areas. Still, 77 percent of all the poor live in metropolitan areas. Poverty is particularly severe in many inner-city neighborhoods, but only a very small percentage of all the poor live in these neighborhoods.

Family Structure

About 74 percent of all the poor live in families, with a significant percentage of the poor living in families headed by a single woman with no husband present. In 1997, almost 38 percent of all the poor lived in one of these female-headed families. The poverty rate for female-headed families is extremely high. In recent years, over one-third of all female-headed families have lived below the poverty level.

The last entries on Table 3.1 show additional information about the impact of family structure on poverty. The composition of families is very important. Married-couple families are far less likely to live in poverty than female-headed households. In 1997 the poverty rate for female-headed households was six times the rate for married-couple families. As Table 3.1 shows, the poverty rate is particularly low for white married-couple families (4.8 percent), and fairly low for black families (8 percent). However, the poverty rate is surprisingly high for Hispanic married-couple families, 17.4 percent in 1997. Still, the poverty rate for female-headed families is always higher, regardless of the race or ethnicity of the mother. The poverty rate for white female-headed families (27.7 percent) is almost six times the rate for white married-couple families. Poverty is even worse for black and Hispanic female-headed families. Almost 40 percent of black and 47.7 percent of Hispanic female-headed families lived in poverty in 1997.

Summary

Some Americans are much more likely to suffer poverty. As Figure 3.1 illustrates, minorities suffer particularly high rates of poverty, as do single-parent families and children in those families. Almost 40 percent of all the poor are children, a problem that in significant measure is related to the very high poverty rate for single-parent families and, as we will see below, the low wage rate of many young, employed family heads. While the poverty rate for Americans 65 and older has declined significantly over the last forty years, individuals sixty-five and older constitute over 9 percent of the poor. Poverty, in the final analysis, is a condition that impacts America's most vulnerable citizens—minorities, members of single-parent families, children, the aged and poorly educated young couples with children.

Chapter 4, which examines the causes of American poverty, provides another way to think about the poor. There we will examine issues such as how long those identified as poor live below the poverty level. Are most of the poor impoverished for a long time, or is poverty more of a temporary problem for many of the poor? Are some people

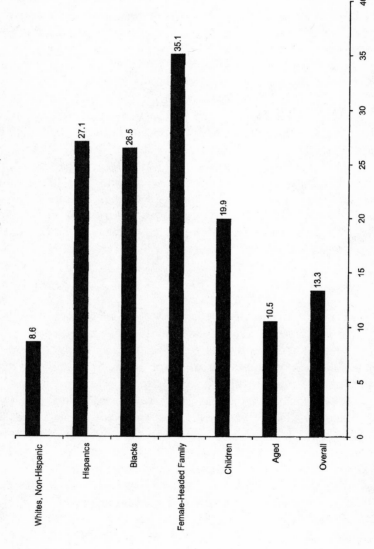

Figure 3.1 Poverty Rate for Individuals in Selected Demographic Groups, 1997

Source: Poverty in the United States, 1997. *Current Population Reports*, Series P60–201, Table A and Table 2.

episodically poor, moving in and out of poverty? Also, what percentage of the poor receives welfare, and what are their use patterns? How many receive assistance for a short period and how many are long-term welfare users? The combination of information about the poor provides important insights into the problems of the various groups that make up the poor and the type of policies required to alleviate poverty.

Why Has Progress in Reducing Poverty Slowed?

As noted previously, despite both an economy that has been quite robust and growing welfare spending over the last twenty years, progress in reducing American poverty has been disappointing. The lack of progress was one of the major reasons that members of Congress cited for the major overhaul of welfare passed by Congress in 1996. As detailed in Chapter 5, critics of the welfare system blamed the lack of progress on evidence of an increasing willingness on the part of Americans to rely on welfare (Hoynes and MaCurdy, 1994), high rates of welfare fraud, drug and alcohol abuse by welfare recipients, and many other problems. While much of what the critics cited may be true, considerable evidence suggests that three major trends played a significant role in slowing and even reversing progress against poverty.

First, over the last thirty years, very significant changes have taken place in American families. One very important change is that single women head an increasing proportion of all families. Figure 3.2 shows the changes that have taken place since the late 1950s. In 1959 a single woman headed less than 10 percent of all families with children. By the 1990s, almost one-fourth of all families with children was headed by a single woman.

The magnitude of the change is extremely important. In 1959 there were about 2.5 million female-headed households with children. By 1997 the number of such households had increased to almost 9 million. Thus, one reason progress against poverty slowed is that a family type most vulnerable to poverty has grown extremely rapidly over the last four decades.

A second problem that has made it difficult to reduce poverty is that wages for many workers have stagnated over the last twenty-five years. Figure 3.3 shows the changes that have taken place in income levels for the lowest 20 percent of all workers, the middle 20 percent,

Figure 3.2 Mother-Only Families as a Percentage of all Families with Children, 1959–1997

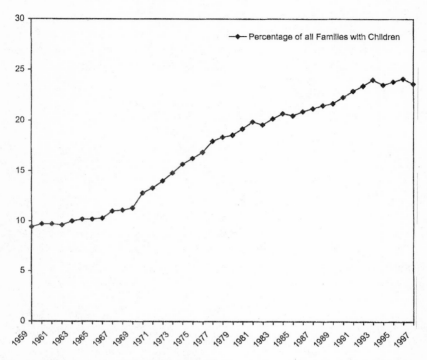

Source: Poverty in the United States, 1997. *Current Population Reports*, Series P60–201, Table C-3.

and the top 20 percent. Notice that between 1975 and 1997 the earning power of those workers at the bottom of the wage scale increased in only the most modest fashion. In fact, between 1990 and 1997 the yearly income of the workers in the lowest group of earners increased by only $37. The middle group of earners fared a little better, especially in 1997, but still made only modest progress. The picture is completely different for the highest fifth of all income earners. This group's income on average increased from $85,131 in 1975 to almost $123,000 in 1997.

Figure 3.4 shows how household earnings accumulate into shares of all income earned by the entire population in a given year. These data reveal that income has become increasingly maldistributed. Figure 3.4 divides all households into five groups, ranging from the low-

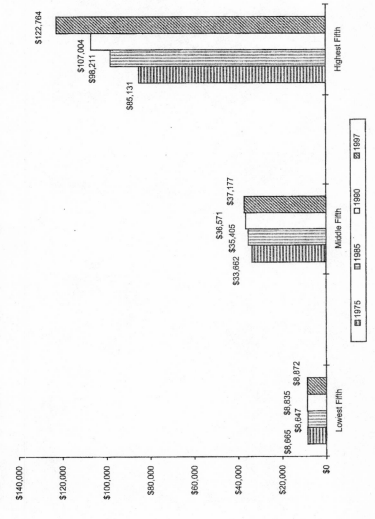

Figure 3.3 Average Income of Low, Middle, and Upper-Income Households, 1975–1997

Source: Money income in the United States, 1997. *Current Population Reports*, Series P60–200, Table B. Income in 1997 dollars.

Figure 3.4 Share of Aggregate Household Income by Quintile, 1975–1997

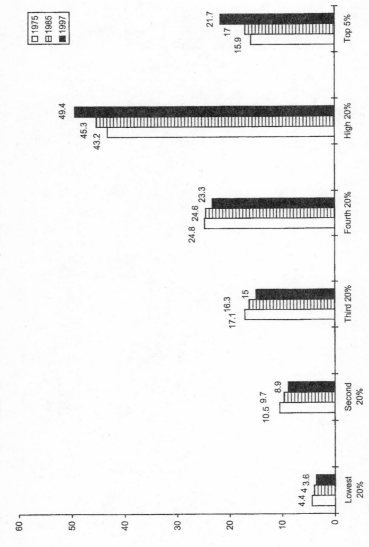

Source: Money income in the United States, 1997. *Current Population Reports,* Series P60–200, Table B. Income in 1997 dollars.

est 20 percent of all households with income to the highest 20 percent. The data show that only the top 20 percent of all households have gained income, and their share of the total pie increased from 43.2 percent in 1975 to 49.4 percent in 1997. The share of all income going to the bottom 20 percent shrank from an extremely modest 4.4 percent in 1975 to a paltry 3.6 percent in 1997. The second, third, and fourth quintiles also saw their share of total income decline.

By contrast, Figure 3.4 selects out the top 5 percent of all households. Notice that their share of all income increased very substantially between 1975 and 1997, increasing from 15.9 percent to 21.7 percent. In 1997 the top 5 percent of all households received far more of the cumulative income than the bottom forty percent of all households, more than the middle 20 percent, and almost as much as the fourth quintile of earners.

Why has income stagnated for most of the workforce, while a small percentage of workers have gotten richer and richer? The basic answer is education. On average, the only workers enjoying real income gains over the last twenty-five years have been the college educated. As American society has changed from a manufacturing economy to a global economy based on information transfer, only the best educated of Americans have been prepared for the most competitive and lucrative jobs (Bound and Johnson, 1992; Juhn, Murphy, and Pierce, 1993; Murphy and Welch, 1993).

Both high school dropouts and high school graduates have suffered a steady decline in inflation-adjusted wages since the late 1970s (Freeman and Katz, 1995; Bureau of the Census, 1998b: Table B). However, workers with post-high school training and college degrees have made significant wage gains over the same period (Blank, 1997, 32–33). This is a trend that will certainly continue. Americans in search of economic gain and security will increasingly find education mandatory.

The last reason for the decline in progress against poverty has been the decreasing effectiveness of welfare programs in helping recipients escape poverty. Welfare spending simply failed to keep pace with increases in the welfare rolls. The percentage of all American families on cash welfare was 1.7 percent in 1960 (Department of Health and Human Services, 1999). The percentage steadily increased to 5.2 percent in 1972, declined modestly during the 1980s, but moved up again in the 1990s. By 1994, 5.5 percent of all families with children were receiving cash welfare. The reform debate in 1995 and the passage of the Personal Responsibility and Work Opportunity Reconciliation act (PRWORA) in 1996 led to substantial drops in the welfare rolls. By March 1999, the percentage of all families with children receiving cash assistance had dropped to 2.6 percent, the lowest caseload since 1968.

As caseloads remained high during both the 1980s and most of the 1990s, spending for the primary cash welfare program, Aid to Families with Dependent Children (AFDC), increased in inflation-adjusted dollars, but not enough to cover the increasing caseload. Thus, spending per AFDC family declined quite drastically between 1970 and 1995. In 1970, for example, the average AFDC family received $734 a month (1996 dollars). By 1996 the average AFDC family received only $374 (Green Book, 1998, Table 7–2). As the real dollar value of AFDC declined, the number of welfare families pushed over the poverty line by these benefits decreased throughout much of the 1980s and early 1990s (Danziger and Weinberg, 1994, 50).

The impact of social welfare spending on poverty rates began to improve in the late 1980s. While AFDC benefits were being eroded, other programs for the poor were improving. The most important improvements were in the Earned Income Tax Credit (EITC). A recent study by the Congressional Budget Office (1995) examined the impact of all cash and near-cash transfer programs on poverty among persons living in families with children under 18 between 1979 and 1994. The analysis included all means-tested cash transfers such as AFDC and Supplemental Security Income (SSI), plus Social Security, unemployment compensation, workers' compensation, food and housing benefits, and the EITC. This study found that these programs lowered the number of poor in these families by 36.6 percent in 1979. As per capita spending per family declined, the antipoverty effectiveness of the programs was greatly eroded. The poverty count was reduced by only 19.1 percent in 1983, slowly recovering to 23.9 percent in 1989, and 26.5 percent in 1993. By 1994, however, the poverty reduction was 32.6 percent, much improved but still below 1979 levels. Thus, welfare spending recovered some of its effectiveness in reducing poverty by the mid-1990s, but still had less antipoverty impact than in the late 1970s.

These major trends that have slowed progress against poverty provide some insights into the challenges involved in making additional progress in reducing poverty. Female-headed families are growing and they are extremely vulnerable to poverty. The PRWORA of 1996 focuses considerable attention on reducing out-of-wedlock births, especially among teenagers, and on forcing both parents to accept financial responsibility for their children. But even if the act is successful in reducing out-of-wedlock births and improving child support, it seems doubtful that divorce and separation will decline in any major fashion over the next decade. Thus, the proportion of all families with children headed by a single woman will remain very high, and perhaps even grow. This means that further poverty reduction depends in part on welfare and social policy ameliorating the major barriers to economic independence for single-parent families.

The declining wages of less educated adults is also a challenge. Again, the forces that have altered the job market are not likely to reverse. In the future, a quality education will become increasingly important to economic security. States simply have to do a better job of educating students while increasing opportunities for adult continuing education.

In later chapters we will examine the PRWORA of 1996 in some depth. One goal will be to determine if the new reform legislation is really responsive to the problems that have stymied progress in reducing poverty over the last twenty years.

Poor Children

The largest single group of poor Americans is children. Since preventing and alleviating poverty among children is critical to the long-term goal of improving the economic security and productivity of American citizens, this group of poor Americans deserves particular attention. Figure 3.5 shows the trend in child poverty rates since 1959. What the data show is that during most of the 1960s and 1970s considerable progress was made in reducing poverty among children. However, over the last fifteen years the rate of poverty among children has generally been increasing, and has remained in the 20 percent range since 1990. Children under six suffer even higher rates of poverty. In 1997 the poverty rate for related children under six was 21.6 percent. If these children lived in a mother-only family, the poverty rate was 59.1 percent (Bureau of the Census, 1998a, vi).

Table 3.2 shows the actual number of poor children by race and

Figure 3.5 Poverty Rate of American Children, 1959–1997

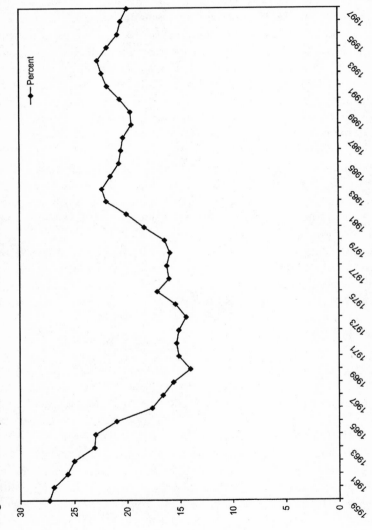

Source: Poverty in the United States, 1997. *Current Population Reports*, Series P60–201, Table C-1.

Table 3.2

Poor Children by Race, 1975–1997

Year	Total (000)	Poverty rate (%)	White (000)	Poverty rate (%)	Black (000)	Poverty rate (%)	Hispanic (000)	Poverty rate (%)
1975	11,104	17.1	6,927	12.7	3,925	41.7	NA	NA
1976	10,273	16.0	6,189	11.6	3,787	40.6	1,443	30.2
1977	10,288	16.2	6,097	11.6	3,888	41.8	1,422	28.3
1978	9,931	15.9	5,831	11.3	3,830	41.5	1,384	27.6
1979	10,377	16.4	6,193	11.8	3,833	41.2	1,535	28.0
1980	11,543	18.3	7,181	13.9	3,961	42.3	1,749	33.2
1981	12,505	20.0	7,785	15.2	4,237	45.2	1,925	35.8
1982	13,647	21.9	8,678	17.0	4,472	47.6	2,181	39.4
1983	13,911	22.3	8,862	17.5	4,398	46.7	2,312	38.1
1984	13,420	21.5	8,472	16.7	4,413	46.5	2,376	39.2
1985	13,010	20.7	8,253	16.2	4,157	43.6	2,606	40.3
1986	12,876	20.5	8,209	16.1	4,148	43.1	2,507	37.7
1987	12,843	20.3	7,788	15.3	4,385	45.1	2,670	39.3
1988	12,455	19.5	7,435	14.5	4,296	43.5	2,631	37.6
1989	12,590	19.6	7,599	14.8	4,375	43.7	2,603	36.2
1990	13,431	20.6	8,232	15.9	4,550	44.8	2,865	38.4
1991	14,341	21.8	8,848	16.8	4,755	45.9	3,094	40.4
1992	14,617	21.9	8,955	16.9	4,938	46.6	3,116	39.9
1993	15,727	22.7	9,752	17.8	5,125	46.1	3,873	40.9
1994	15,289	21.8	9,346	16.9	4,906	43.8	4,075	41.5
1995	14,665	20.8	8,981	16.2	4,761	41.9	4,080	40.0
1996	14,623	20.5	9,044	16.3	4,519	39.9	4,227	40.3
1997	14,113	19.9	8,990	16.1	4,225	37.2	3,972	36.8

Source: Bureau of the Census, 1998. Poverty in The United States, 1997. *Current Population Reports,* Series P60–201, Table C-2.

ethnicity since 1975. The population of poor children has grown considerably during this period, remaining above 14 million since 1991. Child poverty rates vary considerable by race and ethnicity but are high for all groups. The poverty rate is lowest for white children, but non-Hispanic white children numbered 5.2 million in 1997 and were the largest group of poor children. The poverty rate for black and Hispanic children is particularly high, about 37 percent. Millions of additional children live in families with incomes just above the poverty threshold. In fact, over 40 percent of all American children live in families with incomes below 200 percent of the poverty threshold, including over 60 percent of black and Hispanic children (Bureau of the Census, 1998a, Table 2).

Figure 3.6 shows the poverty rate by race and ethnicity for children since the mid-1970s. Between 1976 and 1997 the poverty rate for American children rose from 17.1 to 19.9 percent, an increase of about 20 percent. Most of the increase in child poverty was attributable to rapidly growing poverty among Hispanic children. In 1976 the poverty rate for Hispanic children was 30.2 percent[1]. By 1990 the rate had risen to 38.4 percent, but it declined to 36.8 percent in 1997 (Hauan, 1995; Enchautegui, 1992). Over the twenty-three year period shown in Figure 3.7, the poverty rate of Hispanic children increased by about 30 percent. By 1997 there were 3.8 million more poor children in America than in 1976. Growth in poverty among Hispanic children accounted for 2.5 million of the increase, or about 66 percent of the total change in child poverty[2].

Just as race and ethnicity are strong predictors of poverty among children, family structure also plays an important role. Figure 3.7 shows the poverty rate for children depending upon whether they live in a married-couple family or in a mother-only family. The differences between the poverty rates for children in these family types are stark for all racial and ethnic groups. With the exception of Hispanic families, the poverty rate of children in married-couple families is fairly low. However, the poverty rate for children in mother-only families is extremely high for all racial and ethnic groups. Almost half of all children living in mother-only families live in poverty, and the poverty rate for black and Hispanic children in these families is exceptionally high. In 1997 over 55 percent of all black children living in a mother-only family lived in poverty. For Hispanic children the poverty rate in mother-only families was almost 63 percent.

Figure 3.8 shows the percentage of all poor children living in mother-only families in 1980 and 1997. Over half of all poor children live in mother-only families, with the rate being extremely high for black children. In 1980 over 75 percent of all poor black children lived in a mother-only family, rising to almost 83 percent in 1997. The percentage of all poor white children (including Hispanics) in mother-only families increased between 1980 and 1997, but a slight majority still lived in a two-parent family. The picture is particularly interesting for poor Hispanic children. Between 1980 and 1997 the percentage of all poor Hispanic children in mother-only families declined from 47 percent to 45.5 percent. As noted above, even intact Hispanic families are having increased difficulty escaping poverty.

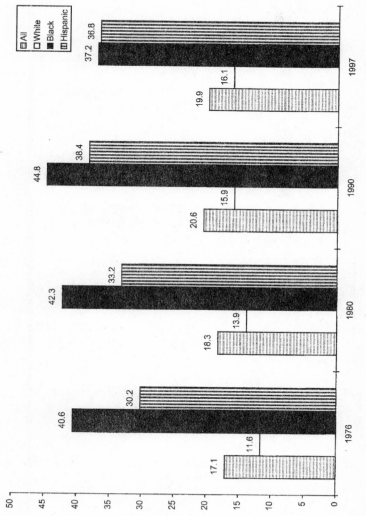

Figure 3.6 Poverty Rate of Children by Race and Ethnicity

Source: Poverty in the United States, 1997. *Current Population Reports*, Series P60–201, Table 2.
Note: Hispanics may be of any race.

Figure 3.7 Poverty Rate of Children by Family Type and Race, 1997

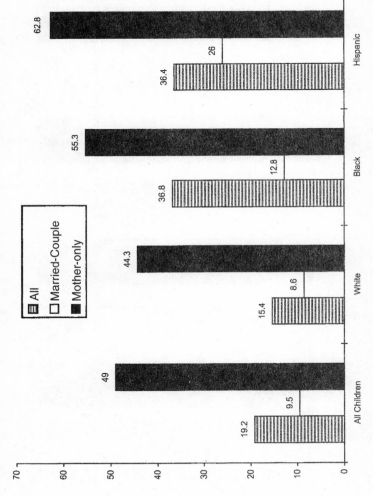

Source: Poverty in the United States, 1997. *Current Population Reports*, Series P60–201, Table 2.
Note: Data are for related children in families.

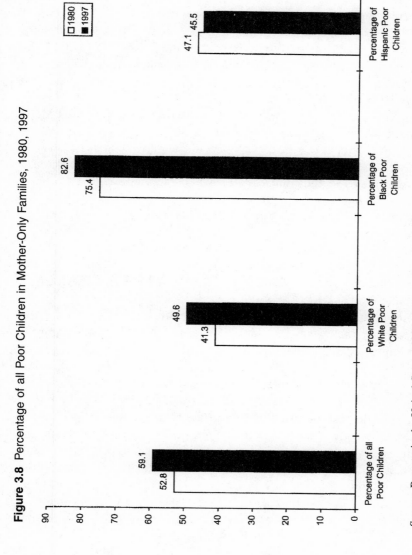

Figure 3.8 Percentage of all Poor Children in Mother-Only Families, 1980, 1997

□ 1980
■ 1997

Source: Poverty in the United States, 1997. *Current Population Reports*, Series P60–201, Table 2.
Note: Data are for related children in families.

How can the high rates of poverty among Hispanic children be explained? There are a number of obvious contributing factors. First, compared to other major racial and ethnic groups, Hispanic adults on average have lower education levels. For example, in 1998 only 55.5 percent of all Hispanics twenty-five and older had a high school degree. This is considerably below the 83.7 and 76 percent levels for whites and blacks, respectively (Bureau of the Census, 1999, Table 1). Hispanics also compare unfavorably with other major racial and ethnic groups on measures of advanced education. In 1998 only 11 percent of all Hispanics twenty-five and older had a college degree. This is about one-third the rate for white, non-Hispanic Americans. Many Hispanic adults, therefore, would seem to be particularly disadvantaged by recent trends in technology, the employment market's shift toward better-educated workers, and the globalization of the economy.

Examining income trends for Hispanic families seems to support this conclusion. Despite a growing economy, median income gains for Hispanics have been elusive over the last couple of decades. In inflation-adjusted dollars, the median income of Hispanic families declined from $27,751 in 1976, to $26,628 in 1997. Median income for Hispanic families declined in each year between 1990 and 1995, but made modest recoveries in 1996 and 1997 (Bureau of the Census, 1998d, Table B-2).

Additionally, within the Hispanic population income is becoming increasingly maldistributed. In 1973, for example, the lowest quintile of families received only 5.3 percent of all income earned by Hispanic families. By 1997 the share of the lowest quintile of Hispanic families had declined to 3.6 percent. During the same period the share of all income received by the highest quintile of Hispanic families increased from 42.3 to 49.5 percent (Bureau of the Census, 1998d, Table B-3).

Compounding these economic problems, divorce and out-of-wedlock births are increasing, resulting in a growing proportion of all Hispanic children living in families headed by single females. As noted in Figure 3.7, the poverty rate for Hispanic children in mother-only families exceeds 67 percent. One last problem is that many of the poorest Hispanics may be recent immigrants with little formal education and struggling with language barriers.

What about poverty among black children? As Table 3.2 shows, poverty among black children has remained stubbornly high over the last couple of decades, although it declined slightly in 1996 and 1997.

In 1975, 41.7 percent of all black children lived in poverty. In 1997 the poverty rate for black children was 37.2 percent. The standard deviation in the poverty rate of black children in twenty-three years was just above 2.0. Given the educational and occupational gains of so many black Americans during this period, it is somewhat surprising that progress has been modest in reducing poverty among black children.

Of course, poverty among black children has been impacted by all three factors that slowed down progress in reducing American poverty. Wage stagnation and real-dollar declines in welfare assistance to poor families made it more difficult to reduce poverty among black families. The robust economy in 1996 and 1997 may account for the small but significant decline in poverty among black Americans in those years. A major barrier to significant progress in reducing black poverty would seem to be related to family structure. The growth of female-headed families has been particularly dramatic in the black population and clearly a major reason for the stubbornly high level of poverty among black children. In 1975, single women headed 42.6 percent of all black families with children. By 1997 the percentage had grown to 54.1 percent. In 1975, 72.2 percent of all poor black children were found in households headed by single women. The percentage has been above 80 in every year since 1985, except for 1989 when it was 79.4 percent. In 1997 the percentage was 82.6 percent. Additionally, more poor black children lived in families headed by single men in 1997 than in 1975. The result was that in 1997 only 11.9 percent of all poor black families with children were headed by a married couple (Bureau of the Census, 1998a, Table C-3).

Family structure has enormous implications for poverty among black children. The poverty rate for black female-headed families with children exceeded 50 percent in every year between 1975 and 1996. In 1997, the poverty rate declined to 46.9 percent. On the other hand, the poverty rate for black married-couple families with children declined significantly since 1975, falling from 16.5 to 9 percent. Between 1975 and 1997 median family income for black, married-couple families increased by about 38 percent in real (inflation-adjusted) dollars. In 1975 the median income of black married couples equaled about 76 percent of the median income of white married-couple families. By 1997 the ratio was 87 percent. By contrast, black female-headed families had a median income of about 42 percent of black

Table 3.3

Poor White, Non-Hispanic Children, 1997

	Number (000)	Poverty rate	% of total related children
All	5,204	11.4%	
Related children			
In families	4,759	10.7%	100.0%
In married couple families	1,852	5.2%	38.9%
In female-headed household, no spouse present	2,551	37.2%	53.6%
In families with male-householder, no spouse present	355	16.4%	7.5%

Source: Bureau of the Census, 1998. Poverty in the United States, 1997. Current Population Studies. Unpublished data. File://D/new2_006.htm.

married-couple families in 1975. Twenty-three years later, median incomes for these families had increased by only 21 percent and had declined to only 37 percent of the median income of black married-couple families.

Significantly reducing poverty among black children, therefore, would seem to depend substantially upon: (a) reducing the proportion of families with children headed by single women, and (b) helping more single mothers to gain economic independence through supported employment.

Table 3.3 separates white and Hispanic children, showing the poverty rate for white, non-Hispanic children in 1997. At 11.4 percent, the poverty rate for white, non-Hispanic children is considerably lower than the rate for black children (37.2 percent) or Hispanic children (36.8 percent); see Table 3.2. Still, with 5 million white, non-Hispanic children living in poverty in 1997, they were about 37 percent of all poor children and the largest single group. Table 3.3 shows how seriously the poverty rate of white, non-Hispanic children is impacted by family structure. The poverty rate for white, non-Hispanic children living with one or more parents was 10.7 percent. If they lived in a married-couple family, the poverty rate drops to 5.2 percent. However, if they live in a female-headed household with no spouse present, the poverty rate is over seven times higher at 37.2 percent. Living with a male head of household with no spouse raises the poverty rate to 16.4 percent.

Not only is the poverty rate extremely high for white, non-Hispanic children living in a female-headed family, a majority of all poor white children live in these families. About 39 percent live in a married-couple family and only 7.5 percent live with a father only. Thus, while white, non-Hispanic children are poor for a variety of reasons, family structure is extremely important. Rising rates of divorce, separation, and out-of-wedlock births have greatly increased the number of white, non-Hispanic children living in high-risk, single-parent families. Many white, non-Hispanic children are also in families with very low, stagnated earning power and families that have found welfare benefits in decline.

Summary

Children are the major victims of American poverty. The overall poverty rate of American children is very high. Only one group of American children has a fairly low rate of poverty—non-Hispanic white children who live in married-couple families. All children, regardless of race or ethnicity, have high poverty rates when they live in a mother-only family. A majority of all poor white non-Hispanic and black children live in mother-only homes, and the percentage is extremely high for black children. The causes of poverty among children vary somewhat by race and ethnicity, but are always complex. Ameliorating poverty among children will require reducing the number of unplanned and unwanted children to parents who are unprepared to take care of them, while providing opportunities for parents in financial trouble to become economic viable. In later chapters, we will assess the possibilities of the PRWORA of 1996 to accomplish these goals.

Mother-Only Families: Growth and Causes of Poverty

Since the growth of mother-only families has played such a major role in the persistence of poverty, and especially poverty among children, this demographic trend needs to be carefully examined. Designing

Table 3.4

Mother-Only Families with Children 18 and Under, 1998

Mother, householder	All	White, Non-Hispanic	Black	Hispanic
Never married	37.8%	20.3%	60.0%	39.4%
Spouse absent	22.2	21.5	18.6	30.4
Widowed	3.4	5.2	3.1	5.1
Divorced	35.6	52.9	18.3	25.1

Source: Bureau of the Census, 1998. Marital Status and Living Arrangements, March 1998, Series P20–514.

policies to remediate poverty among women and children requires insights into why an increasing proportion of all families are headed by a single woman, and why these families are so economically vulnerable.

There are two major reasons for the dramatic increase in mother-only families. The first is greatly increased rates of divorce and separation over the last several decades. The second is significantly higher rates of out-of-wedlock births. Table 3.4 focuses on mother-only families with children eighteen and under. In 1998, having never been married was the reason that almost 38 percent of these families formed. Divorce was responsible for almost 36 percent of these households, while separation accounted for another 22.2 percent. Only 4.4 percent of these families were the result of the mother being widowed.

Figure 3.9 shows how the varying rates of divorce, separation, and out-of-wedlock births by racial and ethnic groups impact the living arrangements of children in mother-only families. In 1998 a majority of all white, non-Hispanic children lived with a mother who was divorced or separated. Only a little over 20 percent lived with a mother who had never been married. The pattern is reversed with black children. Sixty percent live with a mother who has never been married. A majority of all Hispanic children live with a mother who is divorced or separated, but almost 40 percent live with a mother who has never been married.

Until very recently, divorce was the number one reason for the formation of mother-only families with children. Since the late 1980s

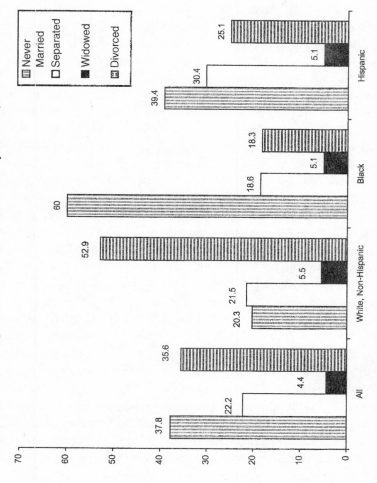

Figure 3.9 Living Arrangements of Children in Mother-Only Families, 1998

Source: Bureau of the Census, Marital Status and Living Arrangements, March 1998, Series P20–514, Table 3.

divorce rates have stabilized, while out-of-wedlock births have continued to rise. During the 1950s and 1960s, the yearly divorce rate per 1,000 women ages fifteen and up was about ten. By the mid-1970s the rate had doubled. The rate continued to increase in the late 1970s and early 1980s but has since leveled off. In 1990 the divorce rate was 20.9. This is still a very high rate of divorce. In recent years about 43 percent of all new marriages have ended in divorce. Since the mid-1970s over a million couples a year have ended their marriages (Bureau of the Census, 1999). Still, in 1996 fewer marriages ended in divorce than in the late 1980s.

Out-of-wedlock births, however, have continued to increase. Figure 3.10 shows the rise in out-of-wedlock births since 1970. In 1970 only 11 percent of all children were born out-of-wedlock. By 1995 the percentage was 32 percent. Out-of-wedlock births have increased for all racial and ethnic groups, but the increase is particularly dramatic for the black population. By 1995 over 70 percent of all black children were born to an unwed mother. The rate was also very high for the Hispanic population, reaching 43.1 percent in 1995.

These patterns are important because the poverty rate for mother-only families vary significantly depending on how they were formed. Table 3.5 shows the poverty rate for children living with both parents, along with the poverty rate for children in mother-only families. The poverty rate for white, non-Hispanic children is low, while the poverty rate for black children in two-parent families is relatively low. Hispanic children have a high poverty rate even in two-parent families, about 26 percent in 1998. All children suffer high poverty rates in mother-only families, but the rates are particularly high for black and Hispanic children. Except for Hispanic children, the poverty rate is somewhat lower in families with a divorced mother. Divorced mothers are on average older than never-married mothers, have more job experience, and may be getting some child support. When the mother is separated from her spouse, the poverty rate is very high. In many instances the separation is the result of abandonment by the spouse and there is no support. The poverty rate for children living with a mother who has been widowed is relatively low for white, non-Hispanic children, but high for black and Hispanic children. The poverty rate for children living with mothers who have never been married is extremely high for all children. It is almost 50 percent for white,

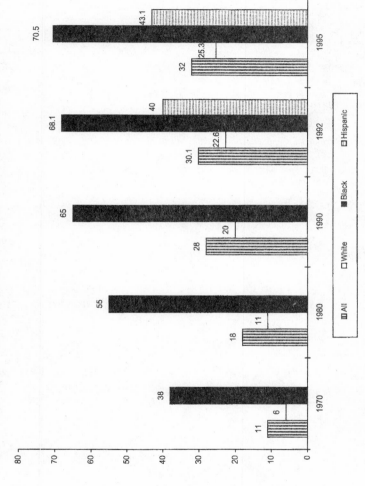

Figure 3.10 Percentage of all Children Born Out-of-Wedlock by Race, 1970–1995

Source: Vital and Health Statistics, Series 21, No. 53. U.S. Department of Health and Human Services, Public Health Service, June 1998.
Note: Hispanic data not available before 1992.

Table 3.5

Poverty Rates of Children in Mother-Only Families by Marital Status, 1998

	All	White, Non-Hispanic	Black	Hispanic
Living with				
Both parents	9.3%	5.1%	12.3%	25.9%
Mother-only	47.5	36.6	54.2	60.4
Mother-only, divorced	35.6	31.0	38.3	51.4
Mother-only, separated	51.0	41.3	56.9	61.1
Mother-only, widowed	27.3	17.4	44.0	30.9
Mother-only, never married	57.8	48.9	58.2	68.3

Source: Bureau of the Census, Marital Status and Living Arrangements, March 1998, Series P20–514, Table 6.

non-Hispanic children, almost 60 percent for black children, and almost 70 percent for Hispanic children.

Why Have Divorce and Unwed Births Increased?

The huge increases in rates of divorce and births to unmarried women over the last thirty years constitute two of the most important demographic changes in American families in the twentieth century. The changes significantly alter life patterns such as sexual roles, parenting, careers, and social interactions. The changes have massive implications for social policy. So why have they occurred? Below we examine the four major reasons most often offered as explanations.

Changing Social Mores

The great social movements of the 1960s have been credited with liberalizing public attitudes toward single parenthood and divorce (Magnet, 1993). Certainly the stigma associated with either behavior has declined significantly over the last thirty years (Garfinkel and McLanahan, 1986, 82), and behavior such as premarital sex is both more common and more accepted (Bane and Ellwood, 1994, 114). Demographic change has also played a role in these changing attitudes. Increasingly mature women of childbearing age are single. Women are entering their first marriage later and divorcing more frequently. In 1950 the average age of first marriage was 20.3; in 1985 it was 23.3; and by 1998 it was 25.0 (Bureau of the Census, 1994b, vii; Bureau of the Census, 1994a, Table 142, Bureau of the Census, 1998b, Table 2). In 1950 only about one-fourth of all twenty- to twenty-four-year-old women had never been married. By 1998 the proportion had risen to almost 70 percent. The growing number of adult, single women, many with careers, therefore, increases the number of women who may decide to have a child out-of-wedlock.

It is reasonable to assume, then, that changing demographics and a more accepting public have made it easier for adults to make choices about both divorce and out-of-wedlock births. However, as we will detail in Chapter 5, the huge increases in out-of-wedlock births over the last couple of decades, especially among teens, seems to have created a backlash that is reflected in the provisions of the PRWORA of 1996. Additionally, the data show some recent declines in out-of-wedlock births among teens.

The Availability of Welfare

While the public tends to believe that the availability of welfare has had a major impact on divorce, remarriage, and out-of-wedlock births, the best evidence suggests that there is a relationship, but it is modest. Danziger et al. (1982), Ellwood and Bane (1985), and Bassi (1987) all found a link between welfare receipt and divorce. Garfinkel and McLanahan (1986) concluded that while welfare receipt delayed remarriage, the implications for divorce and out-of-wedlock births are limited. They found that the increase in welfare benefits between 1960 and 1975 contributed to about 15 percent of the growth in mother-only families, rising to about 30 percent of the increase among the low-income population (Garfinkel and McLanahan, 1994, 211). Moffit's (1992) review of the empirical research reached approximately the same conclusions.

Acs (1993), in a very comprehensive evaluation, found little relationship between state AFDC cash benefit levels and the out-of-wedlock birth rate in the state. States that paid the highest cash benefits did not have higher rates of out-of-wedlock births. In fact, some of the states that paid the lowest cash benefits had the highest rates of out-of-wedlock births. The pattern clearly did not suggest that women were having babies in response to cash incentives. Acs's findings are consistent with the major body of research on this topic (Ellwood and Bane, 1985; Duncan and Hoffman, 1988; Plotnick, 1989).

Some critics, however, have argued that the amount of the state grant is less important than the fact that an out-of-wedlock birth opens the door for impoverished women to enter the welfare system and receive a package of benefits. Additionally, if a woman on welfare has another child, she receives an increase in her cash benefits (which is usually very modest) along with medical coverage, food stamps, and perhaps other benefits for the new child. As Chapter 6 will detail, the PRWORA of 1996, to some extent, accepts the validity of this argument. The new act allows states the option of denying cash assistance to teenagers who have children out-of-wedlock. If the state does provide assistance to single teenage mothers, the teen must live at home or under the supervision of an adult, and must stay in school or job training. Additionally, states may cap benefits to welfare families, providing no additional assistance to women who have children while on welfare. Some states have adopted these options, and we will examine the early evidence on the impact of out-of-wedlock birth rates in Chapter 8.

Female Employment

Another reason often suggested for increased rates of divorce and births to unmarried women is the independence women increasingly enjoy because of their careers and independent incomes. Over the last thirty years women have greatly increased their percentage of all college graduates and their role in the job market (Dechter and Smock, 1994). A slightly larger proportion of single women are employed, but, over the last twenty years particularly, more married women have balanced career and family roles. Low-income single women have not significantly increased their employment rates over the same period, but their level of employment has not declined. In 1997, women workers were 48 percent of all wage and salary income recipients, up from 32 percent in 1947 (Bureau of the Census, 1998c, Figure 1.8b). However, men are much more likely to be full-time year-round employees. In 1997, 71.6 percent of all men 15 and over worked full-time year round. Among women in the same age group, 55.6 percent worked full-time year-round (Bureau of the Census, 1998d, Table A).

The evidence indicates that when women have employment or other independent sources of income, they are somewhat more inclined to leave bad marriages, take longer to remarry, and are more willing to have children outside of marriage (Groeneveld, Hannan, and Tuma, 1983; Garfinkel and McLanahan, 1986; Ellwood and Bane, 1985; Bassi, 1987; Garfinkel and McLanahan, 1994, 211). The impact of employment is modest but often important (see Cain, 1987; Bane and Ellwood, 1994, 109–113).

Male Employment and Earnings

As will be detailed in Chapter 4, Wilson and Neckerman (1986) and other scholars have argued that marital instability and the epidemic of out-of-wedlock births are in part the result of decreasing job opportunities for men, especially inner-city minorities with low skills. Wilson and Neckerman's argument is that when young men cannot earn enough to support a family, they avoid the responsibility of marriage, or may be rejected by women as suitable mates. There is some evidence to support their argument. In a recent poll, 77 percent of young women said that a well-paying job was an essential requirement for a husband (Casey Foundation, 1995, 5). There is also a high correlation between male income levels and their rate of marriage. Among men in their thirties, those earning $50,000 a year or more are almost twice as likely to be married as those earning less than $10,000 (Casey Foundation, 1995, 5).

Yet, the median income of most men is quite low, especially when they are minorities. In 1997 the median income for white men was $26,115; for black men, $18,096; and for Hispanic men, $16,216 (Bureau of the Census, 1998d, Table A). When medians incomes are this low, a significant proportion of all men earn too little to support a family of four above the poverty level. In 1997, for example, men with less than a ninth-grade education had median incomes of $12,157 (Bureau of the Census, 1998d, Table 9).

Many men, especially minorities, have significant periods of unemployment. In 1997, 9.9 percent of all white men were unemployed, averaging a total of 12.4 weeks. For black men the comparable rates were 16.5 percent, with an average of 17.8 weeks of idleness. Among

Hispanic men, 14.1 percent experienced unemployment, averaging 14.9 weeks without a job (Bureau of the Census, 1998d, Table 10). There is also a difference by race and ethnicity in whether men were even in the workforce. In 1997, 71.4 percent of all white men were employed during the year, compared to 64.8 percent of black men and 67.6 percent of Hispanic men (Bureau of the Census, 1998d, Table 10).

The evidence suggests that low median incomes and periods of unemployment for many men are not caused by a shortage of jobs (Jenks, 1992, 127; Blank, 1994, 171). Over the last three decades growth in jobs has exceeded population growth. The problem, as noted above, is a shortage of jobs that pay low-skill workers well and a shortage of entry-level jobs that lead to middle-income employment. This is true regardless of whether those jobs are in service or manufacturing. In America's increasingly international and technologically-sophisticated economy, there are decreasing economic opportunities for low-skilled workers, regardless of race (Gottschalk and Moffit, 1994; Cutler and Katz, 1992). The result is that those workers entering the job market today with a high school education or less can expect lower incomes than their fathers (Blank, 1994). In the 1960s and the 1970s, men between the ages of twenty-five and thirty-four had higher incomes than their fathers. By 1987 this trend reversed, leaving men twenty-five to thirty-four with lower median income than their fathers' generation. In 1997 this was still true (Bureau of the Census, 1998c, Figure 1.12).

The evidence, then, does support the argument that declining wages, high unemployment, and decreasing rates of employment characterizes a larger percentage of all men today than in the past (Bound and Holzer, 1993; Bound and Freeman, 1992; Bound and Johnson, 1992). The question is: what is the impact of these changes on family structure? The evidence is mixed. Wilson and Neckerman (1986) compared the ratio of employed men to employed black women in the same age cohort and found a significant decline since the 1970s. The decrease in employed black men occurred at the same time that marriage rates of blacks were declining quite dramatically. However, Mare and Winship (1991) found that only about 20 percent of the decrease in marriage rates for black men could be explained by their lower rates of employment. Testa (1991), Ellwood and Crane (1990), and Ellwood and Rodda (1991) also concluded that changes in employment patterns of men, white and black, are rather modest compared to the steep declines in marriage rates. Thus, while male earnings and rates of employment and unemployment are related to marriage and perhaps divorce, this is just one factor contributing to the major increase in mother-only families (Lichter, McLaughlin, Kephart, and Landry, 1992; Mare and Winship, 1991). In the next chapter, Cornel West, Professor of African-American Studies at Harvard, offers a quite different explanation for the decline in black marriage rates.

In summary, low wages and high rates of unemployment for many men, especially minorities; the independence provided women by their careers; a more liberal attitude toward premarital sex and single parenting; and the availability of welfare all have contributed to the major increases in divorce and out-of-wedlock births that have taken place over the last thirty years.

Why Are Mother-Only Families So Economically Vulnerable?

There is general agreement that mother-only families suffer low income and high rates of poverty for five reason: (1) unemployment rates are very high among mother-only families; (2) when women do work, their median incomes are low; (3) on average, there are fewer workers in mother-only families than in married-couple families; (4) social welfare programs have not been designed to help single mothers become economically independent; and (5) most single mothers receive no child support or inadequate support.

Poorly Designed Social Welfare Programs

Despite the fact that the dramatic growth in mother-only families is one of the most important demographic changes in the latter half of the twentieth century, public policy has been altered very slowly to begin to accommodate or deal with the reality of this massive change in the American family. Through most of its history, the AFDC program was antifamily, denying assistance to almost all two-parent families. Poor women found themselves in the position of losing all assistance if they married. Poor men often realized that their wives and children would be able to qualify for welfare and be better off if they abandoned the family. Even when AFDC was amended by the Family Support act of 1988, AFDC continued to be a program that primarily provided assistance to single mothers. Under AFDC most mothers could not enter the job market because child care assistance was not provided, and they generally could not afford it given the incomes they could earn. Also, the jobs that AFDC mothers could obtain often did not provide health care, and employment resulted in the loss of Medicaid. The result was that when millions of mother-only families fell below the poverty level, welfare programs discouraged marriage, while failing to help significant numbers of them escape poverty through supported work.

Additionally, as noted above, between 1970 and the early 1990s, the inflation-adjusted value of cash benefits declined quite dramatically. Thus, the welfare program contributed to single-parent families, helped very few of those on welfare become employed, and provided increasingly inadequate assistance over time.

Women's Employment Income

The economic condition of mother-only families is also affected by a series of problems related to employment and wage earnings. Most obviously, unemployment rates for single mothers are very high. In 1997 only 61 percent of all single mothers with children under eighteen worked full-time year-round. The rate of employment varied little by race or ethnicity (Bureau of the Census, 1998a, Table 3). Among single mothers with children under eighteen with incomes below the poverty level, very few worked. In 1997 only about 21 percent of these mothers worked at any time during the year. Some 24 percent of white mothers, 16 percent of black mothers, and 17 percent of Hispanic mothers had any type of employment during the year (Bureau of the Census, 1998a, Table 3).

Even when women are employed, they tend to earn less than male workers. In 1997 the median income for women working full-time year-round was $24,973, compared to $33,674 for men. Similarly, female heads of households with no husbands present had a median income from all sources (i.e., wages, cash welfare benefits, child support, etc.) of $23,040, compared to $51,681 for married-couple families (Bureau of the Census, 1998d, Table 2).

Female workers earn significantly less than male workers for several reasons (Bergman, 1989; Fuchs, 1989). Many more women work only part-time, or part of the year. Women also tend to change jobs and move in and out of the work force more often. Among full-time workers the discrepancy between male and female wages is caused by many factors. First, the mean age of working women is considerably younger than that of male employees (which means that women tend to have less seniority). Second, women employees tend to be concentrated in jobs that are traditionally considered "women's work," and these jobs often pay a rather low wage regardless of the skill or training required. Third, some of the differences reflect "glass ceilings" and other forms of discrimination.

Lack of Adequate Child Support

One of the most obvious factors contributing to the poverty of mother-only families is the low level of child support by absent fathers. Until very recently, only about half of all women with minor children from an absent father have been awarded child support, and of these, only about half have received the agreed-upon amount (Bureau of the Census, 1994a, Tables 604–605). Figures for 1989 provide examples from a typical year. In 1989 there were 9.9 million women with children from an absent father. Exactly 50 percent of these women won court decisions ordering the absent father to make support payments. However, only three-quarters of those awarded support ever received any money, and of those who did, only 51 percent received the full amount. The mean payment received by mothers was $2,995. Thus, most mothers did not receive any support, and those who did tended to receive rather modest amounts.

With the passage of the Family Support act of 1988, considerable new emphasis was placed on identifying absent parents and making them pay child support. The PRWORA of 1996 built on the FSA provisions, and includes major new initiatives to identify absent parents and force them to pay their child support obligations. The provisions are explained in Chapter 6 and evaluated in Chapter 8. As will be detailed in those chapters, paternity establishment has greatly improved along with child support collections. There is every reason to believe that progress will continue in the years to come as the PRWORA provisions are fully implemented. In 1996 over $12 billion was collected in child support, an increase of more than 50 percent since fiscal year 1992. Paternity was established in over one million cases, an increase of more than 100 percent since 1992 (Office of

Child Support Enforcement, 1998). Despite real progress, in 1996 only 24 percent of the families headed by a never-married mother received regular child support payments. Only 54 percent of the families headed by a divorced woman received regular and full payments. Thus, child support has been significantly improving, but most mothers still do not receive the support they are owed, and this contributes significantly to the economic problems of these families.

Conclusions

This chapter has examined trends in the American poverty rate and the demographics of the American poor. Poverty has proven to be an extremely difficult problem to resolve. After thirty years of antipoverty initiatives and expenditures in the trillions, the rate of poverty in 1997 was higher than at any point during the 1970s. The problems that have stymied progress against poverty are considerable, but three broader societal and policy changes played major roles: the growth of mother-only families, declining wages for poorly educated workers, and per capita declines in cash welfare assistance. The growth of mother-only families is the result of increasing rates of divorce, separation, and out-of-wedlock births. Changing social mores, the availability of welfare, the independence women have gained through education and employment, and problems with the employment and earnings of many men have all contributed to the breakdown of the traditional family. Mother-only families tend to be economically vulnerable because of poorly designed welfare programs, high rates of unemployment, low earning power, and lack of adequate child support from absent fathers.

America's poor tend to be its most vulnerable citizens—children, the aged, members of mother-only families, and the poorly educated stuck in jobs that pay wages that increasingly fail to keep pace with inflation. Children constitute about 40 percent of all the poor, and a majority of them live in homes headed by a single mother. The rate of poverty for mother-only families has always been high, and it has not changed drastically over the last fifteen years. What has changed is the number of mother-only families. As this type of household has increased, the high rate of poverty experienced by this type of family unit has greatly increased the number of poor women and children. Minority children are particularly likely to live with mothers who are divorced, separated, or never married, and, consequently, their rate of poverty is extremely high.

Notes

1. The data in Figure 3.6 are for all poor children, not just poor, related children. The Census Bureau started collecting data on poor, related Hispanic children in 1973 and all poor Hispanic children in 1976. Between 1976 and 1996 poor, related Hispanic children represented an average of 97.2 percent of all poor Hispanic children. The other poor Hispanic children are in institutions, foster care, or adopted families.

2. The designation Hispanic denotes ethnicity, not race. Hispanic children may be of any race. Census data separating Hispanic children by race is collected each year, but except in decennial censuses, the sample sizes are too small for reliable estimates. Thus racial breakdowns are not available for the twenty-one years represented in Figure 3.6. The decennial census shows high poverty rates for all major groups of Hispanic children, with rates always above 30 percent. For example, in 1989 the poverty rates by origin were 32.6 percent for Cubans, 35.8 percent for Central/South Americans, 45 percent for Mexicans, 57.9 percent for Puerto Ricans, and 37 percent for other (unpublished census data). Landale and Lichter (1997) provide an excellent analysis of differential poverty rates among Hispanic children and find that local economic conditions explain some of the differences in poverty rates among Hispanic children.

4

Why Are People Poor in America?

hy do we have poverty in a country as rich as America?
While many people, including some scholars, seem to think
the answer is simple, a thoughtful analysis suggests that the
antecedents of poverty are quite complex. The first complication is
that the poverty population is much more diverse than many people
imagine. The poverty population is a elaborate mix of people who
vary by age, race, sex, geographic location, and family structure. The
poor are generally stereotyped as primarily single women and their
children, illegitimate or otherwise, along with street people. But,
among the poor can be found the elderly, often living alone, married-
couple families with children in which one or sometimes even both
parents are employed, young healthy males who may or may not be
in the labor force, single or married adults without children, and farm
workers following crop rotations across the nation. The poor can be
found in every state, in central cities, in suburbs and rural areas in
every region of the nation. Does it seem reasonable that the same
factor or factors are responsible for the poverty of all these diverse
groups of people? Is an eighty-five-year-old widow poor for the same
reasons as an eighteen-year-old single mother or an alcoholic derelict?

Not likely. The most common mistake in thinking about the causes
of poverty is to generalize based on one group among the poor. If we

think that poverty is basically only a problem related to teenagers having children out-of-wedlock, or adults who abuse alcohol or drugs, we are not likely to ever understand the complexities of the broader problem well enough to fashion creative solutions. Our understanding, or even biases, about the causes of poverty have a significant impact on the type of solutions we are willing to support (Schneider and Ingram, 1993; Barber, 1984; Lowi, 1972; Wilson, 1973). Many people who might be willing to sanction adults who refuse to work or teenage mothers who will not attend parenting classes would likely have a very different attitude about a parent who worked full-time but could not escape poverty. It is important, therefore, to achieve as sophisticated an understanding as possible of the causes of poverty.

When all the various types of people who are poor are examined, it becomes obvious that poverty is not a single problem, but rather a series of problems that affect diverse groups within our population. Additionally, being poor does not automatically mean that a person is a welfare recipient. Only some of the poor receive welfare (see Table 5.5). For a variety of reasons many poor people never apply for assistance, and others would find qualifying for aid to be quite difficult because most assistance is reserved for select groups of poor people. Stereotypes of the poor often result from the fact that only some of the poor receive the cash benefits that society thinks of as welfare. Those people who qualify for cash assistance—mostly female-headed families—tend to be thought of as the poor. But they are really a subset of the poor.

Even being cognizant of the diversity and complexity of poverty and the use of welfare by the poor will not solve all our analytical problems. Fashioning public policies to solve poverty would certainly be easier if there was agreement about the causes of poverty. But even when we examine the poverty of a particular person or a specific group of people, individual values impact perceptions of why these people are poor. Think about this example. The poverty rate for married-couple families with children is rather low—about 7 percent. A number of seemingly rather obvious factors make a rather small percentage of these families poor. Some of these families, for example, go through periods of unemployment, and some work full–time but receive very low wages, a not uncommon problem in many central cities and rural areas. Some family heads suffer illness, or become disabled, perhaps because of a job-related injury.

While the basic reasons these families suffer poverty may seem clear, there are many ways to diagnose their problems. If unemployment is a problem, how did the parents become unemployed? Did they fail to take employment seriously? Did they have the misfortune of being downsized? Do the parents abuse alcohol or drugs? Have the parents remained unemployed because they refuse to accept jobs they consider undesirable? Are they willing to relocate to an area with more jobs? Are both parents seeking employment? Is one parent forced to stay home because child care is too high or unavailable? Are the parents at fault for having children despite their low income potential? Have the parents been wronged by employers who fail to offer adequate benefits (e.g., health care or day care) or exhibit too little concern about the on-job safety of their employees?

Depending upon individual values and perhaps the behavior of the individuals involved, there are considerable grounds for differences in perspectives about why these families are poor, whether they should be offered any assistance, and, if so, what type of assistance they should be given. The same is true, of course, for other subgroups of the poor. Thus, agreeing on the causes of poverty is quite difficult.

The Dynamics of Poverty

Before examining specific theories of poverty, it is also helpful to know some additional facts about America's poor population that have relevance to this discussion. An important question is what type of poverty are we dealing with? Does America have a large number of people who are poor for long periods, even a lifetime, or is poverty more likely to be a short-term problem? A permanent poverty class would be more complicated to deal with, and the causes of their poverty would probably be more intricate than that of people suffering from episodic spells of poverty. There are studies that answer this question. Research shows that most Americans who are identified as poor are impoverished for a relatively short period of time. About three-fourths of new poverty spells last less than two years. Gottschalk, McLanahan, and Sandefur (1994, 89) found that a small percentage of all spells—7.1 percent—last seven or more years. The length of poverty spells varies by race. Poverty spells are longer for blacks than for nonblacks. About 63 percent of nonblack poverty spells last less than one year. For blacks the corresponding figure is

48.4 percent. Blacks also suffer a higher rate of longer spells. While only 4.3 percent of nonblacks remain poor seven or more years, the rate for blacks is almost 15 percent (Gottschalk, McLanahan, and Sandefur, 1994, 90).

The above figures are based on Census surveys conducted once a year. Ruggles (1990) studied poverty spells by examining family income on a monthly basis. This research showed even more income mobility among low-income groups. Over 80 percent of those individuals whose income fell below the poverty line in any one month suffered a poverty spell that lasted less than eight months. Examining these families over a two-year period, Ruggles found that only 11 percent were poor all twenty-four months.

If a person does become poor, how long will he/she be poor before moving above the poverty line for a full year? Gottschalk, McLanahan, and Sandefur's (1994, 89) data show that for most of the poor, regardless of race, the answer is less than two years.

For most people, therefore, new poverty spells tend to be short. However, for some people poverty is a more long-term problem. By shifting focus and examining poverty spells in progress, rather than new spells, Gottschalk, McLanahan, and Sandefur (1994, 91) find a more troubled population. About 20 percent of those persons in poverty at any point in time have been poor for seven or more years.

There is additional evidence of income vulnerability that also documents that poverty is more than a fleeting problem for millions of people. Gottschalk, McLanahan, and Sandefur (1994, 91) tracked those individuals who escaped poverty to determine how far they moved above the poverty threshold. They found that most of those who escape poverty remain economically marginal, considerably below middle-income levels. Some 91 percent of those individuals who were poor in one year had incomes less than twice the poverty line in the next year. Living on the margins means that if they encounter any economic adversity, many of the former poor are in jeopardy of falling back into poverty.

The evidence reviewed here reveals that poverty is a transitory problem for most people whose income falls below the poverty line. Most of these people leave poverty, but remain economically vulnerable. However, a significant proportion of the poor live below the poverty line for a long period of time. If this information is correct, we should find three primary patterns of welfare use. First, many people will be poor for too short a period to receive welfare. Second, most of those who do receive welfare should stay on the rolls for a relatively short period. They may, however, cycle through the welfare system several times. Third, some 20 percent of the poor should be long-term users, remaining on the rolls for seven or more years. We examine the facts about welfare spells below.

Welfare Dynamics

Table 5.5 shows that the first pattern above is correct. Only 34 percent of those identified as poor in 1997 received cash welfare assistance, less than half received food stamps, and only a little over half were covered by Medicaid. Many people identified as poor never receive welfare, or benefit only from programs such as the school lunch program for poor and low-income families.

The second pattern is also confirmed by the data. Most welfare spells are short. Gottschalk, McLanahan, and Sandefur (1994, 94) in studying AFDC spells found that for nonblacks 44 percent of cases are closed in one year, while an additional 22.8 percent end in the second year. Spells last longer on average for black recipients, but 33.7 percent ended during the first year, with an additional 16.2 percent ending in the second year. By the end of two years, two-thirds of the spells for nonblacks and half the spells for blacks had closed.

Many recipients who leave welfare return. Recidivism, or multiple spells, significantly lengthens welfare use by many people. Looking at multiple spells over a ten-year period, Gottschalk, McLanahan, and Sandefur (1994, 95) found that 27.7 percent of black recipients received AFDC for only two or fewer years. For nonblacks, 41.3 percent received assistance for two or fewer years over a ten-year period. When multiple spells are added, 34.4 percent of blacks and 18 percent of nonblacks used AFDC for seven to ten years. The average of all stays for recipients, counting multiple spells, is about four years (Moffit, 1992; Bane and Ellwood, 1994, 95–96). About 35 percent of all recipients leave the rolls only to return after losing a job or suffering another financial setback (Brandon, 1995). Rather than transitional users, they are episodic users (Bane and Ellwood, 1994, 41; Pavetti, 1993).

The third pattern is also confirmed by their data. About half of all recipients remain on AFDC for more than four years, while about 25 percent remain on the rolls for ten years or more. Almost 6 percent of the AFDC spells of nonblacks were still in progress at the end of seven years, while 25.4 percent of the spells for blacks were still in progress. One result is that while most of the poor who receive assistance are on the rolls for a relatively short period, most of those persons receiving assistance on any given day have been on the rolls for a long time. This sounds contradictory, but it is not. Most people who receive assistance cycle though the system rather quickly, but a small percentage of recipients become long-term users. In a year's time, short-term users greatly outnumber long-term users. Thus, the typical user is short-term. Still, long-term users dominate the rolls. An example can make this clearer. Suppose you had a hospital room with four beds. Patients who remain in the hospital for the whole year occupy three of the beds. The fourth bed accommodates patients who stay in the hospital on average for one week. At the end of the year the hospital room will have served fifty-five patients, 94.5 percent of whom were short-term users. However, on any given day during the year, 75 percent of the patients in the room would be long-term. This is the way the welfare system works. Most people cycle through, some recycling. A small percentage of users are long-term, constituting the majority of recipients on any given day.

Bane and Ellwood (1994, 35–37) provide some important insights into the differences between long- and short-term users. The long-term users tend to be young, never married mothers, especially those who drop out of school and have little job experience. While only about 14 percent of divorced women remain on the rolls for ten or more years, about 40 percent of all never-married mothers do so (Green Book, 1994, 444). Banes and Ellwood also find that when AFDC recipients remain on the rolls for more than two years, they are in danger of becoming long-term users. On the other hand, when recipients manage to leave the rolls and stay off for at least three years, they usually do not return to AFDC (Hoynes and MaCurdy, 1994).

With this understanding of the poverty population and their use of welfare, we can examine and evaluate some specific theories of the causes of poverty.

Theories of Poverty

Theories of poverty generally fall into one of two categories: cultural/
behavioral or structural/economic. Structural/economic theories usually contain some behavioral component, but argue that the
precipitating factor that causes poverty is a lack of equal opportunities
for all Americans. Cultural/behavioral theories generally make the
case that the only real cause of poverty is the behavior, values, and
culture of the poor. Conservatives generally favor cultural/behavioral
arguments, while moderates and liberals usually emphasize structural/
economic explanations that contain a behavioral component.

Cultural/Behavioral Theories

In *The Dream and The Nightmare* (1993), Myron Magnet articulates
a conservative interpretation of American poverty. Magnet argues that
the basic cause of poverty is the culture and behavior of the poor.
People become poor, Magnet argues, not because they lack social,
political, and economic opportunities, but because they lack the inner
resources to seize the ample opportunities that surround them. Magnet
believes the poverty of the poor is primarily a destitution of the soul,
a failure to develop the habits of education, reasoning, judgment, sacrifice, and hard work required to succeed in the world. To Magnet the
poor are not hardworking, decent people who have fallen victim to
economic problems. Rather, he says, they are people who engage in
school-leaving, welfare abuse, illegitimacy, drug and alcohol abuse,
and often crime.

The primary job of any civilization, Magnet says, is soulcraft: the
transmission of values which combine to develop mature, educated,
honest, hard working, caring, and responsible people. The poor represent society's failures, those who have not inherited the central values of mainstream culture. Magnet believes that the values of today's
poor reflect the revolutionized culture of the 1960s, which taught that
it was legitimate to blame the system for personal failures and expect
government handouts rather than seek success through education, hard
work, and sacrifice. This same 1960s culture also promoted the sexual
revolution, endorsing premarital sex, promiscuity, and illegitimacy,
while degrading marriage, sacrifice, education, and industriousness.

Magnet's concluding point is that an individual's values and behavior determines his/her opportunities, economic or otherwise. Economic opportunity can abound, but if a person lacks the inner resources to take advantage of opportunities, he/she will fail. Giving welfare to those who fail only makes matters worse. Welfare reinforces the belief that people are not responsible for their behavior, that they cannot overcome their problems through hard work, and that welfare is something they deserve.

Moderate and liberal scholars tend to believe that the image of the poor drawn by Magnet and others who accept his point of view is nothing but a narrowly drawn stereotype. This view of the poor, they argue, is based on a subset of the poor, which ignores the complexity of the poverty population, and as noted above, empirical evidence about length of poverty spells and welfare use. Out of a population of 35 to 40 million poor people, Magnet, they argue, bases his theory of poverty on the behavior and welfare use of a few million of the poor, a group often labeled the underclass. Those poor people with obviously dysfunctional habits or lifestyles have long interested society. Often they have been labeled as the undeserving poor, or more recently as the underclass. But what proportion of the poor do they represent?

A considerable body of research has attempted to define and identify the underclass. Scholars who have attempted to identify and count them have used a number of definitions and methodologies. Some studies have tried to define the underclass as those poor who are isolated in inner-city impoverished neighborhoods, essentially separated from the workforce (Bane and Jargowsky, 1988; Gottschalk and Danziger, 1986; Hughes, 1989; Nathan, 1986; Ricketts and Sawhill, 1988). These studies identify a rather small underclass population ranging from under 1 million to about 6 million.

Another group of scholars have tried to identify those long-term poor people, often including those who live in neighborhoods with high concentrations of poverty, who engage in dysfunctional behavior such as chronic unemployment, drug use, out-of-wedlock births, crime, school-leaving, and antisocial attitudes and behavior (Adams, Duncan, and Rodgers, 1988; Reischauer, 1989; Kasarda, 1992; O'Hare and Curry-White, 1992). These studies identify a population that ranges from less than 1 million to slightly more than 8 million, depending upon definitions, methodologies, and number of cities studied.

While these various studies arrive at estimates that differ consid-

erably, they do agree that most of the poor are not the highly dysfunctional people described by Magnet. That proportion of the poor
population that does exhibit serious social problems, however, is considerable, quite visible, and they are expensive users of social services.
It is not too surprising that this group is often thought of as the poor.

Many conservative scholars, on the other hand, are not concerned
about stereotyping the poor because they think Magnet's basic arguments are both correct and should serve as a warning. They believe
that the welfare system is so perverse in design that it has the ability
to spread a contagion of pathologies among the poor. Charles Murray
in his influential book *Losing Ground* (1984) argued that the real cul-
prit of the poor is welfare. Welfare, Murray argues, robs the poor of
initiative, breaks up families by encouraging men either not to marry
the mothers of their children or to desert them, provides an incentive
to women to have children out-of-wedlock, so they can get on welfare
or increase their benefits, and discourages work by providing a combination of cash and noncash benefits that amounts to better compensation than could be obtained through employment.

Murray's arguments have attracted strong critics, in part, because
he proposes a radical solution. Murray argues that the best way to
reduce poverty is simply to abolish all welfare programs. Labeled the
cold turkey approach, Murray's arguments are almost the perfect foil
for those sympathetic towards the poor. But even critics of Murray
often agree that welfare does produce some antifamily impacts. As
noted in Chapter 3, Danziger et al. (1982), Ellwood and Bane (1985),
and Bassi (1987) all found a significant link between welfare receipt
and increased rates of divorce. Garfinkel and McLanahan (1986) concluded that while welfare receipt often delays remarriage, it has a
modest impact on divorce and out-of-wedlock births (Garfinkel and
McLanahan 1994, 211).

Also as noted in Chapter 3, there is little relationship between state
AFDC benefits and state out-of-wedlock birth rates (Acs, 1993; Ellwood and Bane, 1985; Duncan and Hoffman, 1988; Plotnick, 1989).
The out-of-wedlock birth rate, in other words, is not higher in states
that pay high AFDC benefits than the rate in states that pay low benefits. In fact, Mississippi, one of the lowest-paying states in the nation,
has one of the highest out-of-wedlock birth rates. Critics like Murray
countered that the amount of the state grant is less important than the
fact that an out-of-wedlock birth makes a women eligible for welfare

or may increase her benefits, even modestly. Murray argues that if states gave no money to single mothers, especially teenagers, parents would put more pressure on teenagers to avoid pregnancy, and women would expect more of men—and would be more careful about having children with men who did not have the prospect of becoming parental partners.

Other scholars take a somewhat different approach than Murray, but argue that welfare programs play an important role in making and keeping people poor. In a pair of influential books, Mead (1986, 1992) argued that the welfare system had become too permissive, placing too few obligations on the recipients. By not requiring the healthy poor to work, Mead contended, the welfare system undermined both the confidence of the poor and public sympathy for them. One of Mead's theses was that passive poverty, that is an idle poverty population, reflected a welfare-nurtured defeatism on the part of recipients rather than a real lack of economic opportunity. Mead focused, first, on proving that the healthy poor could work and, second, on documenting ample economic opportunity for those with motivation. Mead argued that the poor would be substantially better off economically and psychologically if they were moved into the workforce and that society would be much more positive about helping low-income working families than in assisting passive welfare families. Thus, Mead did not contend that all welfare is wrong or harmful, but rather that welfare, especially long-term, is the wrong solution to the problems of the healthy poor.

James L. Payne (1998) agrees with the fundamental position of conservatives that welfare is harmful to the poor. Payne makes the familiar argument that welfare destroys the integrity of the poor while promoting and prolonging poverty by asking too little in return. Payne advocates what he calls "expectant giving," basing most assistance to the poor on the understanding that they must give something in return. "What the poor actually need," argues Payne, "is to be asked to give, not be given to."(1998, xii). "Expectant giving" requires the poor to engage in constructive efforts to help themselves. The best assistant programs, Payne argues, are those that require the greatest contribution from the poor.

Payne takes the conservative argument one step further. He contends that government can never pass or administer effective welfare reform. The reason, he argues, is that governments will always yield to a handout mentality, based on the belief that the poor, regardless of why they are poor, deserve help. "Expectant giving" requires judgments about why people are poor, what they need, what they should give in return, and whether they have lived up to the terms of their agreement or contract. Effectively helping the poor, Payne argues, requires that they be treated selectively or unequally, a role government is unsuited to play. With heavy caseloads, endless, inflexible rules, and a bias toward uniformity, government programs, he says, will always drift to handouts. The best alternative, Payne suggests, is to turn welfare over to private, voluntary efforts that can be more flexible and creative. Only then, says Payne, can we avoid the extremes of indulgence and cruelty that exacerbate America's poverty problems.

The cultural/behavioral approach, in summary, basically places responsibility for America's poverty problem on the personal inadequacies of the poor, welfare in general, or the design flaws of welfare programs.

Structural/Economic Theories

As noted, moderates and liberals generally explain poverty in terms of limited economic or political opportunities, changes in government policies, and sometimes racial and/or sexual discrimination. An important theory offered by William J. Wilson in *The Truly Disadvantaged (1987)* examines the impact of civil rights laws on changes in economic opportunities. Wilson's theory focuses on the growth of poverty and social problems in urban black ghettoes. Blacks, Wilson notes, migrated from the South to the major cities of the Midwest and North in search of economic opportunities. Because of housing discrimination, almost all black people, regardless of education or skills, became concentrated in central city ghettos. By the 1970s, Wilson maintains, important changes were taking place in American society that would have major impacts on black ghettos. Wilson explains these dynamics with four hypotheses.

First, Wilson hypothesizes that changes in the employment market harmed low-income, low-skilled blacks, especially black men living in central cities. These changes involved the general decline of manufacturing jobs, which paid good wages for low-skill work, and the migration of hundreds of thousands of these same types of manufacturing jobs from central cities to the suburbs. Replacing these manufacturing jobs in the central cities were clerical and white-collar jobs. However, these jobs tended to require more postsecondary or specialized skills than many ghetto residents possessed. Wilson labels these changes as slow economic growth, skills mismatch, and spatial mismatch. Slow economic growth reduced the number of manufacturing jobs; the jobs that increased in urban areas were those that many poor blacks were unqualified to fill, while those jobs they could perform were increasingly located in suburbs.

Second, Wilson hypothesizes that increased joblessness among inner-city men encouraged many of them to turn to idleness and hustling, including criminal activities such as the drug trade. The combination of unemployment and crime among so many men left ghetto women with fewer qualified or desirable partners, significantly reducing the marriage rate while increasing the incidence of out-of-wedlock births and the use of welfare.

Third, the civil rights laws passed in the 1960s played an important role in making these problems worse. Civil rights and affirmative action laws extending equal employment opportunities, and fair housing increased the income of the most educated and skilled ghetto residents and allowed them to move to the suburbs. Wilson calls this selective out-migration.

Fourth, Wilson theorizes that selective out-migration harmed the ghetto community in important ways. Those who migrated had been the communities' best role models and civic leaders. Gone were those community leaders who had championed the importance of education, quality schools, and high academic standards while resisting crime and illegitimacy. In turn, those left behind had less education, skill, and motivation. This produced what Wilson labels a contagion effect, the degeneration of aspirations, morals, schools, and the general health of the community—leading to ever-increasing rates of poverty and other social problems.

Wilson's theory is interesting and important because it provides a tightly reasoned theory of the growth of the black underclass in American ghettos. Wilson emphasizes a loss of low-skilled, decent paying jobs as the precipitating event in increasing poverty in ghettos, but there is also a behavioral component. Wilson does not deny that many poor people engage in behaviors that make and keep them poor. He believes, however, that economic problems set off the chain of events that increased poverty and social problems in central cities.

Wilson's theory has attracted opposition on two points. First, some scholars condemn Wilson, a black scholar, because he places no emphasis on racial discrimination as a cause of ghetto poverty. Wilson, in fact, believes that racism plays a declining role in black poverty (Wilson, 1980). Other scholars have argued that racism is the primary reason for the increasing marginalization of black males (Massey, 1990; Darity and Myers, 1983). Second, other scholars fault Wilson for not crediting welfare with making any real contribution to ghetto poverty. Scholars such as Mead, Murray, and Payne, of course, believe that welfare played a pivotal role. Mead (Wilson and Mead, 1987) criticizes Wilson's theory by pointing out that low-skill immigrants have a history of maintaining high employment levels, often doing so despite language barriers. Mead believes that immigrants sustain high employment levels because they were not raised in welfare families. Blacks, on the other hand, Mead says, often grew up in or around welfare families and are, therefore, more willing to turn to welfare rather than accept low-paying jobs that they consider unpleasant, demeaning, or unrewarding or obtain the education or job skills required for better employment.

Mickey Kaus in *The End of Equality* ([1992] 1995) takes a somewhat different position. Kaus argues that welfare might not be the actual cause of poverty, but that it is the welfare system that sustains it. Kaus raises the question of why ghetto blacks did not follow low-skill jobs as they moved to the suburbs. Wilson's answer is that for many ghetto residents the jobs, once increased transportation and housing costs were factored in, do not pay enough to make them feasible. Kaus finds that answer suspect. He notes that blacks left the South in large numbers and traveled long distances in search of employment opportunities, but they often failed to follow jobs as they moved to the suburbs. Why, asks Kaus, did they travel a thousand miles to seek improved economic opportunities but fail to follow jobs that were 25 miles away? His answer is welfare. Blacks migrated from the south, he says, because they had no choice. The welfare system did not exist and was not an option. However, when urban jobs migrated to the suburbs, black citizens often had an option. Rather than follow the jobs, they could qualify for welfare and become idle. And, that, Kaus says, is exactly what many of them did.

There is empirical evidence to support some of Wilson's hypotheses. Considerable research supports Wilson's skills-mismatch and spatial mismatch hypotheses. Kasarda (1988, 1989, 1990) and Johnson and Oliver (1991) have documented the recent loss of decent paying manufacturing jobs to the suburbs, especially in the major cities of the Northeast and North-Central regions. Holzer (1991) found that when jobs left the central cities for the suburbs, blacks lost more jobs and employment opportunities than did whites or suburban blacks. Research also documents a general decline in the wages of low-income workers. Since the mid-1970s wage increases have primarily taken place only in jobs that require higher levels of skill and education.

The empirical literature provides no support for Wilson's hypothesis that lack of economic opportunity explains the declining black marriage rate (Wilson and Neckerman, 1986). The marriage rate for blacks has been declining at least since the 1950s, seems to be little impacted by fluctuating black male employment levels, or the skill-level, education, or income of black males (Ellwood and Crane, 1990; Lerman, 1989; Hoffman, Duncan, and Mincy, 1991). As we will note below, Cornel West has a completely different explanation for the decline in black marriage rates.

Wilson's out-migration hypothesis is generally supported by empirical research (Gramlich and Laren, 1991). Wilson's contagion hypothesis has not been rigorously tested, but there is some evidence in support. Jencks and Mayer (1990) found that peers significantly effect academic achievement. Students perform better when they attend schools with peers who take education seriously and perform at higher levels. Hoffman, Duncan, and Mincy (1991) found that the higher the proportion of single welfare mothers in a neighborhood, the higher the rate of teenage pregnancy. Anderson (1990), Jarret (1990), and Fagan (1992), all found that young ghetto men turn to hustling when good jobs are unavailable.

In summary, much of Wilson's theory is supported by empirical and ethnographic research, although the role that welfare and racism do, or do not play, is seriously contested, and there is little support for the marriage hypothesis.

Culture as Structure

Another prominent black scholar offers a structural theory of black poverty, which includes some of the fundamentals of Wilson's theory.

Wilson basically believes that black poverty stems from economic problems, and he believes that economic reform would go a long way toward reducing the poverty and social problems of the ghetto. But Cornel West in his book *Race Matters* (1993) argues that while there is an economic antecedent, the problems of the black population are more complex than Wilson imagines. West agrees with Wilson that many black people, especially those who live in central city ghettos, engage in self-destructive behavior. But West argues that this dysfunctional behavior has complicated antecedents, reflecting problems not just of the economy, but also of America's culture, and, thus, cannot be reversed simply by economic reform.

West attributes the poverty and social problems of poor blacks to four factors:

- First, the economic decline that has taken place within the inner cities of America and the change in compensation for low-skilled jobs. His analysis of economic problems that have harmed the black population is very similar to Wilson's.
- Second, a history of racism along with continuing discrimination that West believes has done great emotional harm to millions of black people.
- Third, a prevailing American culture that stresses materialism and material gain to the exclusion of other, more important values, especially intellectual, moral, and spiritual growth. Materialism, West argues, is such a dominant value in American society that it is the core of American culture. As such, says West, it should be admitted that this perverse culture is a form of structure, much like the economy and the political system (12). When mainstream culture is so shallow that it reflects primarily market moralities, he argues, it misdirects and teaches low value, thus keeping people from becoming fully developed, successful humans with culture and meaningful values.
- Fourth, a lack of quality black leadership. West is extremely critical of black leadership, arguing that most black leaders are unprepared to transcend narrow racial issues, be examples of moral and spiritual growth, and lead with real vision and courage (23).

West believes that the combination of base cultural values, racism (past and present), economic problems, and poor leadership has produced battered identities in much of black America. These battered identities express themselves in two ways. First, West contends, many black people suffer from nihilism, a disease of the soul that manifests itself by producing lives of "horrifying meaninglessness, hopelessness, and (most important) lovelessness (14) . . . Life without meaning, hope, and love," West concludes, "breeds a cold-hearted, mean-spirited outlook that destroys both the individual and others" (14–15). Second, is racial reasoning. Racial reasoning, West says, is not moral reasoning. "The humanity of black people," says West, "does not rest on deifying or demonizing others" (28). Racial reasoning leads to a closing-ranks mentality that takes the form of inchoate xenophobia (poorly thought out fears and dislikes about foreigners), systematic sexism (which West says contributes significantly to the declining black marriage rate), and homophobia.

West believes that racial reasoning must be replaced with moral reasoning, which would produce mature black identities, coalition strategies that cross race lines, and black cultural democracy. Mature blacks could be honest about themselves and other black people, would be willing to work with other groups to achieve collective goals, and would promote a society in which black people treated everyone with respect, regardless of race, ethnicity, sex, or sexual orientation.

West's recommended solutions go beyond reducing black poverty, and they can be summarized in four parts. First, West believes that black people need a love ethic that would confront the self-destructive and inhumane actions of black people. Second, black people, he says, must also understand that the best source of help, hope, and power is themselves. The combined power of mature blacks must be focused on the public square. Black people, in other words, must participate in the debate, shaping, and passage of enlightened public policies design to advance good values and stable, prosperous families. Third, government programs to aid low-income and poor people must be increased. And last, there needs to be a new generation of black leadership with genuine vision and courage and a commitment to uphold ethical and religious ideas.

West's theory is provocative and challenging. He is basically arguing that just improving the economic opportunities will not solve the fundamental problems of millions of black people. He believes that millions of poor blacks suffer from battered identities, destructive reasoning, perverse cultural values, and inadequate black leadership. Solving the problems of many poor blacks, he argues, requires an alteration in the basic values of our culture, along with enlightened public policies and better leadership.

Tobin's Structural Theory of Poverty

The economist James Tobin (1994) offers another structural theory, one much more purely economic in nature. Tobin's theory rests first on his empirical research on the relationship between the yearly rate of poverty in America and the health of the economy. Tobin finds that in those years in which there have been real (inflation adjusted) increases in wages and reductions in unemployment, poverty has declined (148). The performance of the economy, in other words, is important. Tobin's findings are consistent with those of a considerable body of research (Bartik, 1991; Blank, 1997; Cutler and Katz, 1991; Fitzgerald, 1995; Harris, 1993; Hoynes, 1996; Moffit, 1992). However, as Tobin documents, between 1973 and the early 1990s the economy often performed less well, and poverty rates were less responsive during those periods when the economy prospered (149).

Tobin believes that there are five reasons for the decreased impact of economic performance on poverty rates:

1. An expanding proportion of the population is excluded from the more viable sectors of the market economy because they do not have the increasingly sophisticated skills required by employers (161).
2. Jobs, especially good-paying low-skill jobs, are increasingly located outside the central cities (160).
3. Wage rates have been held down because corporations can export jobs to low-wage markets in other nations and because corporations must spend more on fringe benefits. Tobin points out that corporations think about labor costs in terms of the total expense, rather than just in terms of wages. As the cost of fringe benefits (especially health care) have increased, employers have tried to hold down wages to cover some of the increasing expense of fringes. However, fringes, says

Tobin, go mostly to better-paid workers. The lowest-paid workers often do not benefit from fringes, but their wages still suffer.

4. The welfare population has changed over time, being increasingly composed of female heads of households and poorly educated unattached males, with both groups less willing or able to take advantage of economic opportunities (155).

5. The Federal Reserve has allowed the economy to grow too slowly (164).

Tobin believes that the Federal Reserve's fiscal policies have been too conservative, overregulating the growth of the economy. Tobin argues that fundamental changes have taken place in the economy that allow faster growth without setting off inflation. The major changes Tobin sees are the increasing globalization and deregulation of the economy. Globalization increases available labor and product markets. The increase in labor pools and products reduces the chances of product or labor shortages that tend to set off inflation. Since consumers have access to more markets for goods, there is less chance of consumption producing shortages and thus inflation. Global markets also hold down prices by restraining labor costs and labor demands because employers have options in other nations. Deregulation lowers business costs while allowing companies to be more creative, reducing costs and improving productivity.

Tobin believes that these changes allow the economy to grow faster than in the past, without setting off inflation. He recommends that the Federal Reserve consent to the economy growing at a rate of about 3 to 3.5 percent a year, one percentage point higher than in the past. If the economy were allowed to grow faster, Tobin says, more jobs would be created, employees would pay their employees better because they would be making better profits and labor markets would be tighter, and companies would be more willing to invest in their employees by giving them more training and more opportunities.

The economic history of the United States in the 1990s would seem to bear out Tobin's arguments. The economy has grown faster than the Federal Reserve intended without setting off inflation. Additionally, in the last few years, a healthy economy has reduced the poverty rate, dropping the black poverty rate below 30 percent for the first time in American history.

Tobin's theory is about as pure as structural theories ever are, but even his theory recognizes that some poor people do not take advantage of opportunities as they become available and that other poor people need considerable help to get into and stay in the job market.

What Do These Theories Tell Us About Poverty and Welfare Reform?

What insights do we gain from this review of theories? There are several and they are important. First, poverty is not a single problem; it is a series of rather complex problems. There are both cultural/behavioral and structural/economic causes of poverty, which vary by the subgroups of people found among the poor. Culture and structure are also connected. Opportunities influence culture, which influences behavior, which influences opportunity, which influences culture, ad infinitum.

Even when the same set of factors cause poverty, the problem of poverty varies because of the differential reactions of those who become poor. Some single mothers, for example, might seize the chance to obtain job training, and transitional health and child care to allow them to enter the workforce, while others may use every excuse possible to avoid accepting responsibility for themselves. Therefore, both variations in causes and reactions to poverty make the problem complex.

Second, the economy is important. The economy must be kept healthy and growing to provide quality opportunities for low-income and poor people. Third, many families cannot take advantage of economic opportunities without a better education or advanced job training. Fourth, similarly, many of today's poor people, especially parents, cannot work without child care and healthcare assistance. Fifth, some people will need extra help, encouragement, even sanction, to make the transition to employment. These people will need not only education and skill training, but also help with interpersonal skills, self-esteem, hope, and confidence before they believe in themselves enough and interact with others well enough to benefit from assistance and become self-sufficient. Some people will need help more than once. When they fail, they will need a second or even third push to get on their feet. Some people will need assistance in overcoming alcohol and drug dependency problems before they can be helped into the job market.

Sixth, discrimination based on sex, race, or ethnicity cannot be tolerated. Assistance programs and the employment market must be free of bias. Last, poverty, especially among the elderly, would be greatly reduced if the government sponsored more programs designed to help people save during their employment years.

5

The American Welfare System

Of all the major Western industrial nations, the United States has always been the most conservative about social welfare policy. America's welfare programs are the most recent in origin and the most limited in design, coverage, and cost among the major Western powers (OECD, 1976; Smeeding, 1992a, 1992b; Wilensky, 1975, 11). Despite their comparative modesty, American welfare programs rest on tentative public support (Feagin, 1975; Shapiro, Patterson, Russell, and Young, 1987). The American public philosophy stresses freedom over equality (Bobo and Smith, 1994). Americans believe that everyone should be given an opportunity to succeed, that opportunity in America is bountiful if not always equal, and that failure generally reflects personal shortcomings. While public surveys show that Americans are generally sympathetic toward the poor, they are not comfortable with welfare programs. The public fears that welfare programs are wasteful and that they reward, support, and encourage indolence and even immoral behavior (Bobo and Smith, 1994). Thus, for the most part, the public supports giving assistance only to those who cannot be expected to support themselves, along with temporary assistance to help the able-bodied become established in the workforce. This philosophy has shaped the establishment and evolution of the American welfare system.

The Historical Context

Decades after the other major western industrial nations had begun developing welfare programs, the United States established its first very limited and modest programs in response to the Great Depression, which began in 1929 (Katz, 1986; Piven and Cloward, 1971). The economic collapse brought about by the depression was so massive that by 1933 one-fourth of the nation's adult men were unemployed, millions of families were losing their homes, and thousands stood in bread lines each day. Millions of those who suffered from the economic crisis had formerly been solid members of America's middle class (Rodgers, 1979, 43–72).

When Franklin D. Roosevelt (FDR) became president in 1933, he was ambivalent about using public funds to directly assist those individuals devastated by the economic crisis. Still, under the Federal Emergency Relief Administration, President Roosevelt sent billions of dollars to the states to help them aid their citizens. The states handed out most of this money in the form of cash assistance and public service jobs, many of which were considered "make-work." Roosevelt, however, became alarmed when the relief rolls continued to grow. In 1935 some 20 million Americans were receiving assistance. In his State of the Union address in 1935, Roosevelt warned Congress that relief undermined the character of the public:

> . . . dependence upon relief induces a spiritual and moral disintegration fundamentally destructive to the national fiber. To dole out relief in this way is to administer a narcotic, a subtle destroyer of the human spirit. . . . I am not willing that the vitality of our people be further sapped by the giving of cash, of market baskets, of a few hours of weekly work cutting grass, raking leaves, or picking up papers in the public parks. We must preserve not only the bodies of the unemployed from destitution but also their self-respect, their self-reliance and courage and determination (Roosevelt, 1935).

Rather than direct relief, Roosevelt convinced Congress to pass the Works Progress Administration (WPA), a program designed to employ over 3 million people in jobs such as housing and highway construction, slum clearance, and rural electrification. The able-bodied would be hired in these jobs, while those unable to work would continue to receive relief.

The WPA provided jobs to millions of needy citizens, but most of the able-bodied unemployed still could not find work. It has been estimated that the WPA provided jobs to only one in four applicants and that some 8 million able-bodied males could not find any type of work (Piven and Cloward, 1971, 98). Those millions who could not find work, along with the aged, the handicapped, and orphans, turned to state and local governments for assistance. Many states, however, could not handle the burden. Some cut the size of grants so more of the needy will receive some assistance; others abolished all assistance. New Jersey offered the indigent licenses to beg (Piven and Cloward, 1971, 109).

The Social Security Act of 1935

The continuing hardship spawned increasing criticism of the Roosevelt administration. Under these pressures, FDR launched what historians refer to as the "second New Deal." This New Deal had three primary thrusts: first, the government would use Keynesian economics to stimulate and, it was hoped, moderate economic cycles; second, assistance to business was increased in hope of promoting an economic recovery; third, to assist many of those who continued to be impoverished by the depression, FDR proposed and Congress passed the Social Security Act of 1935, establishing assistance programs for those who were outside the labor force.

The Social Security Act consisted of five major titles:

- Title I provided grants to the states for assistance to the aged.
- Title II established the Social Security system.
- Title III provided grants to the states for the administration of unemployment compensation.
- Title IV established the Aid to Dependent Children (ADC) program.
- Title V provided grants to the states for aid to the blind and disabled.

The Social Security Act created a new role for the federal government, which, at the time, was quite radical. The federal government had subsidized state and local assistance programs in the past, but this was the first time that assistant programs had been established that would be run by the federal government (Social Security) or in partnership with the states (ADC).

As fundamental a departure as the Social Security Act was, its benefits were originally quite modest. Grants under Social Security were extended only to those who worked in certain occupations and industries, and payments were delayed until 1942. It was not until 1950 that half the retired population received any benefits under the program. ADC was sold as a program for widows and their dependent children, and until 1950 only orphans and poor children received assistance. In 1950 the program was changed to Aid to Families with Dependent Children (AFDC), allowing benefits to one parent (normally the mother) in a family with eligible children.

With the passage of the Social Security Act of 1935, the United States became the last of the major industrial nations to establish a national welfare system—one that by European standards was quite modest. Three features of the act reflected American reservations about welfare, especially to the able-bodied, and had long-term consequences for U.S. social welfare programs. First, benefits under the various Social Security titles were designed for only a select category of the needy rather than all the poor. Even as social welfare programs expanded greatly in the 1960s and 1970s, they continued to be categorical rather than universal, as they are in many other nations.

Second, some of the Social Security titles allowed the states to determine who would receive assistance and how much they would receive. This meant that needy citizens would be treated very differently, depending upon the state in which they lived. As AFDC expanded to become the nation's primary cash assistance program for the non-aged poor, this feature remained. Variations in state coverage and benefits to their poor were huge under AFDC, with some states providing much more generous assistance than others. Titles I and V also allowed a great deal of local autonomy in funding assistance to the aged and the blind.

Last, the Social Security Act did not include health insurance. By 1935 most other western industrial nations already had health insurance programs. Roosevelt considered including health insurance in the Social Security Act but eliminated it because opposition from the

American Medical Association and southern members of Congress was so intense.

State control over the benefit levels under Titles I, II, IV, and V of the Social Security Act substantially limited growth in these programs through the 1950s. By 1960 only 787,000 families (1.7 percent of all families) were receiving benefits under AFDC, and only 144,000 blind and disabled citizens were receiving assistance under Title V. Thus, by 1960, twenty-five years after the original act, U.S. welfare programs were still extremely modest, and, as events would prove, poverty was severe.

The Civil Rights Movement

Just as the Great Depression had served as the necessary catalyst for the establishment of the nation's first major social welfare programs, the civil rights movement and the ghetto riots of the 1960s served as the stimulus for the next substantial expansion of the welfare state. The civil rights movement, which matured in the late 1950s and the early 1960s, focused attention on the economic conditions of millions of U.S. citizens. Civil rights workers often charged that many U.S. citizens of all races were ill-housed, ill-clothed, medically neglected, malnourished, and even suffering from hunger. Most of the nation's public leaders simply dismissed the latter charge, but slowly the evidence of acute poverty, malnutrition, and poverty-related diseases began to be documented (Rodgers, 1996, 72–73).

In 1967 the Senate Subcommittee on Employment, Manpower, and Poverty held hearings on U.S. poverty. The testimony of many civil rights leaders contained graphic allegations of acute poverty and hunger in the South. Again, these charges were largely dismissed, but the testimony convinced two liberal members of the subcommittee—Robert Kennedy (D, NY) and Joseph Clark (D, PA)—personally to tour the Mississippi Delta. The tour turned into a major media event that documented severe hunger and malnutrition among Mississippi's poor.

The subcommittee's initial investigation also encouraged the Field Foundation to send a team of doctors to Mississippi to investigate the health of children in Head Start programs. The team issued a report documenting extensive poverty, poverty-related diseases, and malnutrition among the children and their families (Kotz, 1971, 8–9; Kotz, 1979).

The most publicized documentation of severe poverty was yet to come. In the mid-1960s the Field Foundation and the Citizen's Crusade against Poverty joined to establish the Citizen's Board of Inquiry into Hunger and Malnutrition in the United States. After hundreds of on-site investigations and hearings, the Citizen's Board reported its findings in late 1967 and 1968. The findings confirmed the worst suspicions of welfare reform advocates. Investigators had discovered, within the larger population of the United States, a population that might best be described as an underdeveloped nation. They reported "concrete evidence of chronic hunger and malnutrition in every part of the United States where we have held hearings or conducted field trips" (Citizen's Board of Inquiry, 1968, iv).

These widely-publicized findings contributed powerfully to pressures on Congress for improvements in and expansion of welfare programs. As leaders of the civil rights movement lobbied for assistance for the poor, their arguments were bolstered by the outbreak of hundreds of riots in U.S. cities between 1965 and 1969 (Downes, 1968). The nation was divided as to the causes of the riots (Hahn and Feagin, 1970), but a national commission identified the source as pervasive racism against black Americans (Kerner Commission). Congress concluded that both new civil rights laws and expanded social welfare programs were needed. Thus, with the cities on fire and media attention focused on the struggles of the black population and the poverty of millions of U.S. citizens, Congress passed major civil rights acts in 1964, 1965, and 1968. Congress also expanded existing welfare programs and created new ones. The changes included:

1. In 1961 the AFDC program was amended to allow states to provide support to families where both parents were unemployed (less than half the states adopted this option).
2. The food stamp program was formally established in 1964 (initially only twenty-two states opted to participate).
3. The Medicare and Medicaid programs were enacted in 1965.
4. Congress adopted national standards for the food stamp program in 1971, which were extended to all states in 1974.
5. The Supplemental Security Income Act (SSI) was passed in 1972, effective in 1974.

The 1960s and early 1970s, then, saw the second significant installment in the development of American social welfare programs. Still, American welfare programs retained much of the initial design imposed by the Social Security Act of 1935. Assistance remained categorical, and only some of the poor qualified for most of the assistance (Moynihan, 1992). Those who did qualify were primarily single mothers and their children, the aged, and the handicapped. AFDC benefits varied greatly by state, and Medicaid benefits were tied to welfare. If a welfare mother left the rolls for a job, her family lost Medicaid coverage and often other critical support.

Ironically, in supporting expansion of the welfare system, President Lyndon Johnson campaigned for a system that reflected the Roosevelt philosophy. Johnson distrusted the dole* and wanted to help the poor become independent through work. Johnson's proposals focused on job training, education, legal aid, and community action (Lemann, 1991, 164–169; Moynihan, 1970; Patterson, 1986, 138–141). The theme of his "War on Poverty" was a "hand up, not a hand out." In signing the "War on Poverty" legislation in 1964, President Johnson announced that "the days of the dole in this country are numbered"(Lemann, 1991, 149).

But, as we will see below, for over three decades welfare moved in exactly the direction that Roosevelt, Johnson, and other presidents decried. Welfare became a huge program that supported millions of families headed by single mothers who were unattached to the work force. There are several reasons why welfare moved in this unintended direction. First, was the unexpected explosion in the growth of single-parent families, largely the result of unprecedented rates of out-of-wedlock births and increasingly high rates of divorce (Moynihan, 1992). Second, since the expectation was that the programs would serve only a rather small number of mother-only families, little emphasis was placed on job training or support services to help single mothers leave welfare and become established in the workforce. In fact, the main cash welfare program, AFDC, discouraged work by linking critical services such as health care with welfare. Third, welfare became a method of assisting many minorities who had been victims of racism. Welfare became an extension of civil rights, a

---

*"The dole" is welfare, from the phrase "doling out money to the poor."

method of compensating and aiding people who had been mistreated. Fourth, when the welfare rolls grew to unexpected levels, public officials realized that, at least in the short run, moving welfare recipients into the job market would be quite expensive. Welfare recipients would often need education, job training, child care, health care, and many others expensive services to make the transition. Until the cost of Medicaid became extremely expensive in the mid-1980s and 1990s for both the states and the federal government, it seemed cheaper to just leave most welfare recipients at home and on the dole. But, by the mid-1980s, the size and costs of the welfare system forced Congress and the executive branch to rethink the nation's antipoverty programs.

Trends in Welfare Program Growth, Use, and Spending

The welfare system that evolved from the Social Security Act of 1935 is extremely complex and expensive. In fiscal year 1996 the Congressional Research Service (CRS) identified seventy-eight programs that provide means-tested cash and in-kind assistance to low-income citizens (Burke, 1998; Tin, 1996). The rest of this chapter will provide an overview of these programs, an analysis of their costs at both the federal and state levels since the late 1960s, and an in-depth description and critique of some of the major programs that serve the poor (see Table 5.7).

Table 5.1 shows that the seventy-eight income-tested programs identified by the CRS cost $367,711 billion in fiscal 1996, $261,311 in federal funds and $106,401 in state dollars. Federal expenditures accounted for 71 percent of the total cost, and were 16.7 percent of the total federal budget in fiscal 1994 (Green Book, 1998, 1413). Expenditures in fiscal 1994 were twenty-three times as great as in 1968. Controlling for inflation, expenditures increased by about 400 percent over the twenty-eight-year period shown in Table 5.1, a period in which the U.S. population increased by 32 percent (Green Book, 1998, 1414). Per capita welfare spending grew in constant 1996 dollars from $367 in fiscal 1969 to $1,434 in fiscal 1995. In 1996 spending declined to $1,386 (Green Book, 1998, 1416). The total cost of the programs between 1968 and 1996 exceeded $5 trillion dollars (in 1996 dollars).

The most expensive programs are those that provide medical services. In fiscal 1996, medical programs accounted for 48.3 percent of

Table 5.1

Expenditures for Income-Tested Benefits, 1968–1996
(millions dollars)

Fiscal year	Federal	State/Local	Total spending current dollars	Constant 1996 dollars
1968	$ 11,406	$ 4,710	$ 16,116	$ 73,755
1973	26,876	10,054	36,930	134,259
1975	39,461	14,753	54,214	162,851
1976	49,954	16,990	66,944	187,684
1977	55,113	18,892	74,005	192,884
1978	63,964	20,151	84,115	204,824
1979	70,172	21,304	91,476	202,183
1980	89,043	24,633	104,676	203,595
1981	87,936	29,045	116,981	204,752
1982	88,977	31,706	120,683	196,834
1983	93,830	33,982	127,812	201,291
1984	99,151	36,191	135,342	204,651
1985	105,064	38,230	143,294	209,161
1986	107,775	40,811	148,586	211,527
1987	114,789	43,364	158,153	218,938
1988	125,047	46,580	171,627	228,247
1989	134,715	51,587	186,302	236,454
1990	151,478	61,064	212,542	256,965
1991	177,899	73,943	251,842	289,845
1992	208,211	88,130	296,341	331,016
1993	223,528	88,736	312,264	338,594
1994	246,302	102,396	348,698	368,346
1995	258,382	108,212	366,594	376,763
1996	261,311	106,401	367,712	367,711

Source: Burke,V. 1997. Cash and noncash benefits for persons with limited income: Eligibility rules, recipient and expenditure data, fiscal years 1994–1996 (98–226 EPW). Congressional Research Service. Green Book, 1998, Table K-1.

all outlays, while aid in the form of cash, food, housing, and energy represented 46 percent of the total. Education and job programs were less than 6 percent. Medical services were almost 70 percent of state–local expenditures, and almost 40 percent of federal costs. Cash benefits were the most expensive programs at the federal level until 1980, when medical expenses became predominant.

Table 5.2 breaks down federal and state–local spending for income-tested programs by program type. In 1996 inflation-adjusted dollars, federal expenditures increased by 401 percent between fiscal 1968 and

Table 5.2

Federal and State-Local Spending for Income-Tested Benefits, 1968–1996 (millions of constant 1996 dollars)

Fiscal year	Medical benefits	Cash aid	Food benefits	Housing benefits	Education benefits	Jobs/ training	Services/ other	Energy aid	Total
Federal spending									
1968	$ 12,544	$23,052	$ 4,087	$ 3,583	$ 3,936	$ 3,245	$ 1,753	$0	$ 52,200
1973	24,209	31,174	14,015	12,208	6,620	3,356	6,126	0	97,708
1975	28,792	38,266	19,342	13,019	6,548	6,455	6,113	0	118,535
1976	30,685	41,833	21,653	14,887	10,356	12,913	7,634	$79	140,051
1977	34,352	40,912	20,215	15,742	9,062	14,134	8,439	787	143,644
1978	35,469	39,075	20,720	17,876	9,903	23,620	8,428	665	155,756
1979	36,272	37,424	22,936	18,696	10,633	20,480	8,074	581	155,096
1980	37,731	36,912	25,458	18,684	9,511	16,776	7,265	3,347	155,684
1981	38,949	36,686	27,460	19,007	8,379	13,155	6,761	3,516	153,914
1982	37,578	35,189	25,564	19,218	12,697	6,506	5,061	3,308	145,121
1983	37,127	35,279	28,499	19,653	11,690	7,098	5,203	3,222	147,773
1984	37,567	35,962	28,300	19,408	12,113	8,131	5,200	3,245	149,926
1985	40,695	35,741	28,262	20,600	13,890	5,685	5,183	3,300	153,358
1986	42,386	37,481	27,251	18,884	14,314	5,162	4,826	3,125	153,428
1987	48,588	38,013	27,539	18,289	13,522	5,236	4,993	2,729	158,907
1988	51,345	40,315	26,885	19,551	14,824	4,984	5,970	2,426	166,300
1989	53,805	42,090	26,444	20,212	15,845	4,842	5,675	2,068	170,980
1990	60,680	44,062	28,860	21,216	16,637	4,806	4,938	1,939	183,138
1991	71,813	48,651	32,231	21,822	17,106	5,051	5,992	2,079	204,744
1992	87,817	54,416	36,648	24,487	15,194	5,605	6,524	1,882	232,574
1993	92,151	57,848	37,704	25,975	15,520	5,173	6,341	1,663	242,376
1994	98,891	66,969	38,142	25,506	15,462	5,135	8,051	2,025	260,181
1995	104,149	69,807	37,818	25,640	15,557	4,754	6,179	1,645	265,550
1996	103,568	69,637	37,116	25,096	15,320	3,955	5,452	1,167	261,311

State and local spending

Year	State and local spending								Total
1968	$ 9,432	$11,395	0	0	0	$197	$531	0	$21,555
1973	15,142	19,257	0	0	0	204	1,949	0	36,551
1975	19,859	20,279	$1,679	0	$430	117	1,953	0	44,316
1976	21,879	21,504	1,775	0	437	109	1,929	0	47,633
1977	23,168	21,307	2,119	0	482	149	2,015	0	49,239
1978	23,769	20,459	2,126	0	577	153	1,985	0	49,069
1979	24,613	18,951	873	0	555	172	1,923	0	47,087
1980	25,674	18,956	889	0	556	158	1,679	0	47,911
1981	27,357	19,248	1,015	0	511	147	2,559	0	50,837
1982	28,634	18,222	1,173	0	439	122	3,099	$24	51,712
1983	29,739	18,600	1,233	0	476	124	3,307	39	53,518
1984	31,045	18,730	1,436	0	457	118	2,873	65	54,724
1985	31,470	19,195	1,502	0	663	118	2,810	45	55,803
1986	32,840	20,104	1,570	0	705	104	2,705	71	58,099
1987	34,064	20,516	1,616	0	707	98	2,741	288	60,031
1988	36,113	20,471	1,515	0	723	96	2,793	235	61,947
1989	39,363	20,928	1,475	0	692	123	2,665	228	65,474
1990	44,244	21,532	1,493	0	760	323	5,324	150	73,827
1991	54,621	22,271	1,510	0	630	505	5,435	130	85,101
1992	63,846	23,577	1,612	$2,569	686	532	5,522	98	98,442
1993	62,896	23,260	1,698	1,442	831	609	5,405	77	96,218
1994	71,545	24,214	1,881	1,706	954	691	7,105	81	108,166
1995	75,249	24,332	1,881	2,389	981	833	5,464	83	111,214
1996	74,007	22,036	1,921	2,113	955	612	4,684	73	106,401

Source: Burke, V. 1997. Cash and noncash benefits for persons with limited income: Eligibility rules, recipient and expenditure data, fiscal years 1994–1996 (98–226 EPW). Congressional Research Service. Green Book, 1998, Table K-2.

Table 5.3

Share of Federal Budget Used for Income-Tested Aid, Selected Years
(in percent)

Fiscal year	Medical aid	Cash aid	Food aid	Housing aid	Education aid	Jobs/ training	Energy	Services
1968	1.54	2.83	0.50	0.44	0.48	0.48	0.00	0.22
1973	2.71	3.49	1.57	1.37	0.74	0.38	0.00	0.69
1978	3.18	3.50	1.85	1.60	0.89	2.11	0.06	0.75
1983	2.92	2.77	2.24	1.54	0.92	0.56	0.25	0.41
1988	3.63	2.85	1.90	1.38	1.05	0.35	0.17	0.42
1990	4.00	2.91	1.90	1.40	1.10	0.32	0.13	0.33
1991	4.71	3.19	2.12	1.43	1.12	0.33	0.14	0.39
1992	5.69	3.53	2.37	1.59	0.98	0.36	0.12	0.42
1993	6.03	3.79	2.47	1.70	1.02	0.34	0.11	0.41
1994	6.40	4.34	2.47	1.65	1.00	0.33	0.13	0.52
1995	6.69	4.48	2.43	1.65	1.00	0.31	0.11	0.40
1996	6.64	4.46	2.38	1.61	0.98	0.25	0.07	0.35

Source: Burke, V. 1997. Cash and noncash benefits for persons with limited income: eligibility rules, recipient and expenditure data, fiscal years 1995–1996 (98–226 EPW). Congressional Research Service. Green Book, 1998, Table K-3.

Note: In fiscal year 1978, jobs and training benefit outlays were $9.7 billion of this total; $5.8 billion, employment and training services.

fiscal 1996. Between 1983 and 1995 federal spending increased ever year but declined by 1.6 percent in fiscal 1996. Between 1968 and 1996 state-local spending increased by 392 percent (1996 dollars). Between 1983 and 1996, state-local expenditures almost doubled, with 80 percent of the new dollars going to medical services.

Table 5.3 shows the share of the total federal budget expended on various types of income-tested programs between 1968 and 1996. In 1968 income-tested programs constituted 6.4 percent of all federal expenditures. By 1995 these costs had climbed to 17.1 percent of the total budget, declining to 16.8 percent in 1996. Much of the overall increase in costs (5.1 percent of the 10.4 percent increase) was accounted for by mounting costs for medical services. In 1968 medical programs accounted for only 1.54 percent of the total federal budget. By 1996 they were 6.64 percent of the federal budget. Cash assistance also increased substantially in costs, driven by increases in the percentage of all families receiving cash assistance, and the introduction and growth of both the Supplemental Security Income (SSI) program and the Earned Income Tax Credit (EITC). Food assistance also increased as a percentage of the federal budget while housing aid was fairly stagnant after the early 1970s, as was aid to education. Expenditures for job training declined.

The cost of income-tested programs, then, increased very substantially over the last thirty years. As a percentage of both federal and state–local budgets, means-tested programs expanded greatly. But, as we will see below, the poverty rate often increased during periods in which programs and welfare use were expanding and expenditures were escalating.

Welfare Rolls

Table 5.4 shows the number of recipients of the nation's major cash welfare program for the non-aged between 1960 and September 1998. As national attention was focused on civil rights issues and hunger in the 1960s, the AFDC rolls grew substantially. Growth continued in the early 1970s, exceeding 5 percent of the population between 1972 and 1977. The rolls declined somewhat after 1978, but averaged 4.6 percent until 1991. Five percent of the population received means-tested cash assistance in 1991, and the rate remained above 5 percent until 1996. With the debate and passage of the Personal Responsibility

Table 5.4

Recipients of AFDC/TANF, 1960–1998

Year	Recipients	Percent of population	Poverty rate	Percent of poor receiving cash
1960	3,005,000	1.7	22.2	7.5
1961	3,354,000	1.8	21.9	8.5
1962	3,676,000	2.0	21.0	9.5
1963	3,876,000	2.0	19.5	10.6
1964	4,118,000	2.1	19.0	11.4
1965	4,329,000	2.2	17.3	13.0
1966	4,513,000	2.3	14.7	15.8
1967	5,014,000	2.5	14.2	18.0
1968	5,705,000	2.8	12.8	22.4
1969	6,706,000	3.3	12.1	27.8
1970	8,466,000	4.1	12.6	33.3
1971	10,241,000	4.9	12.5	40.1
1972	10,947,000	5.2	11.9	44.7
1973	10,949,000	5.2	11.1	47.7
1974	10,864,000	5.1	11.2	46.5
1975	11,165,185	5.2	12.3	43.1
1976	11,386,371	5.2	11.8	45.6
1977	11,129,702	5.1	11.6	45.0
1978	10,671,812	4.8	11.4	43.6
1979	10,317,902	4.6	11.7	39.6
1980	10,597,445	4.7	13.0	36.2
1981	11,159,847	4.9	14.0	35.1
1982	10,430,960	4.5	15.0	30.3
1983	10,659,365	4.5	15.2	30.2
1984	10,865,604	4.6	14.4	32.2
1985	10,812,625	4.5	14.0	32.7
1986	10,996,505	4.6	13.6	34.0
1987	11,065,027	4.6	13.4	34.3
1988	10,919,696	4.5	13.0	34.4
1989	10,933,980	4.4	12.8	34.7
1990	11,460,382	4.6	13.5	34.1
1991	12,592,269	5.0	14.2	35.3
1992	13,625,342	5.3	14.8	35.8
1993	14,142,710	5.5	15.1	36.0
1994	14,225,591	5.5	14.5	37.4
1995	13,652,232	5.2	13.8	37.5
1996	12,648,859	4.7	13.7	34.6
1997	10,936,298	4.1	13.3	30.7
1998	7,613,000	2.8	12.7	22.0

Source: Enrollment data are from Health and Human Services web page: www.dhhs.gov.

Note: Figures for 1998 are for December.

and Work Opportunity Reconciliation Act (PRWORA) of 1996, welfare rolls began to decline. Between August 1996 and September 1998, the rolls dropped by 35 percent. In September 1998, only 2.9 percent of the population was receiving Temporary Assistance for Needy Families (TANF), the program that took the place of AFDC when the new reform bill was passed in August of 1996. In a very short period of time, the percentage of the population receiving assistance from the nation's major cash program had dropped back to the 1968 rate. In Chapter 7 we examine in more depth the causes and implications of this rapid decline.

Table 5.4 also shows the poverty rate and the percentage of all the poor receiving cash assistance by year. These data show the extent to which cash assistance is provided to only a subset of the poor. It was not until 1968 that slightly more than 20 percent of the poor received cash assistance. The percentage of the poor receiving cash welfare rose to 40.1 percent in 1971 and stayed above 40 percent until 1978. Since the late 1970s, less than one in four of the poverty population has received assistance from AFDC or TANF.

Table 5.5 provides a more comprehensive examination of welfare assistance in one year, 1997. The data show that a significant percentage of all American households receive at least one form of means-tested assistance. In 1997, 24.3 percent of all households received assistance that was income tested. However, only 8.6 percent of all households received cash assistance, and 8.7 percent received food stamps. Of those below the poverty level, 69.4 percent received some type of means-tested assistance. This means that slightly over 30 percent of those counted among the poor received no assistance. Only 34 percent of the poor received any type of cash assistance (TANF, General Assistance, SSI, etc.), and less than half received food stamps. A slight majority received Medicaid benefits, and only 19.2 percent received housing assistance.

Since American welfare programs are designed to serve only subsets of the poor, the rate of assistance varies significantly, depending upon family composition (Blank and Ruggles, 1996). Notice that female-headed households with related children under eighteen are the most likely to receive assistance. Over 89 percent receive some type of means-tested assistance in 1997. This is the only family type among the poor in which a slight majority received some type of cash assistance: 53.7 percent, and the only group in which over 60 percent

Table 5.5

Program Participation of Households by Poverty Status and Family Structure, 1997 (in percentages)

		Households that received			Households in which at least one person is covered by medicaid	Lived in public or subsidized housing
	means-tested assistance	means-tested assistance, excluding school lunches	means-tested cash assistance	food stamps		
All income levels	24.3	19.3	8.6	8.7	16.2	4.2
Below poverty level:						
Total	69.4	61.4	34.0	43.6	53.2	19.2
65 and over	43.8	43.0	21.4	19.7	32.7	15.8
In families	77.9	67.6	37.6	50.9	59.9	21.1
Related children under 18	85.3	73.8	42.5	58.2	66.4	24.5
In married-couple families	68.8	54.7	22.4	36.0	47.4	9.7
Related children under 18	79.5	61.8	25.3	42.5	54.7	11.3
In families with female householder, no spouse present	86.4	79.3	51.4	64.2	71.5	31.4
Related children under 18	89.2	81.6	53.7	68.2	74.2	33.4
Unrelated individuals	43.4	42.0	22.9	21.5	32.5	14.6

Source: Bureau of the Census, 1998. Unpublished Census Data. File D3–001.

receive food stamps. Interestingly, only about 74 percent of these households received Medicaid benefits, and only 33.4 percent received any assistance with housing.

Thus, a significant percentage of the poor receive no assistance, and among those who do receive aid, an even smaller percentage receives cash assistance or food stamps. Only about 23 percent of poor unrelated individuals (mostly single and elderly) along with about 25 percent of married-couple families with children living in poverty received cash assistance. Even among mother-only families with children living below the poverty level, only a slight majority received cash assistance.

Antipoverty Effectiveness of Means-Tested Programs

Until the reforms of 1996, American welfare programs were not designed to move most recipients out of poverty. Thus, the great majority of recipients of welfare continued to be poor. Table 5.6 shows the effectiveness of cash and noncash transfers in reducing poverty in selected years between 1979 and 1996. Table 5.6 includes social insurance (Social Security, Unemployment Compensation, and Workman's Compensation); three programs that are not means-tested. Social insurance is included to contrast its impact against that of means-tested programs. What the data show is that social insurance programs remove a large number of recipients from poverty each year. In the 1990s about 18 million people a year were moved over the poverty line by social insurance benefits. About 30 percent of all recipients of social insurance benefits are moved over the poverty line.

By contrast, means-tested cash programs (AFDC/TANF, SSI, and General Assistance) move less than 3 million recipients a year out of poverty. In percentage terms, only 5.1 percent of all recipients of means-tested cash assistance were lifted over the poverty line in 1996. Food and housing benefits lifted another 7.5 percent of recipients over the poverty line in 1996. And, as the Earned Income Tax Credit (EITC) has grown over time, it has increasingly played a role in moving recipients over the poverty line. In 1996 it elevated about 1.7 million recipients out of poverty. In 1996 the means-tested cash programs, food and housing programs, and the EITC combined removed some 9 million recipients over the poverty line. This is a nontrivial number, but a small percentage of all recipients.

Table 5.6

Antipoverty Effectiveness of Cash and Noncash Transfers, 1979–1996

Year	1979	1983	1987	1989	1993	1995	1996
Number of persons removed from poverty due to							
Social insurance	14,179	15,772	15,299	15,227	18,182	18,034	17,769
Means-tested cash	2,680	1,898	1,834	2,291	2,982	2,891	2,930
Food and housing benefits	4,378	3,333	3,542	3,892	4,500	4,720	4,278
EITC and federal payroll and income taxes	−669	−2,226	−1,396	−1,299	152	1,402	1,713
	20,568	18,777	19,279	20,111	25,816	27,047	26,690
Percent of persons removed from poverty due to							
Social insurance	33.1	29.9	30.8	31.0	30.1	31.4	31.0
Means-tested cash	6.3	3.6	3.7	4.7	4.9	5.0	5.1
Food and housing benefits	10.2	6.3	7.1	7.9	7.4	8.2	7.5
EITC and federal payroll and income taxes	−1.6	−4.2	−2.8	−2.6	0.3	2.4	3.0
	48.1	35.6	38.8	41.0	42.7	47.2	46.6

Source: Green Book, 1989. Table H-23, 1341.

Why do the very expensive income-tested programs play such a modest role in reducing poverty? First, for the most part, the programs are not designed to move people over the poverty line. When we examine the AFDC/TANF program below, we will see that none of the states set cash benefits at a level that would move families over the poverty line. In fact, in most of the states AFDC/TANF benefits are quite modest. Even adding the value of food stamps, the fungible value of health care benefits and housing does not add up to a package of benefits generous enough to push recipient families over the poverty line. This does not mean that the programs are not helpful. AFDC/TANF families receive much needed cash, food stamps clearly improve nutrition, and medical benefits certainly improve the health of recipients.

Still, by the early 1990s there was growing skepticism about the efficiency of welfare expenditures. The nation's governors, members of Congress, presidents, and much of the public was increasingly raised the question of whether or not welfare programs could be better designed to improve their antipoverty effectiveness. To better explain the context within which this debate took place, eventually resulting in the welfare reform act of 1996, an overview of the major welfare programs is provided below.

Major Welfare Programs

Table 5.7 provides a comprehensive overview of federal and state–local income-tested programs in fiscal 1996. There were 78 programs, with a total cost of almost $368 billion. The programs vary greatly in size, cost, and recipient base, and while all are of some importance, major welfare programs are a subset of the total. Below we discuss a handful of programs that constitute the core programs in the nation's struggle to deal with poverty.

Aid to Families with Dependent Children (AFDC)

From 1935 to 1996 Aid to Families with Dependent Children (AFDC) was the core cash-welfare program for poor families with children. In passing the Personal Responsibility and Work Opportunity Reconciliation Act (PRWORA) of 1996, Congress repealed AFDC and replaced it with Temporary Assistance to Needy Families (TANF). TANF is a

Table 5.7

**Income-Tested Programs, Federal and State-Local Costs:
Fiscal Year 1996** (in thousands of dollars)

Medical aid

Medicaid	$159,357
Medical care for veterans without service-connected disability	8,687
General assistance (medical care component)—no federal dollars	5,429
Indian Health Services	1,984
Maternal and child health services block grant	1,105
Community health centers	615
Title X family planning services	193
Medical assistance to refugees and Cuban/Haitian entrants	131
Migrant health centers	65

Cash aid

Supplemental Security Income (SSI)	$30,367
Aid to Families with Dependent Children (AFDC)	23,677
Earned Income Tax Credit (EITC)	21,566
Foster care	5,853
Emergency assistance for needy families with children	3,185
Pensions for needy veterans, their dependents, and survivors	3,086
General assistance (nonmedical care component)—no federal dollars	2,880
Adoption assistance	897
Cash assistance to refugees and Cuban/Haitian entrants	64
General assistance to Indians	61
Dependency and indemnity compensation (DIC) and death compensation for parents of veterans	37

Food aid

Food stamps	$27,344
School lunch program (free and reduced price segments)	4,784
Special supplemental nutrition program for women, infants, and children (WIC)	3,688
School breakfast program (free and reduced price segments)	1,088
Child and adult care food program	945
Nutrition program for the elderly	691
Summer food service program for children	258
Commodity supplemental food program	87
The emergency food assistance program	80
Food distribution program on Indian reservations	70
Special milk program (free segment)	1

Housing aid

Section 8 low-income housing assistance	$15,015
Low-rent public housing	4,710
Home investment partnerships program	3,136
Rural housing loans (section 502)	2,716
Section 236 interest reduction payments	651
Rural rental assistance payments (section 5210 on 521)	538
Rural rental housing loans (section 515)	151

Home Ownership and Opportunity for People Everywhere (HOPE) programs	79
Rural housing repair loans and grants (section 504)	61
Section 101 rent supplements	59
Section 235 home ownership assistance for low-income families	31
Farm labor housing loans (section 514) and grants (section 516)	25
Rural housing self-help technical assistance grants and site loans (sections 523, 524)	14
Indian housing improvement grants	13
Rural housing preservation grants (section 533)	11

Education aid	
Federal Pell grants	6,144
Head start	4,461
Subsidized federal stafford loans	3.339
Federal work-study program	617
Supplemental educational opportunity grants	583
Federal trio programs	463
Chapter 1 migrant education program	305
Perkins loans	158
State student incentive grant program	127
Fellowships for graduate and professional study	33
Health professions student loans and scholarship	32
Migrant high school equivalency program	8
Ellender fellowships	3
College assistance migrant program	2

Other services	
Social services block grant (Title XX)	6,095
Child care for recipients and ex-recipients of AFDC	1,737
Child care and development block grant	935
At-risk child care	487
Community services block grant	436
Legal services	278
Emergency food and shelter program	100
Social services for refugees and Cuban/Haitian entrants	69

Job training aid	
Job opportunities and basic skills training program	1,280
Job corps	1,094
Adult training	850
Summer youth employment and training program	625
Senior community service employment program	446
Youth training	127
Foster grandparents	94
Senior companions	51

Energy aid	
Low-income home energy assistance program	*1,064*
Weatherization assistance	*175*

Source: Burke, V. 1997. Cash and noncash benefits for persons with limited income: Eligibility rules, recipient and expenditure data, fiscal year 1996. (98–226 EPW). Congressional Research Service.

very different program than AFDC program. Under TANF, states are given more discretion in selecting recipients, are allowed to experiment with various ways of helping poor families, must move most TANF heads into the workforce within a relatively short time frame, and have stronger powers to sanction recipients for noncompliance. TANF is also a budgeted program, as opposed to an open-ended entitlement, most recipients are allowed to receive benefits for sixty or fewer months, and states are required to help most recipients move into employment by providing transitional child care and medical coverage and any necessary education or job training.

All states plus the District of Columbia, Puerto Rico, Guam, and the Virgin Islands participated in the AFDC program. Over most of its history, AFDC was a program for one-parent families with children living in poverty. After amendment in 1961, states and other jurisdictions could at their option offer AFDC benefits to some two-parent families under the AFDC-UP (Unemployed Parent) program. Twenty-six states chose to set up these programs. On October 1, 1990, the law changed to require all states to offer AFDC to children in two-parent families with incomes below the poverty level if the main wage earner was unemployed but had a history of work. Those states that did not have an AFDC-UP program before the change in the law were allowed to limit benefits to as little as six months in any thirteen-month period. Despite this change in the law, over 90 percent of all AFDC families continued to be headed by single women. In 1996, for example, 4.5 million families received AFDC. Only 302,000 (about 7 percent) were unemployed parent families (Green Book, 1998, Table 7–6). Additionally, children were always the major group of AFDC recipients. Of 12.6 million recipients of AFDC in 1996, some 68 percent were children (Green Book, 1998, Table 7–6).

Table 5.8 provides an overview of the AFDC program, showing changes in costs and benefits in selected years back to 1936. The number of families served grew quite rapidly during some periods, increasing by 264 percent between 1970 and 1994. In 1994 over 5 million families received AFDC benefits, one in every seven American families with children. Even controlling for inflation, the cost of the program increased substantially over its history. In 1970 AFDC benefits (not counting administrative expenditures) cost about $17 billion, increasing to over $24 billion in 1994. As enrollments declined in

1995 and 1996, AFDC costs also declined. Even though expenditures increased with the huge enrollment expansion between 1970 and 1994, they did not increase enough to keep up with the explosive growth in caseloads. In 1996 dollars, average monthly benefits increased between 1950 and 1970, but declined steadily thereafter. In 1996 the average family received only $374 in monthly assistance, compared to $734 in 1970. This represented an almost 50 percent decline in benefits.

The primary reason that poor families became eligible for AFDC was that the father was absent. Until the early 1980s, divorce or separation was the major reason for the absence of the father. By 1983 the primary reason was an out-of-wedlock birth. By 1995, almost 60 percent of all AFDC family heads were unmarried mothers, while only slightly more that 24 percent were divorced or separated (Green Book, 1998, Table 7–19). The huge increase in unwed mothers and their children was the most significant and unexpected change in AFDC recipients in the history of the program.

Not only did never-married women and their children become the majority of all AFDC recipients, a growing percentage of all AFDC families resulted from births to teen mothers. Between 1976 and 1995, over 40 percent of all women receiving AFDC were teenage mothers. In any given year teen mothers represent only a modest percentage of the AFDC caseload, but families started by a teen have become the major pipeline into the welfare system. In 1995, for example, only 6.1 percent of all AFDC heads were less than twenty years old (Green Book, 1998, Table 7–19). However, women who first gave birth as a teenager headed another 38 percent. Families started by teenagers are much more difficult to help because teen mothers tend to be poorly educated and are less likely to continue their education; they generally have poorer work histories and earn less when they work, and since they start earlier, they have larger families. As a consequence, families started by teens tended to stay on AFDC much longer than families that qualified because of divorce or separation (GAO, 1994a, 1994b, 1994c). The cost of teen families to society is very high. It has been estimated that in 1990 the federal government spent about $25 billion supporting families started by teenagers (GAO 1994b, 9).

AFDC families also changed in other ways over time. The average

Table 5.8

AFDC Summary Data, Selected Fiscal Years, 1936–1996

Measure	1936	1940	1950
Average monthly no. (thousands)[4]			
Families	162	372	651
With unemployed parents	(6)	(6)	(6)
Recipients	546	1,222	2,233
Children	404	895	1,661
Benefit expenditures (millions of dollars)[1]	23	123	520
In 1996 dollars[2]	260	1,373	3,419
Federal share (percent)	7	33	44
Administrative cost (millions of dollars)[3]	.4	9.5	40
In 1996 dollars[2]	4.5	106	263
Average AFDC family size[5]	3.37	3.28	3.43
Average monthly family benefit	28	28	67
In 1996 dollars[2]	322	312	440
AFDC enrollment, as percent of U.S.			
families with children	NA	2.1	3.2
Total population	.4	.9	1.5

Source: Congressional Research Service. Reported in Green Book, 1998. Table 7–2.

[1]Benefit expenditures for 1936–1960 are from U.S. Department of Health and Education (DHEW), expenditures for public assistance payments and for administrative costs, by program and source of funds, fiscal years 1936–1970 NCSS Report F-5; 1936 data are for 5 months only. Later data are from Table 7–3, prepared by the U.S. Department of Health and Human Services (DHHS), but unlike that table, exclude foster care payments made in 1980.

[2]The Consumer Price Index (CPI-U) for all urban consumers was used to adjust current dollars for inflation.

family size declined significantly. Counting the mother in the household, the average family size declined from around 4.0 in 1936 to 2.8 in 1995 (Table 5.8). Mothers shifted from abandoned and widowed women to poorly educated, never-married women who mostly had no income other than welfare. In 1995, 77 percent of all AFDC families had no non-AFDC income (Green Book, 1998, Table 7–19). By the 1960s black women constituted over 40 percent of all family heads, declining to 37 percent in 1995. The percentage of all mothers who were Hispanic increased from about 13 percent in 1973 to about 21 percent in 1995 (Green Book, 1998, Table 7–19).

1960	1970	1980	1990	1994	1995	1996
803	1,909	3,574	3,974	5,046	4,869	4,553
(6)	78	141	204	363	335	302
3,073	7,429	10,497	11,640	14,226	13,619	12,649
2,370	5,494	7,220	7,755	9,590	9,275	8,673
1,021	4,082	11,540	18,539	22,797	22,032	20,411
5,407	16,806	22,445	22,414	24,082	22,643	20,411
60	54	54	55	55	55	54
109	881	1,479	2,661	3,301	3,521	3,266
577	3,627	2,877	3,217	3,487	3,619	3,266
3.83	3.89	2.94	2.88	2.82	2.80	2.78
106	178	269	389	376	377	374
559	734	523	470	397	387	374
3.1	6.6	11.5	12.3	14.8	14.2	13.3
1.7	3.7	4.6	4.6	5.5	5.2	4.8

[3]For years before 1980, administrative costs include some expenditures for services.

[4]Enrollment data for 1936–1960 are December numbers from the 1970 Social Security Annual Statistical Supplement (Table 136). For later years data are fiscal year monthly averages from Table 7–5, prepared by DHHS, but, unlike that table, exclude foster care recipients in 1980.

[5]Calculated by dividing total recipients by the number of families. This understates actual family size for 1936–1950 because the mother or other caregiver was not included as a recipient until after fiscal year 1950.

[6]Program did not exist.

NA—Not available.

AFDC/TANF Benefits

There were no standard cash benefits under the AFDC program, and this continues under TANF. Each state determines the financial needs of its poor families and then decides how much of that need to fund through AFDC/TANF to qualified families. Over its lifetime, AFDC costs were shared between the federal and state governments. Administrative costs were shared 50–50, while the federal government reimbursed states for benefit costs using a formula that varied by the per capita income of the state. The reimbursement rate varied from

78 percent for states with low per capita income to 50 percent for states with the highest per capita income. On average in the 1990s the federal government paid about 55 percent of all benefit costs.

Federal law established maximum asset limits for AFDC recipients ($1,000) that states could lower. Homes, the equity value of a car up to $1,500 (or a lower state limit), and some items of personal property were generally not counted. AFDC heads were required to report all income coming into the household, assign all awarded child support to the state, and cooperate with the state in establishing the paternity of each child in the family. By law the first $50 a month in child support received went to the family head and was not counted as income. Payments above this amount were assigned to the state. Some educational loans and grants were not counted as income, and the earnings of dependent children were not counted as long as the dependent was a full-time student or was involved in certain job training programs. Despite these legal income disregards, if the gross income of the family exceeded 185 percent of the state's determined need level, the family could not receive any AFDC benefits.

When AFDC was transformed into TANF, the states gained the option of altering the cash benefit levels that they pay to qualified poor families. Most states have made very little change. All the states continue to calculate TANF benefits using the same basic formula they used for AFDC. Table 5.9 shows state calculations and how substantially AFDC/TANF benefits vary by state. The states differ greatly in where they set the need level for families of various sizes, how much of that need they fund, and the combined value of AFDC/TANF and food stamps. A quick inspection of Table 5.9 reveals that state differences are more substantial than variations in the cost of living. In 1997 maximum AFDC/TANF benefits for a three-person family varied from a low of $120 a month in Mississippi to a high of $923 a month in Alaska. Eighteen states set AFDC/TANF maximum benefit levels for a family of three at 30 percent or less of the poverty level for families of three. At the high end, two states set maximum grant levels for a three-person family at 66 and 56 percent of the poverty threshold (Alaska and Hawaii), while seven other states set benefits levels in the 50 percent range. The maximum stipend across the nation for this family size averaged $377, or $126 per recipient per month. Basically, then, in most states cash benefit levels are quite modest, and some states, particularly in the South and West, provide very minimal cash assistance to their poor.

About 85 percent of AFDC/TANF families receive food stamps (Green Book, 1998, Table 7–19). Food stamps are not counted in calculating cash benefits, but AFDC/TANF awards are considered in determining food stamp grants. The result is that food stamps are higher in states that pay the lowest average cash stipends, compensating in part for low grants. Table 5.9 shows the combined worth of AFDC/TANF and food stamps in each state and their value in relation to the 1997 poverty threshold for a family of three. The combined value averaged $692 nationally, varying from a low of $435 in Mississippi to a high of $1,246 in Alaska. On average, the combined value of AFDC/TANF and food stamps equaled 62 percent of the poverty level for these families. In no state did the combined benefits lift a family over the poverty line, and in many states families that received maximum AFDC/TANF and food stamp benefits in 1997 were left far below the poverty level.

AFDC Employment: Incentives and Disincentives

As originally designed, the intent of the program that became AFDC was to provide funds to widows so that they could stay home with their children. As noted, over time two things changed: (a) AFDC expanded to become a program that mostly enrolled unwed and divorced mothers; and (b) most women, including mothers, joined the work force. These changes prompted considerable interest in encouraging, even requiring, AFDC mothers to work. For the most part, all policy efforts failed.

Beginning in 1967 the federal government required the states to establish Work Incentive Programs (WIN) to provide job search assistance and in some cases job training to work-eligible mothers with children over six. As an employment incentive for mothers, the law required the states to exclude the first $30 per month in earnings, one-third of all additional income, plus work expenses in calculating benefits. When Ronald Reagan was elected President, he argued that subsidizing people who work was bad policy. President Reagan urged Congress to require all able-bodied mothers to work in exchange for benefits and to amend the income disregards. Congress did not pass compulsory work requirements, but the earning disregards were al-

Table 5.9

Need Standard and Maximum AFDC/TANF and Food Stamp Benefits, One-Parent Family of Three Persons,[1] January 1997

State name	Gross income limit (185% of need standard)	100% of "need"	Max. AFDC grant[2]	Food stamp benefit[3]	Combined benefits as a dollar amount	Combined benefits as a % of 1997 poverty guidelines[4]	AFDC benefits as a % of 1997 poverty guidelines[4]
Alabama	$1,245	$673	$164	$315	$479	43	15
Alaska	1,955	1,057	923	323	1,246	90	66
Arizona	1,783	964	347	315	662	60	31
Arkansas[5]	1,304	705	204	315	519	47	18
California	1,360	735	565	261	826	75	51
Colorado[5]	779	421	356	315	671	60	32
Connecticut	1,613	872	636	239	875	79	57
Delaware[5]	625	338	338	315	653	59	30
District of Columbia[5]	1,317	712	398	311	709	64	36
Florida	2,002	1,082	303	315	618	56	27
Georgia[5]	784	424	280	315	595	54	25
Guam[5]	1,245	673	673	434	1,107	100	61
Hawaii[5]	2,109	1,140	712	472	1,184	93	56
Idaho[5]	1,833	991	317	315	632	57	29
Illinois[5]	1,830	989	377	315	692	62	34
Indiana[5]	92	320	288	315	603	54	26
Iowa	1,571	849	426	302	728	66	38
Kansas	794	429	429	302	730	66	39
Kentucky	973	526	262	315	577	52	24
Louisiana	1,217	658	190	315	505	45	17
Maine	1,023	553	418	305	723	65	38
Maryland	956	517	377	315	692	62	34
Massachusetts	1,045	565	565	261	826	74	51

Michigan							
Washtenaw County	1,151	622	489	292	752	68	41
Wayne County	1,084	586	459	284	772	70	44
Minnesota[5]	984	532	532	271	803	72	48
Mississippi	681	368	120	315	435	39	11
Missouri	1,565	846	292	315	607	55	26
Montana	1,032	558	438	299	737	66	39
Nebraska	673	364	364	315	679	61	33
Nevada	1,423	769	348	315	663	60	31
New Hampshire	3,210	1,735	550	265	815	73	50
New Jersey[5]	1,822	985	424	303	727	65	38
New Mexico[5]	720	389	389	314	702	63	35
New York							
New York City	1,067	577	577	257	834	75	52
Suffolk County	1,301	703	703	219	922	83	63
North Carolina	1,006	544	272	315	587	53	24
North Dakota[5]	797	431	431	301	732	66	39
Ohio	1,758	950	341	315	656	59	31
Oklahoma	1,193	645	307	315	622	56	28
Oregon	851	460	460	292	752	68	41
Pennsylvania[5]	1,136	614	421	304	725	65	38
Puerto Rico[5]	666	360	180	NA	180	16	NA
Rhode Island[5]	1,025	554	554	264	818	74	50
South Carolina	999	540	200	315	515	46	18
South Dakota	938	507	430	301	731	66	39
Tennessee	1,252	677	185	315	500	45	17
Texas	1,389	751	188	315	503	45	17
Utah	1,051	568	426	302	728	66	38
Vermont	2,226	1,203	639	238	878	79	58
Virgin Islands[5]	555	300	240	405	645	58	22
Virginia[5]	727	393	354	315	669	60	32
Washington[5]	2,281	1,233	546	266	812	73	49

Table 5.9 (continued)

State name	Gross income limit (185% of need standard)	100% of "need"	Max. AFDC grant[2]	Food stamp benefit[3]	Combined benefits as a dollar amount	Combined benefits as a % of 1997 poverty guidelines[4]	AFDC benefits as a % of 1997 poverty guidelines[4]
West Virginia[5]	1,833	991	253	315	568	51	23
Wisconsin	1,197	647	517	275	792	71	47
Wyoming	1,247	674	360	315	675	61	32
Median AFDC State[6]	—	—	377	315	692	62	34

Source: Table prepared by the Congressional Research Service from information provided by a telephone survey of the states. Reported in Green Book, 1998, Table 7–8.

Notes: Puerto Rico does not have a food stamp program; instead a cash nutritional assistance payment is made.

[1]In most states these amounts apply also to two-parent families of three (where the second parent is incapacitated or unemployed). Some, however, increase benefits for these families.

[2]In states with area differentials, figure shown is for area with highest benefit.

[3]Food stamp benefits are based on maximum AFDC/TANF benefits shown and assume deductions of $384 monthly ($134 standard household deduction and $250 maximum allowable deduction for excess shelter cost) in the 48 contiguous states and the District of Columbia. In the other four jurisdictions these maximum allowable food stamp deductions are assumed: Alaska, $663; Hawaii, $546; Guam, $573; and the Virgin Islands, $302. If only the standard deduction were assumed, food stamp benefits would drop by about $75 monthly in most of the 48 contiguous states and in the District of Columbia. Maximum food stamp benefits from October 1996 through September 1997 are $315 for a family of three, with these exceptions: (urban) Alaska, $401; Hawaii, $522, Guam, $464; and the Virgin Islands, $495.

[4]The 1997 poverty guidelines for a family of three are: $1,111 per month for the 48 contiguous states and the District of Columbia; $1,389 for Alaska; and $1,278 for Hawaii.

[5]These jurisdictions did not yet have TANF plans in effect on January 1, 1997.

[6]Ranked by size of maximum benefit among the 50 states and the District of Columbia.

NA—Not available.

tered in 1982. Work expenses were capped at $75 per month, and child care expenses were capped at $160 per month per child. The $30 and one-third disregard was limited to four consecutive months. Congress made some additional changes in 1984, basically trying to encourage AFDC mothers to move into the job market by providing them with limited subsidies to make work attractive during the transition from welfare to employment.

By the late 1980s it was clear that short-term subsidies had little impact on AFDC mothers' employment. The Family Support Act of 1988 (FSA) tried another approach by requiring all the states to replace WIN with a program designed to provide job training and education to AFDC mothers. By October 1, 1990, all states were required to establish a Job Opportunities and Basic Skills (JOBS) training program, which over time would enroll almost all able-bodied recipients with no children younger than three. Under JOBS, mothers were to be given the training and/or educational skills required to obtain employment and then be provided with transitional support while they became established in the work force. Medical benefits and child care were to be made available during the first year of employment. Unfortunately, as detailed in Chapter 6, the FSA was so poorly funded that the states were able to extend these services to only a small percentage of their caseloads.

The result of the long history of inadequate education and job training for AFDC heads, along with the limited availability of child care and medical coverage, was that AFDC mothers were usually unemployed. By 1983 only 1.5 percent of all AFDC heads were employed full time with another 3.4 percent working part-time. The employment status of AFDC heads changed little over the next dozen years. In 1995 a total of 9 percent of all AFDC heads were employed, either full- or part-time.

Problems with AFDC

As the major cash-assistance program for the poor in the United States, AFDC was fundamentally flawed. A very large percentage of all the nation's poorest families with children were never served by the program. Those families that were served, even when they received benefits from multiple programs, continued to live below the poverty level. The program played no significant role in preventing poverty, nor did it really help those it served escape poverty. When mothers left welfare, it was rarely because of AFDC services, and often it was in spite of the program.

Most of those families who received benefits under AFDC were enrolled for a short time, but a rather small percentage (about 20 percent) remained on the rolls for ten or more years. It was this latter group of recipients that composed most AFDC families on any given day, they were the group upon whom most AFDC funds were spent, and the group most in need of education and job training services that they never received.

At a time when most women were employed, including most mothers, over 90 percent of all AFDC heads were unemployed, often for very long periods of time. Education, job training, and transitional support were made available to only a small percentage of AFDC heads, even after passage of the FSA of 1988. The result was that most AFDC heads were poorly prepared for decent paying work and were made poorer by employment because they generally lost medical coverage and had to pay for child care and other work-related expenses. Work, in other words, usually did not pay. Young children in AFDC families were also neglected. Most were not enrolled in any type of preschool program. Instead, they stayed home with mothers who were idle and poorly educated. Most started school educationally far behind their middle-income peers, with little chance of ever really catching up.

The wonder of AFDC is that it lasted as long as it did. In the next chapter, we will examine in some depth the changes that have been brought about by PRWORA of 1996.

Food Stamps

Established on a pilot basis in 1964 and expanded to a nationwide program in 1974, the food stamp program has become one of the most important welfare programs. The program is designed to help low-income households purchase a nutritionally adequate diet. Participating families are expected to contribute 30 percent of countable income to food purchases. Food stamps are intended to make up the difference between the family's contribution and the estimated cost of an adequate low-cost, nutritious diet. The maximum food stamp benefit varies by family size and is based on the Thrifty Food Plan, a diet designed by the Department of Agriculture. A family with no count-able income receives the maximum food stamp benefit, while a house-hold with countable income receives a lesser amount based on a 30-cent reduction in the maximum benefit for each counted dollar of income.

Benefits are available to most households who meet income and asset standards. Households in which all members of the family are eligible for TANF, Supplemental Security Income (SSI), and state gen-eral assistance are normally automatically qualified for food stamps. Most noncitizens are barred from the program, along with strikers (unless eligible before the strike), most post-secondary students, most persons living in institutional settings, and anyone found guilty of committing fraud against the program or failing to comply with any program rules.

Generally, the food stamp program is administered by the same state welfare agency that runs TANF and Medicaid programs. These agencies screen applicants for eligibility, determine benefit levels, and issue food stamps, either in the form of coupons redeemable at ap-proved food stores, or in the form of electronic benefit transfers (EBTs). Generally, food stamps can only be used to purchase food. They may not be used to purchase nonfood products such as soap, paper goods, tobacco, alcohol, or hot foods intended for immediate consumption. There are a few exceptions, including seeds and plants to grow vegetables for consumption, and some prepared meals for elderly and handicapped recipients.

Households become eligible for food stamps either by qualifying for TANF, SSI, or state general assistance, or by low monthly cash income. In recognition that not all income is available for food con-sumption, a household's counted (or net) income is determined by use of some standard deductions. These deductions include a standard de-duction that does not vary by family size ($134 a month in 1997), child support payments, 20 percent of earned income, an allowance for child care, an allowance for high shelter costs, and, in the case of elderly or handicapped applicants, some out-of-pocket medical ex-penses. Net income cannot exceed the poverty level for the household. Except for households with an elderly or handicapped person, the gross income of the family cannot exceed 130 percent of the poverty line. Households without an elderly member cannot have liquid assets above $2,000. The asset level for households with an elderly member is set at $3,000. The fair market value of a car above $4,650 is counted as liquid assets.

There are work requirements for able-bodied adult recipients of food stamps. Recipients are required to register for work, accept any suitable job offered, fulfill any required job training or job search obligations, and not quit a job without good cause or reduce their work hours below 30 hours a week. Until the welfare reforms of 1996, to be discussed in the next chapter, most states were not very well prepared to offer job training or placement to most adult food stamp recipients. In 1996 about 3.3 million adults were obligated to participate in some type of job training or job search. About 1.5 million participated in some type of employment activity, while almost 600,000 were sanctioned for failure to meet requirements.

Recent changes in food stamp rules allow states to test variations that might improve the program or help recipients become established in the job market. Some projects have been approved that allow states to "cash-out" food stamp benefits for the elderly, SSI recipients, and some households that are part of state welfare reform efforts. Additionally, the 1996 reforms allow states to use food stamps as a wage supplement, and states can "cash-out" to working families to help them escape welfare. Last, states may run workfare programs in which recipients must accept employment or training in return for food stamps.

The federal government pays most of the costs of the food stamp program. States pay about half the administrative costs, which were about $1.8 billion in 1996 (Green Book, 1998, 927). As Table 5.5 shows, 8.7 percent of all families received food stamps in 1997, about 21.5 million recipients. This included only 43.6 percent of all households below the poverty level. A majority of all those counted as poor never receive these benefits, and early evidence shows food stamp rates declining quite significantly in 1998. Preliminary data show less than 19 million recipients in 1998, down from 28 million a year between 1993 and 1995 (www.fns.usda.gov/fsp).

Table 5.10 shows the growth of the program over its history and average monthly participation. The food stamp program was implemented nationwide in 1974. It was a fairly large program from the beginning, serving some 13 million people a month in 1974. The program grew rather rapidly exceeding 20 million recipients by 1980, and reaching levels that exceeded 28 million recipients by the early

Table. 5.10

Historical Food Stamp Statistics, 1972–1996

Fiscal year	Total federal spending (in millions)[1]		Avg. mo. participation (in millions of persons)	Avg. mo. benefits (per person)		Four-person max. mo. allotment[2]
	Current dollars	Constant (1996) dollars[3]		Current dollars	Current (1996) dollars[3]	
1972[4]	$1,871	$7,072	11.1	$13.50	$49.30	$108
1973	2,211	8,048	12.2	14.60	49.20	112
1974	2,843	9,496	12.9	17.60	49.60	116
1975[5]	4,624	13,872	17.1	21.40	55.00	150
1976	5,692	15,995	18.5	23.90	57.80	162
TQ[6]	1,367	3,705	17.3	24.40	58.60	166
1977	5,469	14,274	17.1	24.70	57.30	166
1978	5,573	13,598	16.0	26.80	56.80	170
1979[7]	6,995	15,459	17.7	30.60	58.10	182
1980	9,188	17,917	21.1	34.40	60.90	204
1981	11,308	19,789	22.4	39.50	64.00	209
1982	11,117	18,121	22.0	39.20	61.20	233
1983	12,733	20,118	23.2	43.00	66.20	253
1984	12,470	18,830	22.4	42.70	64.10	253
1985	12,599	18,395	21.4	45.00	66.20	264
1986	12,528	17,790	20.9	45.50	65.50	268
1987	12,539	17,304	20.6	45.80	62.70	271
1988	13,289	17,674	20.1	49.80	66.20	290
1989	13,815	17,545	20.2	51.90	64.40	300
1990	16,512	19,980	21.5	59.00	69.00	331
1991	19,765	22,730	24.1	63.90	71.60	352
1992	23,539	26,364	26.9	68.50	76.70	370
1993	24,749	26,729	28.4	68.00	74.80	375
1994	25,525	27,057	28.9	69.00	73.80	375
1995	25,676	26,446	28.0	71.30	73.40	386
1996	25,494	25,494	26.9	73.30	73.30	397

Source: Compiled by the Congressional Research Service. Reported in the Green Book, 1998, Table 15–11.

[1]Spending for benefits and administration, including Puerto Rico.

[2]For the 48 contiguous states and the District of Columbia, as in effect at the beginning of the fiscal year in current dollars

[3]Constant dollar adjustments were made using the overall Consumer Price Index for Urban Consumers (CPI-U) for spending and the CPI-U "food at home" component for benefits.

[4]The first fiscal year in which benefit and eligibility rules were, by law, nationally uniform and indexed for inflation.

[5]The first fiscal year in which food stamps were available nationwide.

[6]Transitional quarter (July through September 1976).

[7]The fiscal year in which the food stamp purchase requirement was eliminated, on a phased in basis.

1990s. Program costs also escalated over time, rising to over $27 billion in 1994. The average recipient received $73.30 in benefits in 1996, an average of $397 for a family of four. Recipient benefits are rather modest, but as Table 5.9 shows, when food stamp benefits are added to TANF benefits, the overall purchasing power of families is considerably enhanced.

Medicaid

The other companion program to TANF and food stamps is the Medicaid program. Added by amendment in 1965 to the Social Security Act, Medicaid has become one of the nation's largest and most expensive welfare programs. Medicaid provides medical assistance to low-income people who are aged, blind, or disabled, most TANF families, and some pregnant women and their children. Each state runs its own Medicaid program, within restrictions established by federal guidelines. The flexibility allowed states means that there is substantial variation among the states in coverage and payment levels for services.

The passage of TANF in 1996 severed the automatic link between welfare and Medicaid. Still, most states offer coverage to TANF families, and the states are required to continue to serve individuals who would have been qualified for AFDC in July of 1996, even if they do not qualify for TANF. States must also provide transitional assistance to families made ineligible for Medicaid because of earnings or earned income. States are permitted to deny assistance to nonpregnant adults and heads of households who do not comply with work rules, but their children must be covered.

In the late 1980s and early 1990s Congress passed a number of acts that extended Medicaid to low-income pregnant women and children. States are required to provide medical services to all women and children under age six with family incomes below 133 percent of the poverty threshold. The mothers receive services related only to pregnancy or complications of pregnancy, while the children receive full Medicaid coverage. Since 1991 states have been required to provide services to all children under age nineteen who were born after September 30, 1983, if their family income is below 100 of the poverty level. By 2002 all children in families below the poverty level will be covered. States also have the option of providing services to pregnant

women and infants under the age of one if the family income is no
more than 185 percent of the poverty level.

Under federal rules states may opt to cover other groups with incomes above 185 percent of the poverty level, and a few have chosen
to do so. Normally, SSI recipients qualify for Medicaid. States may
also provide Medicaid to individuals who are not receiving SSI, but
instead are receiving state-only supplementary cash benefits. States
have the additional option of providing Medicaid to disabled SSI recipients with incomes up to 250 percent of the poverty level. These
recipients can "buy into" Medicaid by paying a sliding scale fee based
on their income.

States are required to provide some Medicaid coverage to "qualified
Medicare beneficiaries "(QMBs). These Medicare recipients are aged
and disabled persons with incomes below 100 percent of the poverty
level. States must pay Medicare part B premiums and often part A
premiums for QMBs, as well as required Medicare co-insurance and
deductibles. If individuals would qualify to be a QMB except for the
fact that their income is between 100 and 135 percent of the poverty
level, the state must pay part B premiums for them. States have the
option of providing full Medicaid benefits to qualified QMBs rather
than just Medicare premiums and cost sharing. States are also required
to pay part A premiums for individuals who formerly received Social
Security disability and Medicare and have incomes below 200 percent
of the poverty level.

The law gives the states the discretion of setting a different Medicaid income limit for institutionalized persons. The income cutoff can
be set at 300 percent of maximum SSI benefits to a person who is
living at home. States may also provide Medicaid to individuals who
would qualify for SSI if they were not institutionalized. Likewise,
states may provide Medicaid to individuals who would qualify for
benefits if they were institutionalized. This includes children being
cared for at home, persons who are ventilator-dependent, and persons
receiving Hospice care.

Forty states and several jurisdictions provide Medicaid services to
the "medically needy." These are low-income families with limited
resources who have income above 100 percent of the poverty level,
but below a maximum of 133 percent. If a state covers any medically
needy citizens, children under eighteen and pregnant women who meet
income and asset requirements must be covered.

Enrollment

Medicaid services were provided to 12 percent of the total population in 1996, including about 45 percent of those individuals living below the poverty level. Children are more likely than any other group to be covered, but only about 71 percent of those five and under in families with incomes below the poverty line were covered in 1995 (Green Book, 1998, 957). About half of children eleven to eighteen in poor families were covered. Among poor adults nineteen to forty-four, 33.4 percent were enrolled. Some 30 percent of the aged poor were covered. Young children, especially those five and under, are the most likely to receive assistance when their families have income below 185 percent of the poverty level. About 47 percent of all children in families with income between 100 and 133 percent of the poverty level received assistance under Medicaid in 1995.

Services

The medical services that states must provide to those groups that must be covered is quite comprehensive. States must provide inpatient and outpatient hospital services, physician services, nursing facilities for those over twenty-one, home health services, early and periodic screening, diagnosis and treatment for those under age twenty-one, and family planning. States may cover other services including drugs, eyeglasses, and psychiatric care for individuals under twenty-one and over sixty-five.

States have considerable discretion in the services provided to the medically needy, but if they cover any groups, they must cover children and prenatal and delivery services for pregnant women. If the state covers institutional care for any needy group, it must also provide ambulatory services for this group.

Financing

Medicaid is a state managed program operated under federal rules and paid for by both the federal and state governments. The federal government's contribution is based on a formula that is adjusted yearly. The federal payment rate varies according to the per capita income of the state, ranging from 50 percent to a theoretical high of 83 percent of all costs. In 1997 the highest rate paid was 77.2 percent, and eleven states and the District of Columbia received the minimum rate of 50 percent. Most administrative costs are shared 50–50 between the federal and state government.

Table 5.11 provides an overview of the costs of the Medicaid pro-

Table 5.11

History of Medicaid Program Costs, 1966–1998

Fiscal year	Total		Federal		State	
	Dollars (in millions)	Percent increase	Dollars (in millions)	Percent increase	Dollars (in millions)	Percent increase
1966[1]	$1,658	—	$789	—	$869	—
1967[1]	2,368	42.8	1,209	53.2	1,159	33.4
1968[1]	3,686	55.7	1,837	51.9	1,849	59.5
1969[1]	4,166	13.0	2,276	23.9	1,890	2.2
1970[1]	4,852	16.5	2,617	15.0	2,235	18.3
1971	6,176	27.3	3,374	28.9	2,802	25.4
1972[2]	8,434	36.6	4,361	29.3	4,074	45.4
1973	9,111	8.0	4,998	14.6	4,113	1.0
1974	10,229	12.3	5,833	16.7	4,396	6.9
1975	12,637	23.5	7,060	21.0	5,578	26.9
1976	14,644	15.9	8,312	17.7	6,332	13.5
TQ[3]	4,106	NA	2,354	NA	1,752	NA
1977	17,103	[4]16.8	9,713	[4]16.9	7,389	[4]16.7
1978	18,949	10.8	10,680	10.0	8,269	11.9
1979	21,755	14.8	12,267	14.9	9,489	14.8
1980	25,781	18.5	14,550	18.6	11,231	18.4
1981	30,377	17.8	17,074	17.3	13,303	18.4
1982	32,466	6.8	17,514	2.6	14,931	12.2
1983	34,956	7.7	18,985	8.4	15,971	7.0
1984	37,569	7.5	20,061	5.7	17,508	9.6
1985[5]	40,917	8.9	22,655	12.9	18,262	4.3
1986	44,851	9.6	24,995	10.3	19,856	8.7
1987	49,344	10.0	27,435	9.8	21,909	10.3
1988	54,116	9.7	30,462	11.0	23,654	8.0
1989	61,246	13.2	34,604	13.6	26,642	12.6
1990	72,492	18.4	41,103	18.8	31,389	17.8
1991	91,519	26.2	52,532	27.8	38,987	24.2
1992	118,166	29.1	67,827	29.1	50,339	29.1
1993	131,775	11.5	75,774	11.7	56,001	11.2
1994	143,204	8.7	82,034	8.3	61,170	9.2
1995	156,395	9.2	89,070	8.6	67,325	10.1
1996	161,963	3.6	91,990	3.3	69,973	3.9
1997[7]	174,310	7.6	98,503	7.1	75,807	8.3
1998[7]	184,712	6.0	104,384	6.0	80,328	6.0

Table 5.11 *(continued)*

Source: Budget for the U.S. Government, fiscal years 1969–1998 and Health Care Financing Administration. Reported in Green Book, 1998, Table 15–13.

Note: Totals may not add due to rounding.

[1]Includes related programs which are not separately identified, though for each successive year a larger portion of the total represents Medicaid expenditures. As of January 1, 1970, federal matching was only available under Medicaid.

[2]Intermediate care facilities (ICFs) transferred from the cash assistance programs to Medicaid effective January 1, 1972. Data for prior periods do not include these costs.

[3]Transitional quarter (beginning of federal fiscal year moved from July 1 to October 1).

[4]Represents increase over fiscal year 1976, i.e., five calendar quarters.

[5]Includes transfer of function of State fraud control units to Medicaid from Office of Inspector General.

[6]Temporary reductions in Federal payments authorized for fiscal years 1982–84 were discontinued in fiscal year 1985.

[7]Current law estimate

NA—Not available.

---

gram since its origin, and the division of these costs between the federal and state governments. Growth in the costs of the program has been enormous, growing at rates significantly in excess of the rate of inflation. By 1998 the Medicaid program was predicted to cost about $185 billion, with the federal government paying about 56 percent of all costs. The states were predicted to have costs of about $80 billion in 1998, making Medicaid the most costly welfare program for the states.

Medicaid and Managed Care

To broaden services while dealing with the very high costs of Medicaid, states are increasingly turning to managed care systems. By 1996 over 13 million Medicaid recipients (about 40 percent of the total) were enrolled in a managed care system. Under managed care, providers agree to provide a contracted range of services for a fixed cost. The Balanced Budget Act of 1997 allows states more flexibility in enrolling most of their Medicaid beneficiaries in managed care systems. States now have the option of contracting with managed care organizations serving only Medicaid beneficiaries and to "lock" recipients into the same plan for up to twelve months. This new law also attempts to safeguard the quality of care provided under managed care.

Supplemental Security Income (SSI)

The Supplemental Security Income (SSI) program was passed by Congress in 1972 and became effective in 1974. SSI is a guaranteed income program for the aged, disabled, and blind. The program was designed to establish a national minimum level of income for this select group of Americans. It is a guaranteed income program of last resort. That is, the aged, disabled, and blind are guaranteed a certain level of monthly income. If they have less income than the guaranteed amount, SSI pays the difference.

SSI has become a very important welfare program. It not only provides over 6 million recipients a month with cash benefits, but SSI recipients are also frequently enrolled in Medicaid and other welfare programs such as the food stamp program. Table 5.12 provides an overview of the program. SSI has grown from about 4 million recipients in 1974 to some 6.6 million in 1996. In 1996 the program cost over $28 billion, with most of the costs associated with assistance to the disabled.

The income level guaranteed to SSI recipients is adjusted yearly. In 1996, for example, the guaranteed income level for a single individual was $470, and $705 for a couple. As Table 5.12 shows, the average recipient received less than the maximum payment because they had income from other sources. The average recipient in 1996 received $339.24. Most recipients have income of some type, often from Social Security, general assistance, and even modest earnings. In 1996, for example, 37 percent of SSI recipients were receiving Social Security benefits, over 12 percent had other unearned income, and 4.4 percent had earnings. Forty-three states subsidize the benefits of some SSI recipients, mostly those with high shelter costs. In 1996 about 37 percent of all SSI recipients received a state supplement, which ranged from a very modest amount to several hundred dollars.

SSI recipients who live in a Medicaid institution (mostly nursing homes) are limited to very modest benefits. In 1996 SSI recipients residing in a Medicaid institution received a maximum benefit of $30.

Table 5.12

Supplemental Security Income Summary, Selected Years 1974–1996

Item	1974	1978	1980	1984	1986
Recipients[1]					
Aged	2,285,909	1,967,900	1,807,776	1,530,289	1,473,428
Blind	74,616	77,135	78,401	80,524	83,115
Disabled	1,635,539	2,171,890	2,255,840	2,418,522	2,712,641
Total	3,996,064	4,216,925	4,142,017	4,029,333	4,269,184
Annual payments (in millions of 1996 dollars)	$16,696	$15,767	$15,119	$15,663	$17,295
Monthly federal benefits rates					
Individual	$140.00	$177.80	$208.20	$314.00	$336.00
Couple	210.00	266.70	312.30	472.00	504.00
Average Federal SSI payments[1]					
All recipients	$95.11	$111.98	$143.35	$196.16	$215.40
Aged individuals	78.48	91.22	112.45	143.24	151.38
Aged couples	93.02	120.48	157.56	221.98	246.07
Average federally administered[1]					
State supplementation	$70.92	$75.00	$99.15	$97.61	$115.41
Percent of recipients with other income[1]					
Social Security benefits	52.7	51.7	51.0	49.6	48.9
Other unearned income	10.5	11.5	11.0	11.2	12.1
Earnings	2.8	3.1	3.2	3.5	3.9
Average amount of[1]					
Social Security benefits	$130.01	$156.50	$196.94	$250.61	$263.29
Other unearned income	61.10	66.93	74.35	84.56	86.40
Earnings	80.00	99.32	106.95	126.47	142.17
Poverty thresholds (age 65 and over)					
Individual	$2,364	$3,127	$3,949	$4,979	$5,255
Couple	2,982	3,944	4,983	6,282	6,630
Federal benefit rate as a percent of poverty					
Individual	74.1	72.7	72.3	75.6	76.7
Couple	88.1	86.4	86.0	90.2	91.2

Source: Social Security Administration (1995 and various years) and unpublished data. Reported in Green Book, 1998, Table 3–1.

[1]December data.

NA = Not available.

1988	1990	1992	1993	1994	1995	1996
1,433,420	1,454,041	1,471,022	1,474,852	1,465,905	1,466,122	1,412,632
82,864	83,686	85,400	85,456	84,911	83,545	82,137
2,947,585	3,279,400	4,009,767	4,424,022	4,744,470	4,984,467	5,118,949
4,463,869	4,817,127	5,566,189	5,984,300	6,295,786	6,514,134	6,613,718
$18,284	$19,926	$24,869	$26,050	$27,389	$27,835	$28,252
$354.00	$386.00	$422.00	$434.00	$446.00	$458.00	$470.00
532.00	579.00	633.00	652.00	687.00	687.00	705.00
$227.49	$261.47	$329.74	$317.41	$325.26	$334.12	$339.24
159.36	175.29	195.86	204.45	211.55	219.13	227.42
273.18	322.82	448.61	478.42	505.64	534.00	563.39
$122.68	$139.79	$118.08	$108.50	$101.46	$105.24	$104.58
47.8	45.9	41.3	40.1	39.1	37.9	37.0
12.4	13.0	14.5	13.4	13.1	12.8	12.4
4.4	4.7	4.4	4.3	4.2	4.3	4.4
$286.49	$318.57	$335.72	$338.85	$345.20	$354.47	$382.56
85.92	98.13	91.96	100.44	101.13	105.32	112.46
173.09	195.64	207.55	210.22	225.01	234.94	258.42
$5,674	$6,268	$6,729	$6,930	$7,108	$7,309	$7,525
7,158	7,905	8,489	8,741	8,967	9,221	9,491
74.9	73.9	75.3	75.2	75.3	75.2	75.0
89.2	87.9	89.5	89.5	89.5	89.4	89.1

Benefits are also lower if the recipient lives in the household of another person. In 1996 SSI recipients residing in another household were allowed maximum benefits of $313.34 for an individual and $470.00 for a couple. An individual who takes care of one or more SSI beneficiaries is also entitled to assistance. If they care for them in their own home, they receive more than if they care for them in the household of another person. In 1996, for example, an "essential person" qualified for a maximum benefit of $235 if residing in their own household, and $152.57 if care is provided in the household of another (Green Book, 1998, Table 3–3).

SSI benefits generally push recipients closer to the poverty threshold than do TANF benefits. As Table 5.12 shows, in 1996 the SSI benefit rate for an individual was 75 percent of the poverty threshold, while it was 89.1 percent of the poverty level for a couple.

The Earned Income Tax Credit (EITC)

The last major program that is important to understanding the combination of programs available to assist the poor in escaping poverty is the Earned Income Tax Credit (EITC). This program is designed to make work pay better for low-wage earners. Essentially, the EITC subsidizes the wages of adults with children who work but earn low wages. As Table 5.13 shows, the program has grown from providing benefits to 6.2 million families in 1975 to assisting 18.7 million families in 1996. The program cost less than a billion dollars a year until 1979, but outlays rose to over $21 billion by 1996.

The Earned Income Tax Credit (EITC) is designed both to subsidize low-wage workers and to encourage them to earn as much as possible. There are three parts to the EITC: (1) a base with a subsidy rate; (2) a plateau; and (3) a phase-out range. Three examples illustrate how the program works for a family with two children with earnings.

A Base with a Subsidy Rate

A family with two children earns less than the established base for their family size. In 1996 the base for a family with two children was $8,900 (see Table 5.14). For earnings below the base, the family receives a credit worth 40 percent of earnings. For example, if this

Table 5.13

Earned Income Tax Credit, 1975–1996

Calendar year credit applies	No. of families receiving credit (thousands)	Total amount of credit (millions)	"Refunded" portion of credit[1] (millions)	Avg. credit/ family
1975	6,215	$ 1,250	$ 900	$ 201
1976	6,473	1,295	890	200
1977	5,627	1,127	880	200
1978	5,192	1,048	801	202
1979	7,135	2,052	1,395	288
1980	6,954	1,986	1,370	286
1981	6,717	1,912	1,278	285
1982	6,395	1,775	1,222	278
1983	7,368	1,795	1,289	224
1984	6,376	1,638	1,162	257
1985	7,432	2,088	1,499	281
1986	7,156	1,009	1,479	281
1987	8,738	3,931	2,930	450
1988	11,148	5,896	4,257	529
1989	11,696	6,595	4,636	564
1990	12,612	6,928	5,303	549
1991[2]	13,105	10,589	7,849	808
1992[3]	13,433	12,434	9,625	926
1993[3]	14,004	13,239	10,883	945
1994[3]	18,059	19,647	16,549	1,088
1995[3]	18,411	22,806	19,220	1,239
1996[3]	18,692	25,058	21,026	1,341

Source: Joint Committee on Taxation. Reported in Green Book, 1998, Table 16–13.

[1]This is the portion of the credit that exceeds tax liability. It is treated as a budget outlay because it is a direct payment to the beneficiary.

[2]Preliminary.

[3]Projection.

family earned $6,000, they would have received a credit worth $2,400 (40 * $6,000 = $2,400). If the family owed no federal taxes (which would almost always be the case at the lowest income levels), they would receive this $2,400 in the form of a check from the federal government. This would have raised this family's total income to $8,400. The EITC credit check can be in a lump sum at the end of the tax year, or it can be prorated and paid out in monthly payments.

Table 5.14

Earned Income Tax Credit Parameters, 1975–1996

Calendar year	Credit rate (%)[2]	Min. income for max. credit	Max. credit	Phase-out rate (%)	Phase-out range Beg. income	Phase-out range End. income
1975–78	10.0	$4,000	$ 400	10.00	$ 4,000	$ 8,000
1979–80	10.0	5,000	500	12.50	6,000	10,000
1981–84	10.0	5,000	500	12.50	6,000	10,000
1985–86	11.0	5,000	550	12.22	6,500	11,000
1987	14.0	6,080	851	10.00	6,920	15,432
1988	14.0	6,240	874	10.00	9,840	18,576
1989	14.0	6,500	910	10.00	10,240	19,340
1990	14.0	6,810	953	10.00	10,730	20,264
1991						
1 child	16.7	7,140	1,192	11.93	11,250	21,250
2 children	17.3	7,140	1,235	12.36	11,250	21,250
1992						
1 child	17.6	7,520	1,324	12.57	11,840	22,370
2 children	18.4	7,520	1,384	13.14	11,840	22,370
1993						
1 child	18.5	7,750	1,434	13.21	12,200	23,050
2 children	19.5	7,750	1,511	13.93	12,200	23,050
1994						
1 child	26.3	7,750	2,038	15.98	11,000	23,750
2 children	30.0	8,425	2,528	17.86	11,000	25,300
1996[1,2]						
1 child	34.0	6,160	2,094	15.98	11,290	24,395
2 children	40.0	8,900	3,560	21.06	11,620	28,524

Source: Joint Committee on Taxation. Reported in Green Book, 1998, Table 16–11.

[1]Projection.

[2]Credit rates and phaseout rates remain the same for all years after 1996. Income amounts are indexed for inflation.

A Plateau

A family with two children earns above the base, but within the plateau range. In 1996 the base was $8,900 with a phase-out range beginning at $11,620. Earning that fall within this range received a standard subsidy of $3,560. Thus, a worker with two children earning $10,000 in 1996 would have had a total income of $13,560 ($10,000 + $3,560).

A Phase-Out Range

A worker with two children has earnings within the phase-out range. In 1996 this range started at $11,620 and ended at $28,524. The maximum tax credit of $3,560 was reduced by 21.06 cents for every dollar earned above $11,620. If earnings reached or exceeded $28,524, the credit would have been exhausted. Thus, if a worker earned $15,000, they would have had $3,380 in income above the beginning of the phase-out range. These dollars would have been taxed at the 21.06 rate (21.06 * $3,390 = $711.83), reducing the maximum credit by $711.83. Thus this worker would have received a credit of $2,848.17, yielding a total income of $17,848.17 ($15,000.00 plus $2,848.17).

The EITC significantly increases the value of a low-wage job to a worker. The effect of the EITC on a minimum wage job, for example, is substantial. In 1996 a worker with two children earning the minimum wage would have a yearly income of $10,712 ($5.15 * 40 hours * 52 weeks = $10,712). The EITC would provide another $3,560, yielding a total yearly income of $14,274. With the EITC subsidy, the worker's $5.15 an hour job is turned into a job that paid $6.86 an hour, a considerable improvement.

The EITC is critical to the welfare reform approach adopted by Congress in 1996. As explained in the next two chapters, the new reform approach is based on moving welfare recipients into the job market and giving them some support so that they can earn more by work than by welfare. The EITC is a quintessential part of the strategy.

Conclusions

The American welfare system that was founded by the Social Security Act of 1935 developed quite slowly during its first thirty years, but grew dramatically over the next three decades. The unexpected growth in the number of families headed by single mothers fueled much of this growth, as did the nation's decision to provide better assistance to the aged, disabled and blind, and to extend medical care to millions of low-income and poor Americans.

By the early 1990s the combined cost of welfare programs at the federal and state level was considerably in excess of $300 billion. These programs provided valuable assistance to millions of Americans, but increasingly some of the programs were judged to be seriously flawed. The major cash-welfare program failed to play a meaningful role in preventing poverty or in helping those who received benefits, even over long periods, to escape poverty. The result was a growing class of poor Americans who received welfare benefits for long periods with little or no attachment to the employment market.

The obvious flaws in the design of many of the nation's welfare programs led to major reforms in 1996. In the next chapter, the background of this reform movement will be detailed, along with an analysis of the Personal Responsibility and Work Opportunity Reconciliation Act of 1996.

6

Reform: Ending Welfare as We Know It

As noted in Chapter 5, the American welfare system evolved from the Social Security Act of 1935. In many ways, the welfare system that developed over the next sixty years was totally at odds with the original intentions of the creators of the Social Security Act. Roosevelt and his allies feared welfare, believing that it eroded personal responsibility (Israel, 1966). Their goal was to provide work-relief for the able-bodied poor, while offering welfare assistance only to that small group of mothers with dependent children who had lost their spouses. But, with the enormous growth of single-mother families, the welfare system grew in ways that the Roosevelt administration never imagined. Not only did millions of single mothers—many of whom had children out of wedlock—become welfare recipients, but also a small percentage became long-term users. A system that supported poor mothers outside the job market became increasingly unpopular over time, especially since nonpoor mothers were joining the workforce in record numbers (Bernstein and Garfinkel, 1977, 155).

As far back as the Kennedy administration (1961–63), there has been recognition that the welfare system required reform. President Kennedy proposed that Congress pass legislation supporting employment by welfare recipients and the unemployed. Congress passed a number of bills designed both to encourage employment and, during the Nixon administration (1969–74), to make employment mandatory for a larger group of welfare mothers. Believing that the welfare system was too big and wasteful, Nixon campaigned for a version of the negative income tax to take the place of many welfare programs. Under Nixon's version of a negative income tax, a household or individual's income would have been compared to a predetermined income standard. If a family's income was below the standard, the family had a "negative income," and the government would have transferred income to the family. Families below the standard with earnings would have received more assistance than those without earnings. Nixon's plan was twice passed by the House but expired in the Senate.

Although President Nixon's proposal finally failed, for a time it promoted a consensus about the most plausible approach to reducing the number of welfare programs while efficiently assisting the poor. President Ford (1974–77) made a modest effort to recoup Nixon's momentum on the issue by offering another reform package based on the negative income tax. Ford abandoned the effort when the economy turned increasingly sour. President Carter (1977–81) hoped that welfare reform would be a major accomplishment of his administration. He proposed a system based on a negative income tax for those able to work and a guaranteed income for those who were unemployable. President Carter's plan also foundered in Congress.

The defeat of Carter's plan cast a pall over reform for most of a decade. The concepts on which that plan was based had been debated during three administrations, and it seemed clear that Congress was unlikely to embrace reform based on substantial use of the negative income tax or a guaranteed income. The consensus upon which debate centered during three administrations had clearly dissolved (Ellwood 1989, 269).

A New Consensus—Supported Work

President Reagan's (1981–89) approach to welfare reform consisted of three principles: (1) compulsory work programs for the poor; (2) reducing, consolidating, or abolishing as many welfare programs as possible; and (3) convincing the states to assume a larger share of the costs and administrative burdens of those programs that survived. Reagan's philosophy would prove important in shaping both the debate and the reform of welfare in the 1990s. Reagan's most immediate impact on welfare grew out of his success in convincing Congress to cut federal taxes while substantially increasing spending for defense. Reagan's belief was that the tax cuts would stimulate the economy, producing more, not less, tax revenues. Time proved Reagan wrong. The result of Reagan's failed policies was the largest deficits in the nation's history. The huge new national debt made it even less likely that Congress would entertain welfare reforms that significantly raised federal outlays, even temporarily (Tobin 1994). Additionally, in the early and mid-1980s there was no generalized crisis of the magnitude that had spawned programs in the 1930s, 1940s, 1960s, or early 1970s to lend urgency to welfare reform. Poverty increased quite dramatically during the Reagan years, but Reagan argued that welfare programs were to blame, not his economic policies.

By the end of Reagan's presidency, a new approach to welfare reform was developing in Congress and at the state level focusing on supported work for the able-bodied poor, including single mothers. Supported work required programs designed to educate and train welfare adults for employment, backed up by intermediate support in the form of child and health care to help recipients become established in the work force. Supported work basically involved a mutual obligation contract between the recipient and the state. In return for training and assistance, the recipient agreed to engage in a good faith effort to leave the welfare rolls through employment. This approach is substantially different from programs that simply require welfare recipients to work in return for benefits. Supported work assumes that the recipient will receive help in making the transition to self-sufficiency. This new approach accepted Reagan's argument that welfare recipients should leave the rolls for employment, but it obligated the government to help with the transition. In 1988 Congress embraced this philosophy by passing the Family Support Act.

The Family Support Act (FSA) of 1988

Throughout much of the 1960s, 1970s, and 1980s, Congress had increasingly mandated that able-bodied welfare recipients engage in work. But in practice, few welfare recipients were actually placed in job search, education, or job training programs, and recipients who left AFDC for work received little or no support. The FSA was somewhat more comprehensive, but it was not destined to impact a very large percentage of AFDC recipients. The FSA was very modestly financed, and it was phased in over a five-year period. The importance of the FSA was its philosophical foundation in training and support to help recipients become self-sufficient and its assumption that both parents should be responsible for the welfare of their children.

The goal of the FSA was to reduce considerably the time that families remain dependent on AFDC by providing recipients with services such as education, confidence training, and job skills required by the labor force. To make employment a viable option, the bill financed child and health care for enrolled mothers and extended these support services to the family heads for a limited period while they settled into the job market. The bill also placed major emphasis on improving child support from absent parents. The major provisions of the bill were in five titles.

Title I. Child Support and Paternity

Starting in November 1990, all states were required to provide wage withholding of child support orders in all cases in which the custodial parent received public assistance or in those cases in which the custodial parent had asked for assistance in collecting support. By 1994 states were required to institute wage withholding of child support for almost all support orders, even when the custodial parent was not on welfare. More uniform guidelines for all child support awards were required by the bill, and these guidelines were to be reviewed on a regular basis.

States faced penalties if they failed to establish paternity in a certain proportion of all cases of out-of-wedlock children receiving benefits. To help states locate missing parents, the bill provided access to both IRS and unemployment compensation data. Procedures were established to collect child support from noncustodial parents residing in another state.

Title II. Job Opportunities and Basic Skills Training Program (JOBS)

All states were required to establish a JOBS program. All single parents with children over three (or at state option, over one) could be required to participate, unless they were ill, incapacitated, or had some other valid reason for nonparticipation. States were given a great deal of discretion in designing the training programs, but they had to be approved by the Department of Health and Human Services at least every two years. All states were required to have the JOBS program in place by October 1990 and statewide by October 1992.

The FSA required the state agency in charge of AFDC to assess the needs and skills of all AFDC heads. From this consultation an employability plan for each recipient was to be developed, specifying the activities the head would undertake and the supportive services the participant would receive. State programs could include education, job training, job preparedness training, and job placement. Postsecondary education and other approved employment activities could also be offered. Parents under age twenty without a high school diploma were required to participate in an educational program leading to graduation. Some states were also allowed to set up programs to provide education, job training, and placement to noncustodial parents.

In an effort to reduce long-term welfare dependency, the bill required the states to spend at least 55 percent of all JOBS funds on: (1) families that had received assistance for more than thirty-six months during the preceding five years; (2) families in which the head was under age twenty-four and had not completed high school; and (3) families that would lose benefits within two years because of the age of their children.

Title III. Supportive Services

The states were required to provide child care to participants engaged in education, employment, or job training. To help recipients stay in the workforce and leave welfare, the state could assist in child care for up to one year after families left welfare. The cost of the care to the parent was to be based on a sliding scale based on the income of the parent. Families leaving the AFDC ranks because of employment were eligible for Medicaid coverage for up to one year.

Title IV. AFDC Amendments

The FSA required all the states to establish an AFDC-UP (unemployed parent) program to cover two-parent families with an unemployed head. Until the FSA, only about one-half of the states allowed two-parent families to receive AFDC benefits. States new to the AFDC-UP program were allowed at their option to limit benefits to a minimum of six months a year. However, Medicaid benefits would have to be ongoing.

The amount of money that an AFDC family could earn without losing benefits was raised to $90 a month from $75. The amount of child care cost that the family would have disregarded was raised from $160 a month to $175 (or $200 if the child was under age two). Expenditures for child care were not counted as income in calculating AFDC benefits. States were given the option of requiring single parents who were minors to reside with a parent or guardian.

Title V. Demonstration Projects

The bill funded a rather wide range of innovative demonstration projects at the state level to determine how well various experimental programs alleviated problems or promoted certain desirable outcomes. For example, $6 million over a three-year period was allocated to encourage innovative education programs for poor children. Three million dollars was authorized to fund programs to train poor family heads to be child care providers. Eight million dollars was provided to establish programs to improve noncustodial parents' access to their children. Other programs provided counseling for high-risk teenagers and incentives to businesses to create jobs for AFDC recipients.

The Impact of the Act

As noted above, the FSA was very modestly funded. The FSA represented agreement in Congress that welfare needed to change, and it incorporated some clear principles about how welfare should be reformed. But because the bill was so modestly funded, the importance of FSA is primarily in the philosophy it establishes about some of the ways Congress could agree that welfare needed to be reformed. In passing FSA, a majority of conservatives, moderates, and liberals agreed, at least in principle, that AFDC recipients should receive education, training, and supportive services to help them become independent of welfare. There was also broad support for holding both parents responsible for the sustenance of their children. Establishment of paternity and support from the noncustodial parent both increased as a result of the act (Green Book 1994, 500–501). States were slow in establishing JOBS programs. By 1994 only about 13 percent of all AFDC heads were receiving JOBS training.

Perhaps the most important consequence of the FSA has been the innovative welfare reform experiments at the state level established by the bill. The FSA allowed the states to petition the Department of Health and Human Services for waivers to provide them with the flexibility to be creative in the design of their welfare programs or specific experiments. The waivers permit states to treat welfare recipients within the state differently as long as they were participating in an approved experiment. The state had to agree to pay for any additional costs associated with the implementation and evaluation of such experiments. By late 1996, forty-three states had obtained approval to implement and test some ninety innovative programs. A few states, such as Wisconsin, Michigan, Oregon, and Vermont, led the way. The plans these states and others put into effect would later serve as models of how states could reform their welfare systems and would substantially influence the reform plan passed in 1996.

The Clinton Administration Plan

President Clinton (1993–2001) had considerable experience with the welfare system as Governor of Arkansas and included welfare reform in his presidential platform. Clinton believed that the FSA was on the right track but was underfunded and in need of both amendment and expansion. Once elected President, Clinton put together teams of experts to design a new reform plan based on the FSA that would, he pledged, "end welfare as we know it." The resulting plan proposed by President Clinton was based on the continued use of entitlement programs to ensure that all categorically eligible poor were given assistance. The plan rested on six principals:

1. *Make work pay.* Clinton believed that to reform welfare, it had to be more profitable for families to work than to receive welfare. To achieve this end, Clinton favored raising the minimum wage, improving the Earned Income Tax Credit (EITC), and expanding child care and Medicaid coverage for those leaving or avoiding welfare by entering the work force.

2. *Improve child support enforcement.* Clinton believed that the FSA was moving in the right direction on this policy, but that the process by which absent parents were identified and forced to support their children needed improvement. Clinton proposed wage withholding of all child support orders, and penalties for mothers who failed to cooperate in identifying the father(s) of their children, and a number of changes designed to make it easier to identify and track absent parents.

3. *Pregnancy prevention.* Funds would be allocated to help states establish anti-pregnancy programs for teenagers based on counseling, moral suasion, and incentives. To improve the supervision of teen mothers, Clinton proposed that to be eligible for cash assistance, unwed mothers younger than eighteen be required to live with a parent or guardian.

4. *Job assistance for welfare heads.* Building on the FSA, Clinton proposed increased funding for job training, education, and support programs for AFDC family heads. An additional $10 billion would be allocated to job training and child care to move AFDC family heads into the work force and help them to stay employed.

5. *Set time limits on cash benefits.* In a substantial departure for a Democratic President, Clinton proposed that recipients who were born after 1972 and were healthy and able to work be required to accept a combination of education, training, or job placement assistance to enable them to leave the welfare rolls, often within two years. This provision was know as "two years and out" but actually meant a transition to a job, subsidized if necessary.

6. *Public service and subsidized jobs.* If welfare heads could not find employment in the private sector, Clinton proposed that as a last resort, they be placed in either a public sector job or that their employment in the private sector be subsidized. Once employed, the parent would be given child care and Medicaid assistance to help them become established in the world of work.

President Clinton summarized his proposal in a speech to the National Governor's Association in early 1995: "Anyone who can work should do so. Welfare reform should include time limits. Anyone who brings a child into the world ought to be prepared to take financial responsibility for that child's future. Teen pregnancy and out-of-wedlock childbearing are important problems that must be addressed through comprehensive welfare reform."

Clinton's proposals represented a substantial alteration in the welfare system, especially his emphasis on time limits. While Clinton had made welfare reform an important part of his campaign for the presidency, during the first two years of his administration, he concentrated on health care reform, believing that it was a necessary first step. The Republican members of Congress, interested in reducing the size and cost of the federal government, especially welfare, kept the issue on the agenda and by 1995 had raised welfare reform to a central political issue.

The Republican Party Plan

In 1995 the Republican party had a majority in both houses of Congress. One goal of the Republican majority was a thorough overhaul of the nation's welfare system. The Republicans were never united on how to reform welfare, but they did agree that the system needed major renovation. Some of the Republicans were primarily interested in reducing costs, others wanted to move welfare recipients into jobs even if it was initially expensive, others wanted to turn welfare over to the states, and a few just wanted to get rid of welfare because they believed it did harm to recipients (Bryner, 1998, 152). Republicans in the House tended to be more conservative than their colleagues in the Senate. Some Democrats were interested in a fundamental reform of welfare and often joined their Republican colleagues in supporting various reform proposals.

Given the divisions within the Republican party, opposition from many Democrats, and significant differences between the two chambers, the debate was vigorous, emotional, and even hostile. Throughout 1995 the House and Senate debated various reform proposals and struggled to agree on a welfare reform bill. In November 1995, Congress sent President Clinton a reform plan as part of a larger budget reconciliation bill (H.R. 2491). President Clinton vetoed this bill on December 6, 1995. Congress made some minor changes in this plan and sent it back to the White House in late December 1995 (H.R. 4). President Clinton vetoed this bill on January 9, 1996.

After Congress amended its proposal to meet some of the President's objections, on August 22, 1996, President Clinton signed into law the third version of welfare reform passed by Congress. President Clinton made it clear that he did not agree with all the provisions of the bill he signed but wanted welfare reform to pass and stated that he would seek in the future to amend those provisions of the bill he found objectionable. The reform bill finally passed was a true bipartisan compromise. All major public policies result from many compromises, but the new reform bill represented an unusual degree of compromise because the Republicans controlled Congress and because President Clinton's position on this issue was quite moderate. The liberal wing of the Democratic party lobbied and voted against the bill and were very disappointed by its passage.

The major policy differences between the Republican majority in Congress and President Clinton varied during the most intense months of the debate, but some of the most important differences included the following:

1. *Capping welfare spending:* Clinton's reform proposals would have continued to treat major welfare programs as entitlements, meaning that all persons who qualified for assistance under a program would be served. This "open-ended" spending on welfare was a major concern of the Republican majority, especially those interested in realizing cost savings from reform. The Republicans proposed eliminating entitlements by placing a yearly cap on spending for most welfare programs.

2. *Turn welfare programs over to the states.* The Clinton plan envisioned the continued administration of welfare by the federal government. The Republican plan proposed the devolution of these programs to the states. The Republican plan proposed giving the states block grants and then allowing them to use these funds to design their own welfare systems. The nation's governors, represented by the National Governors' Association, vigorously promoted this approach.

3. *Time limits, sanctions, and caps.* Clinton supported time limits, but the Republican proposals were more stringent. The Republican majority bills would have required states to cut off cash benefits to any family that over its lifetime had received assistance for a total of five years. States could exempt up to 15 percent of their caseloads from time limits. Penalties for noncompliance and other time limits

would have also been tougher under the Republican plans. Assistance would have been denied to any adult who refused to cooperate in establishing paternity or who failed to assist a state child support enforcement agency. If a recipient had received a year of education or training, benefits could be terminated. Any adult recipient who received welfare for two years (or a shorter period at state option) would be required to engage in work activity.

In several versions of its plan, the Republicans proposed that both the food stamp and Medicaid programs be capped and turned over to the states in the form of block grants. Agricultural and nutrition lobbies convinced Congress to preserve the food stamp program, while President Clinton forced the Republicans to back away from its plans to give states control over Medicaid. Thus, the reform plan sent to the President in August 1996 allowed recipients who were rendered ineligible for cash assistance by deadlines to retain the right to apply for noncash assistance such as food stamps and Medicaid.

4. *Employment deadlines.* To force states to make substantial progress in moving welfare recipients into the job market, the Republican plan imposed yearly benchmarks. As the Republican plan evolved, states would have been required to enroll half of all caseload family heads in work or training programs by 2001 or suffer a 5 percent reduction in funding. The goal was to require 1.5 million welfare family heads to find employment by the year 2001.

5. *Deny or reduce cash assistance to some families.* While the Senate and House often disagreed on the details, the Republicans proposals significantly increased the opportunities for denying assistance to certain recipients. States would have been allowed to make teen mothers under eighteen ineligible for cash assistance, except in cases of rape or incest. At state discretion, the ban could have been extended to all unwed mothers under twenty-five. Children born to families on welfare could have been denied assistance. The savings realized could have been used to fund orphanages, adoption services, and homes for unwed mothers. States would have been given the option of issuing vouchers to teen mothers and to women who had additional children while on welfare, which could have been used to purchase baby supplies.

6. *Eliminate most aid to legal immigrants.* The Republican proposals varied over time, but all placed major restrictions on assistance to legal aliens. Most legal immigrants would no longer have been eligible for cash assistance, Supplemental Security Income (SSI), social serv-

ices block grant funds, Medicaid and food stamps until they became citizens. The only exceptions would have been refugees, permanent residents over age seventy-five who had lived in the United States for five years, legal immigrants who had honorably served in the U.S. military, and, in some cases, legal immigrants who had lived in the United States for five years. The financial responsibility of immigrant sponsors would have been extended, usually until the immigrant became a U.S. citizen or paid Social Security taxes for ten years.

7. *Change food stamp rules.* As noted, in several versions the Republican plans sought to cap food stamp expenditures but still allow everyone qualified by need to receive assistance. If demand were high, each recipient would have received less. All able-bodied food stamp recipients would have been required to obtain employment within ninety days or enroll in job training or a government-sponsored work program.

8. *Tighten eligibility for SSI.* Adults suffering from alcoholism or drug addiction would no longer have been eligible for Supplemental Security Income (SSI). The definition of a disabled child would have been changed. Under the law in place, a child was defined as disabled if mental, physical, and social functioning was substantially less than that of children of the same age. Under the proposed law, a child would be disabled if he or she had a medically verified physical or mental impairment expected to cause death or last more than twelve months.

9. *Enforce child support orders.* The Republican proposals would have established new state and federal registries to help enforce child support orders. States would have been required to establish a central-case registry to monitor all child support orders. They would have also been required to establish a worker registry to which employers would send the name, Social Security number, and address of all new hires. The states would have been required to put Social Security numbers on most licenses and to suspend licenses of parents who fall behind in child support payments. Federal registries would have been established to track absent parents nationwide.

Clinton's Response

President Clinton seriously disagreed with many of the Republican proposals. He particularly objected to the proposed funding caps or annual budgets for major welfare programs. Clinton was afraid that when the economy was weak, causing more citizens to apply for aid, the programs would run out of funds, leaving eligible applicants without assistance. Clinton was also concerned that if welfare was turned over to the states and financed by block grants, many states would rely only on federal money and cut back on state welfare expenditures. Clinton wanted the law to require the states to continue to spend at current levels or very close to current levels on poverty alleviation.

Clinton also disagreed with the Republican rejection of guaranteed jobs for recipients forced off the rolls by time limits who could not find employment in the private sector. While the Republicans felt confident that the economy would provide ample jobs for serious job seekers, Clinton wanted to guarantee that willing applicants who could not find employment in the private sector could be placed either in a subsidized private sector job or in public sector employment. Additionally, Clinton argued, jobs would be of little value to welfare parents if quality, affordable child care was not available and if the recipients lacked the education or training required to make them qualified for employment. Thus, Clinton pressed Congress to expand funding for child care, education, and training programs. Clinton also objected to Republican plans to cut funding for nutrition programs and the Earned Income Tax Credit (EITC), which were critical to his efforts to make work pay. Last, Clinton felt that the restrictions on assistance to legal aliens were punitive and an attempt to use welfare reform to rewrite the nation's immigration laws. If the new law contained time limits, Clinton argued, there was no reason to treat legal immigrants any different than other recipients.

Compromises

After twice vetoing the welfare reform plans passed by Congress, Clinton was successful in convincing the Republican majority to increase funding for child care, education, job training, and nutrition programs. He was also successful in convincing Congress to set required spending levels for the states. Congress also agreed to continue to fund the food stamp and Medicaid programs as entitlements. The Republican majority, however, convinced Clinton to accept many of its key proposals. In the final bill signed by Clinton, spending for cash welfare and several other programs is capped. Welfare administration is turned over to the states, and states are given considerable discretion in the design of their programs. Stringent time limits are imposed, assistance to legal immigrants is significantly restricted, and states are allowed to impose serious penalties for noncompliance.

The new reform bill, therefore, represents a major set of compromises produced by divided government. Both the President and the Republican Congress won concessions on the design of the new bill, but it is a conservative victory. President Clinton took an unusually moderate posture on welfare reform for a Democratic president, and in the end he signed into law an act that gave the Republicans much of what they wanted. While the new reform's foundation can be traced back to the Family Support Act of 1988, it represents a radical change in the design and administration of welfare in America. Below we will describe the bill in some detail and then in Chapter 7 examine the early evidence on the impact of the new legislation.

Personal Responsibility and Work Opportunity Reconciliation Act, 1996

The Personal Responsibility and Work Opportunity Reconciliation Act was signed into law by President Clinton on August 22, 1996. The major goals of this new welfare reform legislation are to:

- Turn responsibility for welfare administration over to the states, allow states more flexibility in designing their programs, and help states deliver services more efficiently;
- Cap annual federal expenditures for a number of major welfare programs;
- Place the emphasis of welfare programs on helping recipients become independent through employment;
- Sharply limit the time period that most recipients can receive federally-funded cash welfare benefits;
- Increase sanctions for noncompliance;
- Lower the out-of-wedlock birth rate;
- Increase the identification and financial responsibility of absent parents;
- Restrict the ability of legal immigrants to receive welfare assistance.

Major provisions include the following:

1. *Turn welfare programs over to the states.* A number of major welfare programs are consolidated into two block grants to the states. States receive yearly lump sum payments under each of the block grants and are given considerable discretion in designing their own welfare programs. The Temporary Assistance to Needy Families (TANF) block grant replaced four cash welfare and related programs: Aid to families with Dependent Children (AFDC), AFDC Administration, the Job Opportunities and Basic Skills Training (Jobs) program, and the Emergency Assistance Program. The TANF block grant provides cash and other assistance to advance a number of welfare goals, including funds to help needy families support their children while making the transition to work.

The second block grant consolidates four child care programs into the existing Child Care and Development Block Grant, which provides funds to states to improve the quality of child care and to subsidize child care for families on welfare, families becoming established in the workforce, and families who might become dependent without child care assistance.

2. *Cap welfare spending.* Federal funding for the TANF block grant is capped at $16.4 billion annually from fiscal 1996 through fiscal 2001. The block grant approach means that TANF is not an entitlement program. If the states spend all the funds, except under limited circumstances noted below, no additional federal funds are made available even for qualified recipients. States, of course, have the discretion of spending their funds once federal funds are exhausted.

3. *Grant distribution.* Grant dollars are distributed to each state based on its federal funding for AFDC and related programs in either fiscal 1995, fiscal 1994, or the average of fiscal 1992–94, whichever was higher. Additional funds to states include:

(a) Beginning in fiscal 1997, $2 billion in contingency funds were designated for matching grants to states with high unemployment or rapidly growing food stamp rolls.
(b) A $1.7 billion loan fund was made available to states beginning in fiscal 1997. States must repay the loans with interest within three years.
(c) Over four years, beginning in fiscal 1998, $800 million is avail-

able for states with growing populations and low welfare benefits per recipient.

(d) Beginning in fiscal 1998, states that reduce out-of-wedlock births by 1 percent in any year compared with the base year of 1995, while also reducing abortions, receive an additional 5 percent of their block grant. States that reduced such births by 2 percent receive an additional 10 percent.

(e) Beginning in fiscal 1999, $1 billion will be allocated over five years to those states most successful in moving welfare recipients into the workplace.

(f) Four hundred million dollars is made available to states to teach abstinence as a means of birth control.

4. *Maintenance of effort.* States must continue to spend at least 75 percent of the funds they contributed to welfare programs in 1994. States that do not meet mandatory work requirements for welfare recipients must maintain 80 percent of previous funding. To qualify for contingency funds described below, states must maintain spending at 100 percent.

5. *Encouragement of innovation.* States are encouraged to be innovative in designing their welfare policies. Programs may vary across a state, but all qualified families must receive fair and equitable treatment. States are not required to provide cash assistance; instead they may substitute vouchers or services. States may also opt to privatize welfare programs by turning them over to charities, religious organizations, or other private entities. To encourage innovation and flexibility, states are allowed to transfer up to 30 percent of their TANF block grant into the Child Care and Development block grant, or a maximum 10 percent into the existing Title XX Social Services Block Grant. Funds transferred into the Social Services Block Grant may be used only for programs and services to children and families with incomes below 200 percent of the poverty level.

6. *Employment guidelines and goals.* Adult welfare recipients are required to begin work within two years, or a shorter period at state discretion. Work activities are defined to include actual work in the private or public sector, plus, to a limited degree, education, vocational training, and job search. After the year 2000, not more than 30 percent of the required number of work participants can qualify by participating in vocational training or by being teen heads-of-households attending secondary school.

States may take parents of children under one out of the participation rate, but only for a total of twelve months. Parents with children
under six are exempt unless child care is available, but they still count
in the state's participation rate. States must have at least 25 percent
of single adult recipients engaged in work in fiscal 1997, rising to 50
percent in 2002.

To count toward the employment goal, single parents must work at
least twenty hours a week in 1997, rising to thirty hours in 2000.
States may allow parents with a child under six to work twenty hours
a week. Two-parent families must work thirty-five hours a week. The
requirements for single parents are summarized below:

Fiscal yr	Min % of caseload	Min hrs work/wk
1997	25	20
1998	30	20
1999	35	25
2000	40	30
2001	45	30
2002	50	30

States that fail to meet the work requirements will have their block
grant reduced by 5 percent, which will grow by 2 percent per year,
rising to a maximum reduction of 21 percent. The Secretary of Heath
and Human Services may approve "reasonable cause" for failure to
meet the goals.

The work participation rate for two-parent families receiving cash
welfare is considerably higher. The participation rate for at least one
adult in a two-parent family is: in fiscal 1996, 50 percent; in fiscal
1997–98, 75 percent; in fiscal 1999 and thereafter, 90 percent.

7. *Time limited assistance.* Block grant funds can be awarded to
adults for a lifetime limit of five years. States can write their regula-
tions to deny federal funds to assist adults who do not work after
receiving TANF for two years. States may exempt up to 20 percent
of their caseload from these requirements. States may also opt to set
a shorter time limit for all families, or they may opt to continue to
provide assistance after the time limit using only state dollars or funds

transferred from the TANF Block Grant into the Social Services Block Grant.

8. *Sanctions and restrictions on assistance.*

(a) Adults who do not cooperate with work or training requirements or in establishing paternity will have their benefits reduced proportionately, or at state option, will be rejected for assistance.

(b) Individuals convicted of felony drug crimes are not eligible for welfare benefits and food stamps. States can pass a state law to amend this provision if they prefer.

(c) States may deny assistance to children born to welfare recipients or assistance to unwed parents under eighteen. If a state provides assistance to unwed parents under eighteen, they must live with an adult and attend school or other specified work or training programs.

(d) Welfare recipients who move into a new state may, at state option, be limited to those benefits that they would have received in their former state for twelve months.

9. *Federal waivers.* States that have received federal waivers in order to establish experimental welfare programs can continue to carry out those programs until the waivers expire, even if the experimental programs are inconsistent with this bill.

10. *Food stamps.* Eligibility for food stamps is tightened and states are given more flexibility in designing and implementing the program, but it remains an entitlement program. Benefits are adjusted yearly for inflation, although individual allotments are reduced from 103 percent of the Agriculture Department's Thrifty Food Plan to 100 percent. Additionally, benefits are reduced by changes in various deductions that recipients are allowed to count against income, and state and local energy assistance is counted as income. The base fair market value above which the value of a car is counted as an asset is frozen at $4,650, and the housing deduction will be capped at $300 by 2001.

Welfare recipients who fail to comply with work requirements can be denied food stamps. Able-bodied Adults Without Dependents (ABAWDs) between the ages of eighteen and fifty must work an average of twenty or more hours per week or participate in a work program. Those not employed or enrolled can receive food stamps for only three months out of every three years, unless they are laid off or live in a community with high unemployment (10 percent or more). If these conditions exist, the state can apply for a waiver that would allow recipients another quarter of eligibility. Federal funding for food stamps, employment, and training programs is budgeted to increase from $79 million in 1997 to $90 million in fiscal 2002. (In 1997 this provision was amended to allow states to exempt 15 percent of all ABAWDs who have used up their three "free" months of food stamp eligibility. Additionally, funds were provided to enable states to create workfare or subsidized job slots for ABAWDs.)

States are given the option of aligning the food stamp program with their revamped welfare programs by establishing a single set of eligibility requirements for assistance. States were also given the option of converting food stamp benefits to wage subsidies for employers who hire recipients. These recipients will receive wages rather than stamps.

11. *Child nutrition programs.* Child nutrition programs, including the Child and Adult Care Food Program, are reduced by about $3 billion over six years. The act eliminates the option of serving an additional meal or snack to children who are in child care centers for more than eight hours per day. Congress repealed this provision in 1997.

12. *Medicaid.* The act does not establish a block grant for Medicaid. Generally, states must provide Medicaid to families that would have been qualified for AFDC under the eligibility standards in existence on July 16, 1996. Thus, qualified families who lose cash assistance because of employment will continue to qualify for Medicaid unless their income exceeds the old AFDC income limit set by their state. States must continue to provide Medicaid coverage for one year to those individuals who lose their welfare eligibility because of increased earnings (six months of full Medicaid; six months of subsidized Medicaid if family income is less than 185 percent of the poverty level). States may, however, deny Medicaid to adults who lose cash aid by not meeting work requirements and restrictions on many legal aliens are tightened.

13. *Restrictions on assistance to legal immigrants.* Illegal aliens and legal nonaliens are generally ineligible for welfare assistance, except short-term emergency aid. The provisions covering legal aliens in the 1996 law were amended in 1997. After amendment, the reform law

provides that legal immigrants residing in the United States on the date that the bill was signed (August 22, 1996) will continue to be eligible for SSI and Medicaid. States were given the option of making this group of legal aliens eligible for food stamps but at state cost. In 1998 the law was further amended to restore food stamps to this group of legal immigrants, estimated to number about 250,000, including about 75,000 children. The 1997 amendments also allowed the states to decide if they want legal aliens residing in the United States on August 22, 1996 to be eligible for TANF and services provided by Social Services Block Grant funds. Legal aliens residing in the United States on that date achieve regular assistance eligibility when they become citizens or when family members work a total of forty quarters.

Legal immigrants who enter the United States after the new law's enactment are much more restricted. During the first five years, they are barred from receiving most nonemergency means-tested federal help, including child care, food stamps, SSI, nonemergency Medicaid, and TANF. After the first five years, the income of sponsors will be counted in assessing the eligibility of legal immigrants for assistance until the immigrant (or immigrant family) has worked in the United States for forty quarters or has become a citizen. Refugees, American military veterans, and those granted asylum are exempt from these restrictions.

14. *Supplemental Security Income.* The law tightens eligibility for SSI for both adults and children. Previously children could receive SSI benefits if their mental, physical and social functioning was substantially less than children of the same age or if they engaged in age-inappropriate behavior. Under this law a child is disabled only if he/she has a medically proven physical or mental disability that results in marked and severe functional limitations. This disability must be expected to cause death or to last more than twelve months. In 1997 the law was amended to provide continuing Medicaid coverage for any disabled child losing SSI benefits because of changes in the law.

15. *Child-support enforcement.* Over fifty statutory changes were made in existing laws. The reforms pursue five major goals: (a) automating many child support enforcement procedures; (b) establishing uniform tracking procedures; (c) strengthening interstate child support

enforcement; (d) requiring states to adopt stronger measures to establish paternity; (e) creating improved enforcement tools to increase actual child support collections.

States are required to create a central case registry to track all child support orders created or modified after October 1, 1997. Information must be updated regularly and shared with the federal case registry. States were required to establish a new hire registry by October 1, 1997, to collect the name, address, and Social Security number of new hires. States must review information on new hires and order employers to withhold child support payment from delinquent employees. A similar federal registry will track nonpaying parents nationwide. States are given the authority to suspend all licenses held by parents who owe past due child support. All funds collected from parents of children receiving assistance will go to the state.

In 1998 President Clinton supplemented these provisions by signing into law the Deadbeat Parents Punishment Act. This law created two new categories of felonies against parents who seek to evade child support: (1) Any parent traveling across state or country lines to evade child support commits a felony if the amount owed is $5,000 or more and has been outstanding for twelve months or longer; (2) If the child support obligation is more than $10,000 or has gone unpaid for over two years, willful failure to pay this support to a child living in another state constitutes a felony.

16. *Child Care.* The Child Care and Development block grant provides child care for low-income families, funding to improve the quality and availability of child care, child-care services for welfare recipients who accept jobs or enter job training, and child-care assistance to families in jeopardy of becoming welfare recipients.

Federal funding is set at $16 billion through fiscal 2002, starting at $1.1 billion in 1996, growing to $2.7 billion in fiscal 2002. This represents an increase of about $4 billion in funding for child-care. At least 70 percent of the funds must be used to assist welfare recipients, those attempting to leave welfare, and those in danger of needing welfare assistance. Child care services are also funded at the state level by Social Services Block Grant funds. This block grant was cut by 15 percent but states were given the flexibility to use these funds to provide noncash vouchers for children whose parents exceed the five-year time limit on benefits.

17. *Earned-income tax credit.* This tightens eligibility for this program for low-income workers; requires that those who apply use a valid taxpayer identification number to make it easier to track recipients and their income; and expands the types of income counted in determining eligibility and excludes some income losses that were previously taken into consideration.

Additional 1997 Amendments

In 1997 Congress added another amendment to create a $3 billion "Welfare to Work Jobs Challenge" fund. In each year of 1998 and 1999, $1.1 billion will be allocated to the states by formula to help the states move long-term welfare recipients into lasting, unsubsidized jobs. These funds can be used for job creation, job placement, and job retention, including wage subsidies to private employers and other post-employment support services. In each of the two years, $400 million will be available on a competitive basis to fund innovative job programs in high poverty areas recommended by the states.

Additionally, employers are given an additional incentive to hire long-term welfare recipients by providing a credit equal to 35 percent of the first $10,000 in wages in the first year of employment, and 50 percent of the first $10,000 in the second year. The credit is for two years per worker to encourage not only hiring but also retention.

Other Federal Welfare Initiatives, 1997

Mobilizing the Business Community

In May 1997 the Welfare to Work Partnership was launched to encourage businesses to hire people from the welfare rolls. Some 800 companies have accepted President Clinton's challenge to help move those on assistance into jobs in the public sector. In August 1997 the partnership established a toll-free hotline (1–888–usajob1), a web page (www.welfaretowork.org), a "Blueprint for Business" manual to help companies across the nation hire people off welfare, and a city-to-city challenge to help promote innovative and effective welfare to work initiatives in twelve cities with high levels of poverty.

Helping Welfare Recipients Get Off and Stay Off Welfare

Vice President Gore was given authority to direct the Welfare to Work Coalition to Sustain Success, a coalition of civic groups committed to helping former welfare recipients stay in the workforce and succeed. The goal is to tailor services to meet welfare recipients' needs. The Coalition will focus on providing mentoring and other support services. Charter members include the Boys and Girls Clubs of America, the Baptist Joint Committee, the United Way, the YMCA, and fourteen other civic groups.

Federal Government Hiring Initiative

In March 1997, the President directed each head of a federal agency or department to develop a plan to hire and retain welfare recipients in jobs in the government. The goal is to hire 10,000 welfare recipients over four years without displacing current employees.

Transportation

In May 1997, President Clinton announced Department of Transportation grants to twenty-four states to develop welfare-to-work transportation strategies. The President also urged Congress to adopt a six-year, $600 million grant program in his NEXTEA transportation bill that would support flexible, innovative transportation systems in rural, urban, and suburban areas to get people to jobs.

Conclusions

The 1996 welfare reform act was a major alteration in the welfare system that evolved over the sixty-year period since the Social Security Act of 1935. Resting on a fundamentally altered philosophy, it places federal spending for several major welfare programs on a yearly budget and turns welfare administration over to the states. States are given a great deal of discretion in designing and administrating their welfare programs, as long as they focus on moving actual or potential welfare recipients into the job market. The deadlines for moving caseloads into employment are short, especially since most welfare families lose eligibility for federal cash assistance after a lifetime limit of five years.

State governors and conservative politicians won a major victory in convincing Congress and the President to agree to turn welfare administration over to the states. Now, however, the states are faced with a major obligation. They are basically required to convert the welfare system into a supported jobs program. The 1996 act allows states a great deal of flexibility in achieving this goal, but the timelines are tight and states will have to show a great deal of initiative to meet the established deadlines and goals. In the next chapter we will examine the early evidence on the impact of the new law and the quality of the job being done at the state level.

7

State Welfare Plans Under PRWORA

T he Personal Responsibility and Work Opportunity Reconciliation Act (PRWORA) of 1996 has resulted in the most innovative period in the history of American welfare. All fifty states,
the District of Columbia, and several territories have designed new
welfare systems, many of which show a genuine determination to find
ways to help the poor become independent through self-employment.
While the 1996 act places many requirements and restrictions on the
states, it allows state officials considerable flexibility in designing their
new welfare systems. Many states have taken advantage of this discretion. States are experimenting with a wide range of policies designed to move welfare recipients, and would-be recipients, into the
job market, and assist them with support services while they become
established in the workforce. The plans being implemented across the
nation vary frequently even within states where different approaches
are often being tested in one or more counties.

State responsiveness, of course, varies a great deal. Public officials
in some states have been interested in comprehensive welfare reform
for over a decade. Wisconsin, Michigan, Vermont, and Oregon, for
example, were leaders in gaining permission to test innovative policies
in the early 1990s. The Clinton administration had approved demonstration projects (experimental plans) in forty-three states before the

1996 act was passed. This allowed many states to test experimental programs, or even to engage in major welfare reform, years before the new law was passed in 1996. A few states were far enough along to become models for reform.

Most states, however, were still in the early stages of reform when the 1996 law was passed, and some have gotten off to a slow start. An indication of how poorly prepared many states were for reform was the failure of many of them to meet one of the employment and job training deadlines required by the 1996 act. The law required the states to have 75 percent of all of their two-parent welfare families enrolled in jobs or job training by September 1, 1997. States that started their programs after April 1997 were not required to meet the deadline. Of the thirty-three states required to meet the deadline, eighteen failed to do so. One additional state (West Virginia) had collected too little data to be evaluated (www.acf.dhhs.gov/news/press/1998/ wlfrewk.htm). Most of the states did meet the deadline for having 25 percent of all single-parent families enrolled in a "work activity," but many barely met the standard and often did so by lowering the target rate through reductions in their welfare rolls.

While the goal for two-parent families was high, given the flexibility states were allowed in the 1996 act in using benefit dollars as wage subsidies, the substantial additional funds voted by Congress in 1997 for training and jobs (both for food stamp recipients and the Welfare to Work Jobs Challenge), the tax breaks voted for employers, and the support volunteered by companies and private organizations across the nation, the difficulty that most states have had suggests that reorganizing to focus on moving welfare recipients into jobs has been a major challenge. Those states without an early start have found it fairly complicated to set up programs to evaluate recipients and potential recipients and provide them with the range of services required to move them into jobs.

Even though many states have gotten off to a rather slow start, and there are differences among the states in terms of their commitment to reform, the range and combinations of policies that have been adopted suggest that many states are interested in designing effective policies to help healthy adults leave welfare for employment. However, the combination of short deadlines contained within the 1996 act, slow startups by many states, and an extremely healthy economy in 1997, 1998, and 1999 has allowed most states to focus primarily on quickly moving recipients off the rolls directly into jobs. Know as "Work First," this policy allows states to de-emphasize education and job training in favor of job search and job placement. Recipients are simply required to take any job they can get, based on the assumption that the best job training is a job. The primary challenge to states under this approach is in setting up the infrastructure to provide recipients with the support services they require—mostly health care and child care. As will be detailed below, some states have designed programs that are much more sophisticated than the basic "Work First" approach, but most have not. Thus, when the economy falters, many states may be challenged to design much more sophisticated programs. Additionally, the early evidence on the impact of the act discussed in Chapter 8 suggests that to really help ex-recipients prosper through employment, "Work First" may need to be supplemented with on-the-job education and skill training, wage subsidies, and income disregards.

Below we will examine how in the early stages the states have exercised the various options allowed by PRWORA in designing their new welfare policies.

Characteristics and Impact of State Programs

To provide insights into how states are implementing PRWORA, three approaches are taken below. First, we start with a case study of Wisconsin, which is recognized as one of the states that have lead the way in welfare reform. The Wisconsin plan is not typical; it is, in fact, one of the most sophisticated reform plans adopted by any state. A study of the Wisconsin plan is valuable because it provides insights into the various program options allowed by PRWORA. Wisconsin chose among those options to lay out a comprehensive set of programs designed to substitute supported work for welfare for almost all the state's poor and low-income population. Second, the Wisconsin plan is contrasted with the approach being taken in a few other states that have demonstrated a commitment to reform. Third, the major provisions of PRWORA are reviewed to show how the fifty states and the District of Columbia have chosen among the various options to design their welfare plans.

Wisconsin: A Case Study

Wisconsin has designed and implemented one of the most comprehensive welfare plans in the nation. As Table 8.1 in the next chapter
shows, welfare rolls in Wisconsin declined by 82 percent between
January of 1993 and June of 1998. The dramatic drop in recipients is
the direct result of a number of Wisconsin plans going back to the
late 1980s designed to restrict welfare eligibility and to aggressively
move welfare recipients into the workforce and a healthy state economy (Wiseman, 1996). An early leader in reform, Wisconsin experi-
mented with a number of alternatives to traditional AFDC during the
late 1980s and early 1990s, and then became the first state to pass a
fully articulated reform plan under PRWORA (Corbett, 1995). Since
the Wisconsin plan was based on considerable experimentation, and
was overtly designed to require, even force, most able-bodied adults
to accept or find employment rather than receive cash welfare, it has
been very influential in shaping both the welfare debate and the plans
of many other states.

No Entitlement to Welfare

The Wisconsin plan is formally named Wisconsin Works, but it is
known as W-2, a reference to the income tax form reporting wages
received by workers. W-2 was implemented statewide in late 1997.
The basic assumption of W-2 is that there is no entitlement to welfare,
but that those who are willing to work will be placed in jobs that
match their abilities, or they will be given help in finding employment.
Thus, almost all cash assistance is linked to some type of work. Unlike
the state's AFDC program, which was restricted to single parents, W-2
is available to all poor or near-poor adults with incomes below 125
percent of their poverty level and with limited assets. A family is
permitted to have $2,500 in available assets, excluding vehicle equity
of $10,000, and first-mortgage homestead property.

Mutual Obligation Contracts

W-2 is grounded in a mutual obligation philosophy. Applicants for
assistance do not meet with a caseworker as in the past, but with a
Financial and Employment Planner (FEP), who helps them develop

an Employment Plan (EP). Part of the EP is a mutual obligation contract in which the applicant pledges, among other things, to be courteous and cooperative, refrain from certain behaviors (e.g., drug and alcohol abuse), accept responsibility for self-help, and take training, education, and employment seriously. This contracting and planning stage is designed to: (a) discourage applicants who have alternatives to welfare or who do not wish to cooperate; (b) establish ground rules for those who want assistance; (c) creatively help those determined to require services through evaluation, counseling, training and/or education. If necessary, applicants are enrolled in several weeks of supervised job search. During job search sessions, applicants are given remedial instructions in a range of topics including time management (particularly on how to get to work on time), accepting criticism from supervisors, getting along with co-workers, and transportation options. Job search sessions normally last half a day, with applicants spending the rest of the day in actual job interviews.

Employment Ladder

As part of the EP, applicants must lay out their goals and develop a plan of action. This exercise is designed to elevate the morale of applicants by convincing them that they can start out in low-paying jobs and work their way up. The second stage is to place applicants within a four-stage employment ladder, starting them at the top stage if they are qualified. As an incentive, the income of participants increases as they move up the job ladder. The four levels are:

Unsubsidized Employment

This is the highest rung of the ladder, and the one recipients are encouraged to achieve. If qualified and the job can be found, applicants are placed here. Those placed in unsubsidized employment receive no cash welfare, but they are often eligible for the Earned Income Tax Credit (EITC), food stamps, Medical Assistance, child care and job access loans.

Trial Jobs (Subsidized Employment)

If an unsubsidized job cannot be found, but the applicant is willing to work, he/she may be placed in a subsidized job. Employers prepared to hire willing applicants who need three to six months of on-the-job training are given subsidies of $300 per month. The expectation is that after the subsidized training period, the employer will hire the trainee for a regular position. If not, the trainee is placed into another subsidized job. While in a training position, the trainee receives no cash welfare, but is paid at least the minimum wage, and may be eligible for the EITC, food stamps, Medical Assistance, child care, and job access loans.

Community Service Jobs (CSJs)

Applicants who are not ready for regular employment may be placed in community service jobs. CSJs are designed to allow parents to learn work habits and job skills. CSJ participants received a monthly grant of $673 in 1998 for up to thirty hours per week of work activities and up to ten hours a week in education or training. Participants may be eligible for food stamps, Medical Assistance, child care and job access loans, but not for the EITC. Clients who miss any work or training without good cause may be penalized at the rate of $5.15 per hour.

W-2 Transition

The lowest rung of the employment ladder is reserved for those parents who are unable to perform independent, self-sustaining work. Transition participants received a monthly grant of $628 in 1998 for up to twenty-eight hours per week of work or developmental activities and up to twelve hours per week in education or training. Transition participants may also be eligible for food stamps, Medical Assistance, child care and job access loans, but not the EITC.

Parents who are placed in any of the three lowest rungs of the employment ladder (below unsubsidized employment, where there are no time limits) are restricted to twenty-four months in any one category, and a lifetime limit of sixty months in the various work options. Exceptions can be made when local labor markets limit opportunities. The grants for CSJs and W-2 transition jobs do not vary with family size. Uniform grants, or caps, are designed to discourage welfare parents from having children to increase their benefits.

Minor teen parents under W-2 are not directly eligible for cash assistance. They must live with a parent or guardian who will provide their support, and they must remain in an education or training program. Teen parents may be eligible for some in kind support for child care. W-2 participants who fail to live up to the terms of their EP have their benefits reduced or eliminated. Counties that do the best job of placing applicants in jobs receive financial rewards, while the poorest performing counties have their jurisdiction turned over to private contractors.

Under W-2, responsibility for the administration of the employment programs was shifted from the state's Department of Health and Social Services to the state's employment service agency, the Department of Workforce Development. The DWH is responsible for subcontracting employment and training programs with both private and public entities. W-2 specifically charges DWH to open competition for the administration of the work programs to the private sector in hope of improving their administration.

Support Services

Wisconsin officials have given a great deal of thought to the support services that applicants require to be able to enter and stay in the job market, while balancing employment with training, education, and parenthood. The services include:

One-Stop Job Centers

Located throughout the state, Job Centers offer one-stop shopping for employers seeking employees and all job seekers, regardless of income level, in need of counseling, career planning, education and training, and job placement. W-2 agencies are either located within individual Job Centers or linked electronically within a Job Center network. Individuals arriving at a Job Center site are evaluated by a resource specialist to determine the type of assistance they need and then referred to those services within the site. The array of services include information about employment opportunities, career options, and the local labor market, along with testing, training, job skills evaluations, job search, and job placement.

Job Access Loans

Small grants are available to help families meet immediate financial needs that may be preventing them from working. The grants cover such costs as car repairs, required clothing or equipment, and moving expenses. Repayment must begin almost immediately and can be done through cash or a combination of cash and volunteer community service. Generally the loans must be repaid within twelve months, but some exceptions are made.

Transportation Assistance

A variety of transportation options are available to ensure that parents can get their children to day care and themselves to work sites. Public transit services have been expanded to a broader range of communities, and service hours have been extended. Financial support has been offered to employers to finance van and shuttle services and to establish volunteer driver programs. W-2 agencies are also encouraged to develop buyer plans with local car dealers, vehicle repair services with local high schools and technical schools, and free bike programs.

Child Care

Wisconsin has substantially expanded funding for child care assistance. All families with gross income equal to or less than 165 percent of the poverty line and assets below the W-2 standard are eligible. There are no time limits on eligibility. Family heads must cooperate in identifying absent parents and meet these nonfinancial eligibility standards: the parent must be employed; if the parent is twenty or younger, he/she must be enrolled in high school or a high school equivalency program; the parent must be participating in W-2 transition, a Community Service Job, or a Trial Job; the parent is enrolled in job training and has been employed in unsubsidized employment for nine months.

Parents eligible for child care assistance receive vouchers that can be used to place their children in licensed day care centers, licensed family day care homes, or even with neighbors or relatives as long as basic health and safety standards are met. Parents pay a co-payment based on their income and family size, the number of children in subsidized care, and the type of provider. As the income of parents increases, the subsidy may phase out.

Child Support

Both parents are expected to contribute to the support of their children. Child support payments are aggressively pursued, and all collections are paid directly to the custodial parent and do not result in a reduction in benefit payments.

Health Care

Two coordinated networks of Medicaid providers serve W-2 participants. Medical Assistance is a mandatory statewide HMO, which serves most W-2 participants. In seven counties the Primary Care Initiative is a program being tested that allows W-2 participants to be case-managed by physicians who render primary care and are responsible for managing participants' health care by preauthorizing referrals to specialists.

Local Children's Services Networks

A volunteer board runs these local committees from the community. Their goal is to coordinate local community resources that are available to help low-income families.

Community Steering Committees

These committees assist W-2 agencies in creating employment and training opportunities for W-2 participants and work on innovative ways to address child care and transportation barriers on behalf of W-2 participants.

Education and Training

The Wisconsin plan is based on the philosophy that a job is the best training for self-sufficiency that a parent can receive. Still, the plan assumes that parents will often need continuing education and training to perform better on the job and to prepare them for advancement up the employment ladder before they reach the sixty-month time limit for public assistance benefits. The opportunities that may be made available include employment workshops, job search skills, and life skills training.

As noted above, the type of education and training that W-2 parents need is determined when the Financial and Employment Planner (FEP) develops their Employment Plan (EP). The EP details the participant's employment, education, and training goals. Additionally, W-2 parents may voluntarily pursue additional post-secondary education after fulfilling the requirement of their EP. Financial aid provided through the Higher Education Act of 1965 is not counted as income in determining W-2 eligibility.

At each rung of the W-2 employment ladder there are education and training options. At the top two rungs of the ladder, employers have the flexibility to direct the education and training participants require to succeed on the job. Participants may also seek education and training through services offered at Job Centers, and they may compete for scholarships, financial aid, and loans to pursue education after work. The Employment Skills and Advancement Program (ESAP) provides grants of up to $500 for education and training. Applicants must be working forty or more hours a week and must match the state funds. Participants in W-2 community service jobs can be required to spend up to ten hours a week in education or training, while the requirement for W-2 Transition participants is as much as twelve hours a week. W-2 participants and workers earning less than 165 percent of their poverty line who have been in unsubsidized employment for at least nine months are eligible for up to one year of child care for voluntary education and training. In order to receive child care assistance, the client's FEP must approve the education and training.

Conclusions

It is easy to understand why the Wisconsin plan is a national model for welfare reform. The emphasis on work rather than welfare, backed up by education and training programs, child care, medical assistance, transportation assistance, community support networks, job access loans, the job ladder, and many other innovative policies make the Wisconsin plan comprehensive and sophisticated. Clearly, the plan has been very well thought out, and it has brought about a very large reduction in welfare rolls. In late 1998 there were about 10,500 families on welfare, down from almost 80,000 in 1994. Many former recipients have found jobs on their own, but W-2 also moved thousands of poor family heads into employment. Wisconsin's first study of families leaving welfare between January and March of 1998 found that 83 percent had been employed since leaving welfare; however, 38 percent were not employed when interviewed. Of those employed, the average wage was $7.42, and a majority were working forty or more hours a week (www.dwd.state.wi.us/desw2/leavers1.pdf). As positive as this sounds, there have been many problems with the execution of W-2, and they constitute a cautionary tale for other states and the nation.

The primary problems with W-2 seem to have occurred in Milwaukee, Wisconsin's largest city. Problems here are critical because some 87 percent of Wisconsin's caseload is in Milwaukee. One of the most serious problems has resulted from conflict between the private management agencies hired to provide assessment, counseling, training, and job placement of welfare recipients and state agencies that must actually provide approved services, such as child care. In Milwaukee, W-2 is privately managed by five private entities that have exclusive jurisdiction over all welfare clients in specific sections of the city. As part of their work, these private agencies qualify family heads for child care, but state employees must approve the recommendations and actually certify space for the parent's children in a day care center. Communications between the private agencies and state employees have been extremely poor. In as many as 60 percent of all child care referrals in Milwaukee in 1997 and much of 1998, the state failed to approve and certify child care services for welfare families recommended by the private agency managing them. By late 1998 state officials were taking corrective actions.

Second, both the caseworkers hired by the private agencies and the state employees who administer support services such as child care have often been unresponsive to recipients. The private sector caseworkers often have had as many as 150 assigned families, rather than the 50 or so envisioned by W-2. As a result, welfare heads often report that they cannot find anyone within the private agencies or the public agencies who will meet with them or return calls. As the rolls continue to fall, state officials have had increased success in correcting this problem. However, the rolls may be falling because recipients have become discouraged rather than employed.

There is also considerable concern about the jobs that many of those family heads leaving welfare have been able to obtain. One study (Pawasarat and Quinn, 1993) found that some 75 percent of the jobs ended within nine months. Many other recipients have taken two or more part-time jobs because they cannot find a full-time position (www.dwd.state.wi.us/desw2/leavers1.pdf). In Chapter 8 several studies of the employment history of former W-2 participants are reviewed in more depth.

Thus, while W-2 has certainly been very successful in some important respects, bureaucratic and coordination problems have been much more complicated than many state officials anticipated. Wisconsin's efforts to preserve state jobs contributed significantly to the lack of coordination of support services for welfare heads. The five private agencies that won the contracts to administer W-2 in Milwaukee have also sought to keep costs down by understaffing. The fact that the private agencies are paid a flat fee for administering W-2 in their jurisdiction, rather than being compensated for all cases successfully handled, undoubtedly has contributed to this problem. Additionally, the emphasis on removing recipients from the rolls as soon as possible has resulted in many parents leaving the rolls without the support they really need.

In early 1999 the governor of Wisconsin, Tommy Thompson, asked the Clinton administration to consider allowing Wisconsin to use more PRWORA grant dollars to subsidize former welfare recipients who have moved into the job market. The governor pointed out that a large percentage of those who had left the rolls for employment were earning wages that were either below the poverty level or just above it. The governor argued that the long-term solution to helping many of these families was wage and service subsidies to make work really pay. As detailed below, in April, 1999 the Clinton administration agreed and ruled that states can use federal grant dollars to subsidize low-income working families who are not receiving TANF cash benefits, often without counting against time limits for assistance. This is an important change and one that will substantially improve the impact of PRWORA.

State Plans

As noted, the Wisconsin plan is not typical. Wisconsin started welfare reform earlier than most states and had a considerable head start on the vast majority of the states by the time PRWORA was passed in 1996. The system of triaging recipients into a job ladder, while allowing clients to simultaneously work and receive education and training, is considerably more sophisticated than the plans in operation in most states. Still, Wisconsin is not the only innovative state or the only one that got off to an early start. The states of Oregon, Vermont, Michigan, and New Jersey, among others, had given considerable attention to reform well before the passage of PRWORA. Many of the major provisions of the PRWORA were borrowed from these states.

Some states, such as Oregon and Vermont, have small populations and relatively modest welfare rolls, and this has allowed them to experiment with programs that provide more education and job training to welfare recipients both before and after they are placed in jobs. Oregon also raised the state's minimum wage to make work pay better. In 1998 over 98 percent of all welfare recipients in Oregon were working at least 20 hours per week. This was the highest employment rate for welfare recipients in the nation. Additionally, as detailed in Chapter 8, many states have used sanctions under PRWORA in a heavy-handed fashion that often results only in families losing all benefits. Oregon has led the nation in designing a sanctioning process that protects children and is structured to encourage family heads to cooperate with supportive programs. Oregon's plan is one of the most thoughtful in the nation and has had very positive outcomes.

The state of Michigan has designed a reform plan that places considerable emphasis on education, job training, and supportive services. In Michigan, families that cooperate with program requirements and make good-faith efforts to succeed through work are not subject to time limits on state-sponsored support services (USDHHS, 1998). Even when the family can no longer receive the federally-funded portion of TANF, Michigan will fund assistance for cooperating families.

New Jersey was an early leader in job training and experiments with the family cap, a controversial policy (Rutgers University, 1999; Heritage Foundation, 1995). Several states made substantial investments in programs to expand health care coverage to low-income and poverty families, and a few focused on improving public education to enhance the next generation's chances of escaping poverty. The state of Kentucky has carried out a comprehensive overhaul of its public education system with the stated goal of giving every child in the state a better opportunity to be successful. Several states are working on plans to direct investments to poor areas of their state, and a few have plans in place to help poor families relocate to communities with better economic opportunities (USDHHS, 1998).

In 1998 Congress passed the Workforce Investment Act, a comprehensive reform of job-training programs. This new act places considerable emphasis on the type of one-stop centers used by Wisconsin. Several states have adopted innovations based on the one-stop approach (Yates, 1998). Many states are also in the process of developing comprehensive transportation plans (Federal Transit Administration, 1997; Johnson and Meckstroth, 1998), individual development accounts (Sherraden, 1991; Sherraden, 1990), and education and job access loans. Thus, despite the fact that almost all state plans are built around "Work First" and backed up by sanctions for noncompliance, many innovative experiments are under way, and much of what will be learned will shape the future of reform. To explore this topic further, the various options states have chosen under PRWORA are reviewed below.

State Program Options

The decisions states have made in exercising their options under PRWORA create a varied and complex matrix. We review state options by examining a dozen major provisions of PRWORA and discussing the decisions states have made in implementing each of these policies. Since the District of Columbia is treated as a state, the number of entities reviewed is fifty-one if all data are available. These data are summarized from the Department of Health and Human Development's annual report to Congress on the first two years of implementation of PRWORA (USDHHS, 1998).

Individual Responsibility Plans

All the states require TANF applicants and recipients to sign an Individual Responsibility Plan (IRP), although the plans carry many different names. PRWORA mandates that each state assess TANF applicants and recipients in terms of their education and job skills, work experience, and qualifications for employment. The IRPs are the way states meet this requirement. IRPs typically require applicants to pledge cooperation with all aspects of state welfare policy, including avoidance of alcohol and drug abuse, immunization of dependent children, identification of absent parents, and any required job training and education programs. Failure to sign an IRP most often disqualifies an applicant for assistance. Noncompliance with the provisions of the plan results in either disqualification or reduction in benefits. Continued noncooperation generally results in loss of all benefits.

- Thirty-two states deny all benefits to applicants who refuse to sign an IRP or fail to comply with a plan they have signed.
- Fourteen states and the District of Columbia limit the maximum sanction to a reduction in family benefits.
- Four states do not specify sanctions for noncompliance.

Time Limits on Assistance

Under PRWORA families are limited to a lifetime limit of five years (or less at state option) of cash assistance. States may exempt up to 20 percent of their caseload from time limits, and they may use Social Services Block grant funds to provide cash and noncash assistance and vouchers to families that have exhausted the time limit. States may also use their own funds to assist families that have used up their five-year limit in federal funds.

- Twenty-seven states and the District of Columbia have set the time limit at sixty months, consecutive or not.
- Eight states limit aid to twenty-four out of any sixty months, with a lifetime limit of sixty months.
- Eight states have set the limit at less than sixty months.
- Eight states use a variety of other options, with Michigan and Massachusetts having no time limit. Texas varies the limit to twelve, twenty-four, or thirty-six months for adults only, depending upon the education and employability of the head. In Texas an adult who receives benefits for the specified limit may not receive additional assistance for five years.

Exemptions from the Time Limit

States have the option of exempting up to 20 percent of their caseload from the sixty-month limit. Exemptions are generally based on high unemployment rates in a particular area of the state, and the mental and physical ability of the family head or a caretaker. Victims of family abuse, minors, and those actively seeking employment also frequently qualify for exemption.

Extensions of the Time Limit

PRWORA does not provide for extensions, but some states allow non-exempt families that have exhausted the time limit to receive state-financed assistance for an additional period, normally three to sixty months. Extensions are most often given to allow individuals to finish a training program, or to family heads making an honest effort to find work.

Time Frame for Work

Almost all of the states employ "Work First" policies, which require recipients to quickly move into available jobs. PRWORA requires those receiving TANF to engage in work (as defined by the state) when ready or within twenty-four months. States may require shorter timelines.

- Thirty-two states require TANF recipients and applicants to engage in work within six months.
- Sixteen states use the twenty-four-month limit.
- Arizona's plan bases the time limit on the characteristics of the recipient; California requires work participation after eighteen months, but the limit can be extended to twenty-four months by the county; Vermont sets the limit at fifteen months for two-parent families and thirty months for single parents.

Exemption from Work Requirements Based on Age of Youngest Child

States are given the option of exempting single parents with children under the age of one from work requirements, and they may disregard them in calculating work participation rates for a cumulative lifetime total of twelve months.

- Twenty-four states exempt single parents with a child younger than one year old.
- Fifteen states exempt single parents with a child younger than age six months.
- Two states leave this decision to each county.
- Four states provide no automatic option.
- Six states exempt some parents with children older than one year.

Making Work Pay

Under AFDC states were required to follow federal guidelines that specified how earnings were treated in determining eligibility for cash assistance. PRWORA drops this rule and allows states to make their own decisions about earning disregards.

- Forty-two states have specifically enacted policies designed to make work pay better, generally by increasing the amount of money that recipients can earn and still be eligible for TANF and other benefits.
- Nine states still use the AFDC income eligibility test.
- Thirty-eight states have significantly raised the asset level for recipients from the old AFDC limit of $1,000. Many of these states now allow recipients to have $2,000 or more in assets.
- Forty-seven states have increased the vehicle asset limit to help recipients to have a reliable form of transportation. Twenty-four of these states simply disregard the value of one automobile. Other states increased the asset range up to $10,000. The District of Columbia, Mississippi, and North Dakota decided to retain the vehicle asset level set by AFDC. Indiana is the only state to lower the vehicle asset level.

Individual Development Accounts

In one of its most innovative provisions, PRWORA allows Individual Development Accounts (IDAs) to be established by or on behalf of a

TANF applicant or recipient. IDAs are restricted saving accounts that allow recipients to accumulate funds that can be used for specific purposes, such as post-secondary education, purchase of a first home, tools required for employment, or start-up funds for a business. IDA accounts are not considered as assets and are not counted in determining TANF eligibility (Sherraden, 1991).

- Twenty-seven states allow TANF funds to be paid into IDA accounts. The limits for these accounts range from $1,000 to an unlimited amount.
- Arizona, California, Delaware, Georgia, Kentucky, Louisiana, Ohio, South Carolina, and Texas set the limit at $5,000 or more with a specified upper limit.
- Arkansas, Colorado, Illinois, Iowa, Missouri, Montana, New Jersey, New Mexico, New York, Rhode Island, and Utah set no upper limit.

Transitional Medicaid Assistance

PRWORA requires the states to follow the old AFDC rule that Transitional Medicaid Assistance (TMA) be made available for one year to families that lose TANF benefits due to earnings. Families that lose benefits because of child or spousal support are eligible for TMA coverage for four months. States, however, have the discretion to provide TMA for longer periods.

- Twelve states have elected to provide TMA for more than twelve months. The range for these states varies from eighteen months to an unlimited period as long as income is below specified levels.
- The Children's Health Insurance Plan (CHIP) passed in 1997 will extend health coverage for children in low-income families in all participating states.

Transitional Child Care

PRWORA significantly increases funding for child care, providing funds through the Child Care Development Block grant and allowing additional funds to be transferred from other block grants.

- All states provide at least twelve months of transitional child care for families moving off welfare.
- Twenty-nine states provide transitional child care for families moving off welfare beyond the twelve-month timeline.

Family Cap

PRWORA allows the states to decide if they want to increase cash assistance to TANF families after the birth of an additional child.

- Nineteen states decided to provide no additional cash assistance to TANF families when an additional child is born.
- Connecticut and Florida provide a partial increase in benefits.
- Maryland provides the benefits to a third party, while Oklahoma limits the increase to vouchers.

Sanctions for Failure to Comply with Work Requirements

PRWORA allows states to either reduce or end cash assistance to individuals or families that refuse to comply with work requirements.

- Thirty-seven states cut off all cash assistance to individuals or families who do not carry out required work assignments.
- Fourteen states reduce cash assistance.
- Suspensions or reductions in cash assistance generally last until compliance or for six or fewer months. Delaware, Idaho, Mississippi, Pennsylvania, and Wisconsin suspend all cash assistance permanently.

Sanctions for Noncooperation with Child Support Requirements

PRWORA requires recipients to cooperate in establishing paternity and child support orders. Any applicant or recipient who refuses to cooperate can have his/her benefits reduced by 25 percent or be refused cash assistance.

- Thirty-six states end all cash assistance to recipients who are not cooperative in identifying the father of their children.
- All the other states reduce benefits by at least 25 percent.

- Most states restore cash assistance if the parent decides to comply.

Treatment of Families from Other States

TANF rules allow states to treat families that move into the state from another state differently. States may choose to restrict these families to the benefits they would have received in their home state.

- Twelve states pay families that move into the state at the rate they would have received in their home state.
- North Carolina allows its counties to set the benefit rate for out-of-state families.
- Florida and North Dakota use the former state's time limit if it is shorter than their limit.

In May 1999, the United States Supreme Court ruled this provision of the PRWORA unconstitutional. The Court concluded that this provision denied citizens the equal protection of the law as defined by the 14th Amendment (Rita L. Saenz vs. Brenda Roe and Anna Doe).

This review of some of the major options provided the states by PRWORA provides insight into the rich mix of decisions that have been made. State welfare programs vary more now than at any time since the passage of the Social Security Act of 1935. The mix of strategies being employed by the states creates a complex set of policies but, in the long run, should provide considerable insight into the best ways to help able-bodied adults make the transition to employment.

Conclusions

PRWORA has certainly "ended welfare as we know it." PRWORA fundamentally changed the philosophy of welfare policy in America, placing the focus on moving most able-bodied poor into the job market. While some states have been slow to make major alterations in their welfare policies, by 1999 even the lagging states had made substantial changes in their approach to welfare. A handful of states have been very inventive, and many other states are testing innovative policies in at least a few counties.

The review above shows how comprehensively states can overhaul their welfare systems if they wish, and it shows the range of options that states can choose from to design welfare systems that meet the unique needs of their state or even specific geographic regions. PRWORA also allows the states to alter their approach over time, based on experiences in the state or evidence produced by studies of experiments in other states.

In Chapter 8 we will review the early evidence on the impact of the new welfare programs on actual or potential welfare recipients.

8

Early Evidence on the Impact of the 1996 Welfare Reform

In Chapter 6 we reviewed the history of the welfare reform movement over the last thirty years, analyzed how the various forces for reform resulted in the passage of a major change in welfare legislation, and examined the philosophy and major provisions of the PRWORA of 1996. In Chapter 7 we examined how the states have opted to design their new welfare systems within the rather liberal boundaries allowed by the PRWORA. In this chapter we turn to an examination of the impact of the PRWORA, reviewing the latest research on how well those required to leave welfare, and those diverted from welfare, are faring and how well various provisions of the reform law are working. The outcomes of a few of the major provisions of the PRWORA, along with legislation passed to supplement or support the reform legislation, are evaluated in depth. We conclude by discussing the early insights gained by this review about the strengths and weaknesses of the PRWORA and the changes that will be required to enhance the chances for the reform legislation to achieve its goals.

Impact on Welfare Rolls by State

Regardless of the decisions that states have made about how to design their new welfare plans, the debate and changes that have taken place in welfare laws since the early 1990s have resulted in major declines in welfare rolls in almost all the states. In 1993 the AFDC rolls contained 14.1 million recipients, or 5.5 percent of the population. By March of 1999 the AFDC/TANF rolls had shrunk to 7.3 million recipients, or about 2.6 percent of the population. This represented a decline in recipients between 1993 and December 1998 of 48 percent.

Table 8.1 shows the decrease in individuals receiving AFDC/TANF by state since the passage of the PRWORA. The impact of the law on enrollments in a handful of states seems to be modest, but in most states the number of recipients declined by at least 30 percent. In 29 states welfare rolls have dipped by at least 50 percent. In a few states the decline has been extremely high. The greatest declines have been in Idaho (-87 percent), Mississippi (-69 percent), South Carolina (-62 percent), Wisconsin (-81 percent), and Wyoming (-84 percent).

Why Have the Rolls Dropped So Fast?

There is still some uncertainty about why rolls have dropped so fast, but some reasons are obvious. First, under "Work First" most adult recipients are required to move into the job market very quickly. An estimated 1.5 million people who were on welfare in 1997 were working in 1998, and this is a considerable improvement over past years (USDHHS, 1998). A second reason is that some states make it very difficult for applicants to enter the rolls. Often they require a job search before potential recipients can apply for welfare, and many states now simply deny assistance to families that would have previously been qualified for cash welfare. Obvious examples include state laws that reject mothers who cannot or will not identify the father(s) of their children, mothers who cannot prove that they have been looking for a job, or mothers who are judged to have family members they can rely on for support.

Another reason is that some recipients have sized up the new laws written by their states and decided on their own to leave the rolls. These recipients have often cited objections to work, job search, or education requirements, or they have stated that they can find a better job on their own (www.dwd.state.wi.us/desw2/leavers1.pdf). Some of these recipients may have left the rolls because they were working off the books and, therefore, not really available for job training or place-

Table 8.1

Change in Welfare Caseloads Since Enactment of New Welfare Law, by State

State	Total TANF Recipients by State		
	August 1996	March 1999	Percent
Alabama	100,662	46,934	−53
Alaska	35,544	28,020	−21
Arizona	169,442	92,467	−45
Arkansas	56,343	29,340	−48
California	2,581,948	1,818,197	−29
Colorado	95,788	39,346	−59
Connecticut	159,246	90,799	−43
Delaware	23,654	16,581	−30
District of Columbia	69,292	52,140	−25
Florida	533,801	198,101	−63
Georgia	330,302	137,976	−58
Guam	8,314	8,620	4
Hawaii	66,482	45,515	−31
Idaho	21,780	2,897	−87
Illinois	642,644	382,937	−40
Indiana	142,604	109,675	−23
Iowa	86,146	60,151	−30
Kansas	63,783	32,873	−48
Kentucky	172,193	99,560	−42
Louisiana	228,115	111,074	−51
Maine	53,873	34,108	−37
Maryland	194,127	89,003	−54
Massachusetts	226,030	151,592	−33
Michigan	502,354	263,583	−47
Minnesota	169,744	140,128	−17
Mississippi	123,828	38,426	−69
Missouri	222,820	135,383	−39
Montana	29,130	15,508	−47
Nebraska	38,592	34,662	−10
Nevada	34,261	20,283	−41
New Hampshire	22,937	16,090	−29
New Jersey	275,637	175,223	−36
New Mexico	99,661	80,686	−19
New York	1,143,962	828,302	−27
North Carolina	267,326	138,570	−48
North Dakota	13,146	8,355	−36
Ohio	549,312	282,444	−48
Oklahoma	96,201	56,640	−41
Oregon	78,419	45,450	−42
Pennsylvania	531,059	312,364	−41
Puerto Rico	151,023	107,447	−29
Rhode Island	56,560	53,859	−5
South Carolina	114,273	42,504	−62

Table 8.1 *(continued)*

Total TANF Recipients by State

State	August 1996	March 1999	Percent	
South Dakota	15,896	8,445	−47	
Tennessee	254,818	152,695	−40	
Texas	649,018	313,823	−52	
Utah	39,073	26,428	−32	
Vermont	24,331	18,230	−25	
Virgin Islands	4,898	3,533	−28	
Virginia	152,845	88,910	−42	
Washington	268,927	174,099	−35	
West Virginia	89,039	44,367	−50	
Wisconsin	148,888	28,863	−81	
Wyoming	11,398	1,770	−84	
U.S. Total	12,241,890	7,334,976	−38	
Total TANF Families and Recipients				
Families (000)	4,415	2,668	−40	1,747,000 fewer families
Recipients (000)	12,241	7,335	−38	4,906,000 fewer recipients

Source: U.S. Department of Health and Human Services Administration for Children and Families, August 1999.

ment. Other recipients simply are determined not to be coached, coerced, or supervised in any fashion (Pavetti, et al., 1996).

As detailed below, many recipients have left the rolls because they have been sanctioned. One study found that 38 percent of those who left welfare during one three-month period in 1997 did so because of state sanctions (Ferber and Storch, 1998). The new law substantially expands the grounds for sanctioning recipients, and many states may frequently use sanctions for the primary purpose of reducing their welfare rolls. Of those recipients forced off the rolls for noncompliance, many return to the rolls as soon as they are eligible. Last, some legal immigrants may have left the rolls or avoided them because they mistakenly believe that welfare receipt could jeopardize their chances of becoming citizens or result in their being deported. Some legal immigrants also may have illegal immigrants in their families.

What Has Happened to Those Recipients Who Have Left the Rolls?

Most of the states are conducting studies to determine what has happened to recipients who have left the rolls as a result of PRWORA (Blum and Berrey, 1999). However, few states have completed those studies. As noted above, there is evidence that many heads of welfare families have been moved into the job market (USDHHS, 1998). At this time, there is limited data on whether employment rates differ significantly from AFDC exits and less than adequate information about the quality of the jobs that former recipients are obtaining. Most states do not yet have quality data on how many former recipients have found a job, how well these jobs pay, if those employed are receiving basic benefits such as health or child care, or even if the jobs are temporary. There are some dependable studies based on a few states, and they will be discussed below.

Since the economy has been very robust during the early stages of reform, job opportunities seem to be plentiful in most areas of the nation. However, the National Governor's Association reports that in eleven states surveyed, only about half of those leaving welfare reported finding work (NGA, 1998). Most of the jobs former recipients found pay minimum wages, and most recipients reported working fewer than 40 hours a week (Rangarajan, Schochet, and Chu, 1998; Rangarajan, 1998). A study of Wisconsin found that about 80 percent of those who have left welfare have found a job, but almost 70 percent of the employed workers said that they are just barely getting by (Sherman et al., 1998, 7). Loprest (1999), using a national sample of families, found that a majority of those who have left welfare since passage of the PRWORA left to take a job. The jobs "leavers" have found are at the low end of the labor market. About 25 percent of the "leavers" had no job and did not have a partner with a job. These data suggest that while a significant percentage of former recipients have moved into the job market, they may be only marginally better off than they were on welfare.

These finding are consistent with a considerable body of research on the post-welfare work and wages of former AFDC recipients. Bane and Ellwood (1983) found that about 40 percent of those who left AFDC were poor in the year after exit, and a similar number were poor in the next year. Harris (1996) found that 28 percent of women who left AFDC because of marriage or cohabitation were poor one year after exit, compared to 46 percent who left for employment and 75 percent of those who left for a variety of other reasons. Pavetti and Acs (1997) found that only 13 percent of women who left AFDC worked full-time at a "good job" by age twenty-six to twenty-seven. Gritz and MaCurdy (1991) and Cheng (1995) found that the average earnings of former AFDC recipients remained low but improved over time. Burtless (1995) and Harris (1996), however, found little increase in wages over time. Most of these studies found that when recipients left the AFDC rolls, they continued to receive means-tested benefits, and many of the women cycled back into AFDC. Even when they combined work and marriage, they lived below the poverty line.

These basic findings are reinforced by two more recent studies (Cancian, et al., 1998, 1998c; Scrivener, et al., 1998) designed to evaluate the impact of state plans that were implemented under waivers before the passage of PRWORA. A third study that evaluates TANF plans in twelve states provides additional insights into the limitations of supported work programs established under PRWORA (Acs, et al., 1998).

Cancian and colleagues (1998) review three data sets to analyze the impact of welfare reform on recipients who move from welfare to work. The National Survey of Youth (NLSY) database is used to examine the economic status of 984 women who left the welfare rolls before 1987. These data provide information on whether these women received means-tested benefits after leaving AFDC, if they worked, what they earned (if employed), and their poverty status in each year between 1987 and 1992. The authors (Meyer and Cancian, 1996, 1998; Cancian and Meyer, 1998) found that 60 percent of the women received means-tested benefits in the first year after leaving AFDC, declining to 40 percent in the fifth year. About two-thirds of the women worked each year, with the proportion working full-time, year round increasing from 13 percent in year one after exit to 25 percent in year five. Less than 5 percent of the women worked full time, full year in all five years, but most of the women worked. Among those women who worked, annual earnings increased from $6,059 to $9,947 over the five-year period. Poverty rates declined over time, especially when all income in the family (not just the recipient's earnings) are considered. If only the income of the recipient is considered, 79 percent were poor in the first year after exit, declining to 64 percent in the fifth year. However, when all family income is calculated, only 19 percent were poor in all of the first five years, while only 22 percent escaped poverty in all five years. Those women who were the most economically successful were better educated, were married, had fewer children, were more consistently employed, and made job advances.

Cancian, et al.'s second data set consists of a sample of AFDC clients in Wisconsin, including a large group who left the rolls in July 1995 (Cancian, Haverman, Kaplan, and Wolfe, 1998, 1998a, 1998b, 1998c). This sample includes 26,047 "leavers" and 28,471 "stayers." The researchers examine welfare use, employment, and earnings. Many of the leavers continued to receive some means-tested assistance, but the rate declined from 89.2 percent in the first quarter to 29.7 percent in the fifth quarter. During the first year after leaving AFDC, two-thirds of the leavers worked. All leavers who worked made income gains each quarter, with the exception of those employed by temporary agencies. Those leavers who worked were economically better off than they had been on welfare. In fact, leavers were "twice as likely to have incomes above the poverty level as stayers" (Cancian, et al., 1998, 14–15). Still, only about 27 percent of leavers had incomes above the poverty level. As found in the NLYS study, married women with more education, better job skills, and fewer children were more likely to escape poverty.

The third data set analyzed by Cancian, et al., consists of a number of studies of recipients who left welfare in nine states: Iowa, Kentucky, Maryland, Michigan, New Mexico, South Carolina, Tennessee, Texas, and Washington (Cancian, et al. 1998). Analyzing welfare leavers from these states, Cancian et al. found: (a) use of means-tested benefits declines over time, especially the use of AFDC and food stamps; (b) about two-thirds of leavers work, but only a small proportion work full time, year round. Over time the proportion of full-time workers increases; (c) leavers earn between $6.50 and $7.50 an hour, but most do not work enough hours to escape poverty; (d) the percentage of leavers above the poverty line improves over time; and (e) married women with more education and job skills, those with smaller families, and those who work more hours make the best gains.

Scrivener, et al. (1998) add to this literature by evaluating a welfare-to-work experiment conducted in Portland, Oregon. The study evaluates an experiment called Steps to Success, which began in early 1993.

Women applying for AFDC between February 1993 and December 1994 (5,547) were randomly assigned to either a program group or a control group. Women assigned to the program group were offered immediate job assignment or limited education and/or skills training backed up by support services such as child care and courses in life skills. Education and training were short term with the emphasis for all the women in the program group being self-sufficiency and employment in a "good job"—full-time, above minimum wages, with benefits and the potential of advancement. The control group was given no special services but was encouraged to seek education and job training in the community (Scrivener, et al., 1998).

The impact of the experiment was quite positive, in part because of strong case management. Case workers and case managers coordinated to determine which support services women in the program group needed and then helped the clients find the best possible jobs. The experiment set the target wage for jobs at $6.00 per hour and required a corrective plan if this and other goals were not met. After two years the percentage of full-time workers was 13 percent higher among the program group (compared to the control group), and earnings were 35 percent higher (about $1,842 per year). Earnings continued to increase over time for the program group, and use of means-tested programs was 17 percent lower.

The Portland study is interesting and the outcome of the project promising. However, it is not clear how typical these results will be. The Portland program group was primarily white, non-Hispanic (greatly reducing the impact of discrimination), better educated than the average AFDC recipient nationally, lived in a community with low unemployment, and the quality of the support services provided was high and rather expensive. The program was also backed up by strong sanctions.

The research of Acs, et al. (1998) provides another way of thinking about the impact of employment on welfare families. This study examines the financial rewards that TANF families will achieve by moving from welfare to supported work in twelve states. The twelve states examined were Alabama, California, Colorado, Florida, Massachusetts, Michigan, Minnesota, Mississippi, New Jersey, New York, Texas, and Washington. For purposes of comparison, the analysis was based on the impact of reform on a family of three, consisting of one parent and two children. In each state the transition from welfare to work was examined in four stages to ascertain if supported employment is economically more viable for the family than being on welfare. The states varied considerably in terms of basic benefit levels, amount of income from earnings or other sources that could be disregarded in determining benefits, and level at which benefits are phased out (i.e., the Benefit Reduction Rate [BRR]). These program differences substantially impact both incentives to work and how many hours a week a family head might work. The four stages studied were: Stage 1: No Work; Stage 2: Part-time Work at Minimum Wage; Stage 3: Full-time Work at Minimum Wage; Stage 4: Full-time Work at $9.00 per hour.

In Stage 1 benefits from TANF ranged from $120 per month in Mississippi to $577 per month in New York. Total income (including food stamps and taxes) ranged from $435 in Mississippi to $734 in New York.

In Stage 2 income improved if recipients moved into part-time work at minimum wages. Recipients who lived in states that provided the lowest TANF rates (Alabama, Florida, Mississippi, and Texas) saw the most dramatic rise in income in Stage 2. In Mississippi, total monthly income increased 108 percent. Recipient gains at this stage were also better in those states with the lowest BRR, the highest level of earnings disregard, and in states that provide subsidies for the Earned Income Tax Credit (EITC).

Movement to Stage 3 increased median monthly income by 20 percent. Gains were real but rather humble, considering the fact that hours worked increased by 75 percent. Movement from Stage 3 to Stage 4 was even more modest. Moving from full-time work at minimum wage to full-time work at $9.00 per hour increased wages per hour by 75 percent but median income increased only by 16 percent. The reason was that at this wage rate EITC benefits are phased out and taxes increased. This study suggests that to make work pay decently, tax and EITC phase-out levels need to be adjusted.

One last insight into the lives of those who have left cash welfare since the passage of PRWORA is provided by recent food stamp and Medicaid enrollment data. What these data show is that large numbers of families who remain qualified for food stamps and Medicaid are dropping off the rolls. Between 1994 and the end of 1997, the food stamp rolls declined by 5.9 million recipients. Medicaid coverage of single-parent families is also significantly declining. It is not clear why so many eligible families leave the rolls, but many families may believe that once they lose cash benefits, they do not qualify for food stamps and Medicaid. Some states may be failing to inform ex-recipients of their continued eligibility, or, worse, even discouraging them from applying for these benefits.

The decline in food stamp rolls may explain why many families who have left TANF are reporting increased problems with food short-ages and reliance on food pantries. In a Wisconsin study of families that left welfare between January and March of 1998, about one-third of the families reported that they sometimes could not purchase needed food (up from 22 percent of these same families while they were on welfare). One in seven of the families had received food from an emergency pantry (Sherman, 1998, 11).

Summary: What We Know About Those Who Have Left Welfare

The various studies of families that have left welfare provide a number of important insights:

1. When family heads leave cash welfare for employment, work pays. The incentive to move from no work to work is particularly clear. When recipients work, their incomes improve over time, and their reliance on welfare programs declines. Still, incomes do not improve dramatically for most families. Perhaps the most important insight gained from recent studies is that most former welfare families continue to live either in poverty or just above the poverty level. One major reason is that most former welfare recipients do not work full time. The reasons for this have not been carefully studied. If former recipients work part-time because support services (e.g., child care) are not extensive enough or flexible enough to allow family heads to work full time, there is an obvious need for program changes. It may also be true that even in a booming economy, there may be a shortage of quality full-time jobs that provide benefits.

2. States can design programs to help poorly educated and low-skilled recipients find a decent job and stay employed, but it is not easy (Gueron and Pauly, 1991; Bloom, et al., 1993; Blank, 1994; Pavetti, et al., 1997). Considerable research has found that programs that provide basic education and/or job skill training generally have only a modest impact on either employment or earnings. When earnings do increase for recipients who have received these services, it is generally because the recipients work longer hours, not because they find

better jobs (Pauly and Dimeo, 1996). By contrast, programs that focus only on moving recipients into jobs as quickly as possible increase employment and earnings but leave most recipients living in poverty. However, Portland's Steps to Success program and several other similar projects suggest that the most promising strategies are those that move recipients into work and then provide them with help in building job and basic skills (Strawn, 1999; Cancian and Meyer, 1998; Ranagarajan, Schochet, and Chu, 1998; Friedlander and Burtless, 1995; Freedman, et al., 1996). Training and education produce the best results when they are directed at helping recipients gain the skills required to advance in their current jobs or obtain existing better-paying jobs. The training must provide skills that are in demand and employers must be willing to hire or promote people with those skills. Several states have developed promising initiatives to provide education and skill training to recipients on-site during work hours (Strawn, 1999, 10).

3. Many families who leave welfare are not finding any type of steady work. Between 30 and 50 percent of all welfare leavers have no steady employment.

4. Many of those families who have left welfare are having serious problems obtaining shelter, adequate food, and proper medical care.

5. Many former cash recipients are not receiving means-tested benefits (e.g. food stamps, Medicaid) for which they probably qualify.

6. A few states are doing a good job of subsidizing families to make certain that work pays (Sherman, et al., 1998, 4). However, most states need to improve their effort. States have many options to help the working poor. States can improve the value of work by lowering the tax burden on low-income workers, by better designing income disregards, and by raising the eligibility levels for services such as child and health care. The federal government could make work pay better by raising the phase-out range of the EITC and by doing a better job of informing recipients that EITC benefits are available on a monthly rather than only on an end of year, lump-sum basis.

New Rules Designed to Make Work Pay

In April 1999 the Clinton administration did take a major step toward making work pay for low-income families. The Department of Health and Human Services (DHHS) published final rules making it permissible for states to spend TANF funds to support working families with no time limits on assistance (www.acf.dhhs.gov/programs/ofa/exsumcl.htm). DHHS ruled that TANF funds used for transportation, child care, refundable earned income tax credits, and individual development accounts will not count as assistance nor be subject to time limits. Similarly states may also use these funds to subsidize employers so that they can pay higher salaries and to pay for education and training, counseling, case management, and job search. To improve workforce participation, the new rules also allow low-income families to keep child support income while receiving noncash assistance.

Under PRWORA's temporary provisions, if a state provided TANF funds to employers to be used to subsidize wages for welfare recipients, the assistance would count against time limits. However, under these amended rules a state may use TANF funds to directly subsidize employers to help pay wages to eligible family heads without regard to time limits. States may also use TANF funds to help families with nonrecurrent, short-term needs (e.g., rent assistance) for up to four months, and this aid will not count against time limits. These revised rules make it much easier for states to help families that have left welfare or have been diverted from welfare.

These new rules are particularly valuable because some states have a great deal of money that they could spend on such services. Because of rapidly falling welfare rolls, during fiscal years 1997 and 1998, the states accumulated about $3 billion in unspent federal funds. Spending has varied by states, with seventeen states having no uncommitted funds, while another nineteen states have funds equaling at least one-third of their block grant allocation. States have until 2002 to use these uncommitted funds. However, if the funds are used for services (rather than cash aid), they must be used in the fiscal year in which they were allocated. This gives states an incentive to use these funds to help working families.

The evidence shows that generally states are committing their own dollars to reform. As welfare rolls have fallen, states are spending more for support services for recipients who have moved into jobs or job training. Some critics of welfare reform had feared that states would use the new law to "race to the bottom," that is, spend less and less on assistance. But the evidence shows that while state spending for cash welfare has declined with caseloads, spending for work-based support services such as education, job search, training, placement, and employment subsidies have increased by about one-third. Spending on child care has increased by 55 percent. Some states have used money saved on cash welfare to increase child care expenditures even more (USDHHS, 1999).

How Well Are Sanctions Being Used?

To help the states implement PRWORA, states are given much stronger sanctioning powers. The way these sanctions are being used in many states raises troubling issues. PRWORA allows the states considerable discretion in using three types of sanctions: (1) Adult-Only Sanctions; (2) Pay-for-Performance Sanctions; and (3) Full Family Sanctions (Holcomb, et al., 1998). Full-family sanctions result in the elimination of all cash assistance to the family unit. Sanctions may be lifted in return for compliance, or after some specified period, but they may also be permanent. Over thirty states impose full-family sanctions, generally only after less severe sanctions have failed to produce a desired change (Ferber and Storch, 1998; Derr, 1998; Holcomb and Ratcliffe, 1998; Kaplan, 1999).

State officials generally believe that strong sanctions are necessary to convince recalcitrant recipients that they must comply with program guidelines or leave the rolls. In some states as many as half of all recipients have received one or more sanctions (Bloom, 1997; GAO, 1997; Fein and Karweit, 1997). Many recipients seem to be sanctioned because of barriers such as lack of transportation or child care or illness in the family that was undetected during initial interviews. Agency errors also account for a significant percentage of all sanctions. In Milwaukee County, Wisconsin, supervisors reversed 44 percent of the more than 5,000 sanctions issued through August 1996. In Massachusetts, some 47 percent of sanctions appealed through December 1996 were decided in the family's favor (Sherman, et al., 1998). In Tennessee over 30 percent of all sanctioned cases were found to be in error (Sherman, et al., 1998, 11–14).

By contrast, Oregon has designed its program to avoid inappropriate sanctions and to safeguard children in families when benefits are terminated. Before full-family sanctions can be imposed, a caseworker must meet with the noncompliant adult to determine if there are legitimate barriers to employment that can be addressed. Additionally, the caseworker must visit the home and develop a plan with other community agencies that addresses the safety of the children in the family. The plan has to include follow-up home visits. Last, a decision to impose a full-family sanction must be reviewed and approved by management (Holcomb, et al., 1998).

Not surprisingly, families suffering full sanction are often in dire straits. In Michigan a study of sanctioned families found that before termination of benefits 85 percent had income of $400 per month, and none of the households had income of less than $250 per month. After sanction, only 47 percent had income of more than $400 per month, while 15 percent had no known income or employment (Pavetti, et al., 1997). A significant percentage of the sanctioned families reported problems providing sufficient food for the family, insufficient income, and receipt of utility shutoff notices (Colville, et al., 1997). A study of sanctioned families in South Carolina reported similar findings (Sherman, et al., 1998).

The evidence also suggests that many sanctioned families are having difficulty paying for housing (Sherman, et al., 1998). In an Atlanta survey of families in shelters or other facilities for the homeless, 46 percent had lost TANF in the last year. An Idaho study found a similar problem, but at a lower rate (Sherman, et al., 1998). Sanctioned families also frequently report having trouble obtaining medical care (Sherman et al., 1998). Last, a study of sanctioned families found a much higher rate of referrals to Child Protective Services for child abuse and neglect than in nonsanctioned families (Colville, et al., 1997). While sanctions may or may not have contributed to abuse and neglect, it is clear that these families needed to be under supervision.

Sanctioned families seem to be those with the most severe barriers to employment (Sherman et al., 1998). Significant barriers are rather common in welfare families. Olson and Pavetti (1996) have identified eight major personal and family challenges capable of hindering a recipient's transition from welfare to the workforce: physical disabilities and/or health limitations; mental health problems; health or behavioral problems of children; substance abuse; domestic violence; involvement with the child welfare system; housing instability; low basic skills and learning disabilities (Pavetti, 1999).

Based on an analysis of the national Longitudinal Survey of Youth (NLSY), Pavetti and Olson concluded that some 90 percent of twenty-seven to thirty-five-year olds on welfare exhibit one or more potential challenges to employment (low basic skills, substance abuse, health problems, depression, or a child with medical problems). About 50 percent of recipients suffer a more serious form of these barriers (alcoholism, abuse of crack or cocaine, extremely low basic skills, health problems that prevent work) (Pavetti and Olson, 1997).

These early findings suggest that most states are not using sanctions, especially full-family sanctions, in a thoughtful manner. Sanctions clear the rolls of difficult and uncooperative recipients, but unless they are used carefully, they do not bring about desired behavioral responses, and the consequences for the family, especially children, are often far too high. Children are often punished simply because they had the misfortune of being born poor. Sanctions also frequently seem to result from poor assessments of the family's needs. The Oregon model of careful case management, home visits, intra-agency coordination, safeguards for children, and administrative review and approval is a much sounder policy.

Private and Federal Government Efforts to Promote Employment of Welfare Recipients

Under PRWORA and supplemental programs passed soon after the 1996 act, the federal government has pledged to play an important role in expanding job opportunities for welfare recipients. Most directly the Clinton administration set a goal of hiring 10,000 former recipients by FY 2000 without replacing any regular employees. In August 1999 the Clinton administration reported that the federal government had hired 14,000 former welfare recipients (USDHHS, 1999), exceeding its own goal. The Clinton administration also pledged to continue to find good jobs for ex-recipients.

The Welfare to Work Partnership—A Private Sector Initiative

When PRWORA was passed, the private sector was challenged by President Clinton to help make the new law a success. The result was the Welfare to Work Partnership, an initiative heavily promoted by Vice President Al Gore. This project was organized by the Chief Executive Officers (CEOs) of United Airlines, Burger King, Sprint, Monsanto, and UPS. The goal was to encourage businesses to provide good jobs to former welfare recipients. The Welfare to Work Partnership has gotten off to an excellent start. By August 1999 over 12,000 businesses had signed on to hire welfare recipients under the initiative (www.whitehouse.gov/8/1/99). By August 1999 these businesses had hired over 410,000 former welfare recipients, 76 percent in full-time jobs.

The key to the early successes of this program seems to lie in the rewards for both business and government, the alliances with other national and local organizations, and the prudent strategy of placing welfare recipients into long-term jobs that pay decent wages. An important player has been the U.S. Chamber of Commerce. The 4,000 state and local Chambers, representing some 3 million businesses, connect welfare recipients seeking employment with community businesses. The U.S. Chamber has also helped President Clinton implement his City-to-City Challenge. This program has targeted seventeen high poverty cities where good jobs for welfare recipients are in the greatest need.

The Welfare to Work Partnership also works with some thirty trade associations. Member associations are also encouraged to further the partnership's cause by discussing the welfare to work initiative in newsletters, promoting the partnership at conferences, and linking their websites to the Partnership's website, welfaretowork.org.

The Welfare to Work Partnership uses several other tactics to attract Business Partners. The partnership, for example, actively promotes the hiring of welfare recipients as a "Smart Solution" to labor shortages. Noting that an expected 4 million recipients will leave the welfare rolls over the next few years, the partnership sells this new "New Labor Force" as an untapped and viable source of labor. The organization advertises that welfare recipients are ready to work or "nearly ready to work." At a time when businesses often experience a shortage of qualified labor, the Partnership offers a solution by providing access to ready-to-work welfare recipients and by training those who are nearly ready to work.

While the "Smart Solution" campaign is extensive, without the tax credits available to businesses, the Welfare to Work Partnership would likely have been less successful in recruiting partners. In the Partnership's first year, the Balanced Budget Amendment allocated $3 billion for the Welfare to Work Jobs Challenge and an expansion of both the Work Opportunity Tax Credit (WOTC) and the Welfare to Work Tax Credit (WWTC). Both of these credits are given to all employers who hire targeted employees, including Business Partners that hire welfare recipients.

Once a business has been recruited, the Welfare to Work Partnership provides services designed to improve the chances that those employees hired will be successful. New members are furnished with a manual, *Blueprint for Business*: *Reaching a New Work Force*, designed to help employers hire and retain former welfare recipients. Also, through a coordinated effort with IBM, the Partnership has developed a Service Provider database. The Service Providers locate and train local welfare recipients to enter the workforce.

Additionally, a National Welfare to Work Network has been established so that new members can benefit from the counsel of more experienced members. The Partnership also assists members by preparing potential employees to enter the workforce through training workshops. The People Empowerment Workshop, for example, focuses on topics ranging from quality workmanship to workplace etiquette. In conjunction with Welfare to Work Partnership workshops, these programs boost the chance that job candidates will be good workers.

Through newsletters and the website, the Partnership conducts surveys designed to monitor the problems of Partners as well as report on their achievements. When problems are documented, the Partnership takes responsibility for resolving or correcting them. When, for example, a survey of Business Partners revealed that transportation was a major problem for many recipients, the Partnership commissioned a report focusing on ways to solve this problem. Not all problems, however, are easily solved. Partners report that attitude problems, inadequate training, lack of child care, and lack of education make many would-be employees unacceptable. Some Partners have also reported that they cannot find applicants in their area. The Welfare to Work Partnership continues to address these issues, maintaining an open line of communication (1–800–USAJOB1) with members about the challenges facing the program.

Despite some problems, a number of studies have documented very positive results for the Partnership. *The Road to Retention*, a series of sixteen case studies conducted by the Partnership, with companies such as Salomon Smith Barney, Xerox, UPS, United Airlines, and Sprint, sought to determine how well former recipients were performing and if they were being moved into long-term employment. The study found that most former recipients were making good employees, that many were in quality jobs, and that some were staying at the firms longer than other employees. Those with the longest tenure tended to be those former recipients that the company had provided with training and follow-up services.

The National Advisory Council of Governors also commissioned Wirhlin Worldwide to evaluate the progress of the Welfare to Work Partnership in its second year. A random sample of 500 of the Business Partners provided very positive data on the program. Companies tended to be pleased with their new workers, many had received promotions, and 77 percent of the surveyed companies said that recipients had been placed in jobs with a 'promotional track." Companies like the Fleet Financial Group, which provides extensive training and follow-up services, were showing especially strong success with the program.

In summary, the Welfare to Work Partnership has proven to be a very successful program that was set in motion by PRWORA.

The States and Child Care

PRWORA implicitly recognizes the importance of expanding the national inventory of affordable, quality child care. PRWORA consolidates four child care funding programs into one Child Care and Development Block Grant (CCDBG), increases funding for child care, and allows the states the option of transferring funds from the TANF block grant to CCDBG. The National Governors' Association and National Association of State Budget Officers recently estimated that state and federal spending for child care increased from $3.5 billion in 1996 to $4.7 billion in 1997. Their projections estimated 1998 spending at $6.3 billion (NGA, 1998).

While funding and spending have increased, PRWORA broadens the flexibility of states in deciding the amount, type, quality, and cost of child care to be offered to low-income families. State reactions have varied considerably. While most states have expanded child care, a few have actually reduced services (Greenberg, 1998). Even those states that have significantly increased spending have not been able to meet the need. In fact, the Children's Defense Fund recently reported that nine out of every ten children in low-income families are either not getting child care or receiving very poor quality care (CDF,

1999a). This same study found that 43 states reported that they cannot serve all eligible families, and many states have developed long waiting lists of families who need assistance.

In many states the demand far outstrips supply. For example, in Iowa in early 1999 the waiting list contained almost 80,000 families, in Texas 36,000 families, and in California over 200,000 (CDF, 1999a). Even when child care is available, for a number of reasons, it may not adequately serve the needs of parents. Costs or co-payments are often too high for low-income families (Greenberg, 1998), quality is often low, and those services provided are often not available during nontraditional work hours.

The high cost of decent child care is a major barrier for many parents who would like to work. A recent study found that the average annual cost of care for a four-year-old in an urban childcare center exceeds the cost of public college tuition in almost every state (CDF, 1999b). Yet, one out of every three families with young children earn less than $25,000 (CDF, 1999b). Despite these low earning levels, child care is so under-funded in most states that families earning just above the poverty level are often denied assistance (Greenberg, 1998).

Providing an adequate supply of flexible, quality child care at affordable prices then, remains a challenge, one that substantially impedes the goal of moving recipients into the job market and making that work pay. Child care policy is one area of reform that is clearly inadequate. It will take major new initiatives and funding to solve this problem. President Clinton has recommended to Congress a major child care initiative. This initiative would double the number of families receiving child care subsidies, increase tax credits for low and middle-income working families and business, provide after-school care for an additional half million children each year, and fund improvements in child care quality and early childhood programs. This initiative would cost $21.7 billion over five years (www.acf.dhhs.gov/news/press/980107.htm).

Reducing Out-of-Wedlock Births

An important focus of PRWORA is to bring about a significant reduction in out-of-wedlock births. It seeks to achieve this goal in several ways. Under PRWORA, the states are required to review and update their programs designed to reduce teen pregnancy and out-of-wedlock births. The act also attempts to reduce the chances of an additional pregnancy and improve the skills of teen mothers by giving them assistance only if they stay in school and live at home or in an adult-supervised setting. The law also provides funding for abstinence education, with high-risk groups being the target population. As an incentive, up to five states will receive bonuses for having the largest decreases in out-of-wedlock births without raising abortion rates above the 1995 level. If four or fewer states qualify for the bonuses, the bonus will be $25 million per state. Improved child support enforcement is also designed to encourage responsibility among teens and adults of both sexes.

Several provisions of the new law are implicitly and explicitly designed to lower the birth rate of adult women. Most adult women will be required to join the workforce, and working women generally have fewer children. Second, the law allows states to cap welfare benefits, with the hope of convincing single women that they should not take on additional financial responsibilities. Third, the emphasis placed on child support is designed in part to convince men to take more responsibility for birth control. The expectation over time, then, is that both teen births and out-of-wedlock births to adult women will decline.

The emphasis of PRWORA is still more direct where teen births are concerned. PRWORA created a new section 510 of Title V, the Maternal and Children Health Block Grant of the Social Security Act. This section establishes a separate program for abstinence education. For each fiscal year between 1998 through 2002, $50 million a year is available for abstinence education activities.

The Department of Health and Human Services (DHHS) also attempted to give the states guidance in setting up effective antipregnancy programs by offering several models that have shown some successes (USDHHS, 1998), and by publicizing some of the characteristics of programs that have been judged to produce positive results. While funding is provided only for abstinence programs, some of the models are considerably more comprehensive. DHHS has spread the message that effective antipregnancy policies include: (1) active involvement of parents and adults; (2) clear messages stressing abstinence and personal responsibility for one's actions; (3) strategies to help teens understand career options available to those who avoid pregnancy and obtain an education; (4) community involvement to help teens understand how to achieve worthy life goals; (5) strategies to enhance the self-worth and self-esteem of teenagers, ranging from community service to apprenticeships; and (6) sustained commitment over a long period of time (USDHHS, 1998).

If a state decides to accept funding to promote abstinence, the guidelines the state must follow are quite specific. Additionally, the Secretary of the Department of Health and Human Services (USDHHS) is required to rank the participating states on out-of-wedlock birth rates and changes in those rates over time. The Secretary must prepare a report ranking the five best and the five poorest performing states. This provision is designed to share knowledge and pressure poorly performing states.

The Department of Health and Human Services (USDHHS) also launched the National Strategy to Prevent Teen Pregnancy campaign. This campaign is designed to help teenagers make better life choices, including avoidance of sexual activity. The strategy places special emphasis on encouraging abstinence, especially among nine- to fourteen-year-old girls. The campaign is called Girl Power! It includes a national media campaign designed to send a strong abstinence message to young girls.

Many of the states and some private organizations are also carrying out programs that go beyond abstinence education. Safer-sex programs are designed to provide unbiased information about sexuality, human development, and positive relationships. Interactive skills are often stressed, especially how to resist pressure to use drugs and alcohol or to have sexual intercourse. These programs generally include mentors and a support system that teens can turn to when in crisis.

Another component of safer sex programs is often education about contraceptive use. These programs offer information regarding proper and consistent use of contraceptives, counseling about contraceptive availability, and follow-up care. Data show that teen access to contraceptives is often crucial to preventing adolescent pregnancy, but there are many obstacles. These include fear of family members becoming aware, high costs, lack of knowledge about where to go to get birth control services, the belief that contraceptives are dangerous, and lack of transportation to clinics. Many programs try to overcome these barriers. The School/Community Program for Sexual Risk Reduction Among Teens is a program in current use in eleven states. This program provides free and confidential information and services to teens.

The Self Center, a similar program, is being run in seven states. A program called Smart Start is being used in sixteen states. This program provides contraceptive information and services and also addresses the importance of monogamy.

There are clear advantages of safer-sex programs. Safer-sex programs help teens learn about their bodies and their developing sexuality in a nonjudgmental manner. Adolescents are taught basic facts, along with information about the possible emotional and physical consequences of early sexual activity. They are given information about contraceptives, how to obtain them, and how to use them to protect themselves from unplanned pregnancies and the spread of STDs and AIDS. This type of program tells teens to think for themselves, ask questions, gather all the facts, and then make a rational decision based on the facts rather than pressure from others teens or misinformation. Safer-sex programs that rely on Norplant and Depo Provera have proven to be quite effective in reducing pregnancies (Donovan, 1998, 4).

There are also a large number of programs that go beyond abstinence and safer sex. These hybrid programs are much more holistic, focusing on the "whole person." Programs of this type teach sex education only as part of a more comprehensive approach. A broad range of services is offered, designed to enhance the education, self-esteem, career vision, and goals of the student. Typical services include vocational training, academic tutoring, career counseling, part-time employment, community service, and mentors. Generally, a life options curriculum is offered as part of the program. Hybrid programs are offered under a variety of names, including the Teen Outreach Program (TOP), and the Children's Aid Society's Family Life (www.advocatesforyouth.org). Programs of this type are fairly sophisticated and expensive, but they tend to be particularly effective for youth at high risk of out-of-wedlock pregnancy.

It is too early to determine if the 1996 act has had any significant impact on births to teens, but the myriad of programs that states and local organizations are experimenting with do seem to be making a difference. Data are available only through 1996, but teen pregnancy and births are declining (Guttmacher, 1999). Teen pregnancy and birth rates have been decreasing throughout the 1990s. Between 1991 and 1996 the teenage birth rate declined from 62.1 births per 1,000 females aged fifteen to nineteen to 54.4, a reduction of 12 percent. The rate of decline varied by race and ethnicity. For non-Hispanic whites the rate declined 9 percent to 48.1 per 1,000. The rate dropped by 21 percent for black teens to 91.4. The rate of 101.8 per 1,000 for Hispanics represented a decline of 5 percent. Hispanics now have the highest teen birthrate, but significant percentages are married.

Data for adult women are available through 1997. These data are not as encouraging. As the figures below show, there has been no decline in the percentage of all births to unmarried women. The data compare the percent of live births to unmarried women between 1996 and 1997. The rates for 1997 are basically unchanged from 1996 (Monthly Vital Statistics, 1998).

	All Races		White, Non-Hispanic		Black		Hispanic	
	1997	1996	1997	1996	1997	1996	1997	1996
United States	32.4	32.4	21.5	21.5	69.1	69.8	40.9	40.7

While it is too early to determine if the provisions of the PRWORA will accelerate the downward trend in teen pregnancy, it will not be surprising if it has that effect. None of the existing programs seem to have an overwhelming impact, but many of the more sophisticated programs lower teen pregnancies in a meaningful manner. The emphasis on reducing teen pregnancy found in the PRWORA should stimulate enough attention and effort to produce even more gains. The impact of the PRWORA on adult women may be more limited, but the combined impact of several provisions may lower the out-of-wedlock birth rate. As welfare recipients are moved into the job market, birth rates, including out-of-wedlock births, should decline, and aggressive enforcement of child support orders should convince many more men to take fatherhood more seriously.

Improving Child Support Collections

The emphasis of PRWORA on requiring both parents to support their children is resulting in increased child support collections. By 1997 the number of child support cases with collections rose to 4.2 million, a 48 percent increase over the 2.8 million cases in 1993. In 1997 some

$13.4 billion in child support was collected, an increase of 68 percent over the $8 billion collected in 1992.

The National Directory of New Hires started operation on October 1, 1998. This program requires employers to report all new hires to a state agency. The state agency coordinates this data statewide and also sends it to the National Directory. The data accumulated by the National Directory allow the federal Office of Child Support Enforcement (OCSE) to track absent parents across state lines. Almost one-third of all child support cases involves parents living in different states. The goal of OCSE is to compile records on 16 million noncustodial parents who owe support to an estimated 32 million children. By early 1999 the National Directory had already identified about 1.1 million delinquent parents (Myers, 1999). Once noncustodial parents are identified, child support payments are withheld from their wages. In turn, noncustodial parents can use the registry to gain access and visitation to their children and for custody arrangements.

States are using a variety of techniques to improve child support (Myers, 1998). Many states have separated Child Support Enforcement (CSE) from the primary state child welfare agency. This allows caseworkers to handle a larger caseload, and it puts enforcement into the hands of an agency with more enforcement power. States are also running ad campaigns (often involving celebrities) designed to stress enforcement and "shame" parents into compliance. Wanted posters and newspaper lists are also being used. Colorado and Maryland consider their publicity campaigns to be their most effective CSE measures, reporting collections of $48 for every dollar spent on the campaigns (www.ncsl.org). Virginia uses car boots to immobilize the vehicles of delinquent parents, color coding the boots pink or blue depending upon the sex of the unsupported child. This campaign is designed to achieve both enforcement and public support (www.ncsl.org). Massachusetts and North Carolina have programs to honor "good" fathers, while Massachusetts also has a team that handles exceptionally difficult cases (www.ncsl.org).

A study commissioned by the National Conference of State Legislatures ranked the most effective methods of CSE in descending order (Myers, 1998):

1. Income withholding (including income tax refunds)
2. License revocation

3. New hire tracking
4. Shared data for locating parents
5. Paternity establishment
6. Asset seizure.

The partnership between the federal government and the states has clearly resulted in better enforcement. National databases have made it easier for states to locate delinquent parents. However, federal directives have changed often and have frequently been confusing. The result has been delays in both the design and implementation of CSE. Still, a great deal of progress has been made, and many innovations at the state level have contributed to success.

A supportive policy that seems to be working is the establishment of paternities. In 1997 the Office of Child Support Enforcement established 1.3 million paternities, two and a half times the 1992 figure of 510,000. This included 350,000 paternities established under an in-hospital program that encourages fathers to voluntarily acknowledge paternity at the time of the child's birth.

The success of CSE depends at least in part on three strategies. First, child support orders must exist. Paternity must be established, judicial access must be available for the custodial parent, and information on the employment and assets of the noncustodial parent must be available. Second, the absent parent must be located and targeted for compliance. Job search and training programs should be available for noncustodial parents to help them improve their ability to pay. Third, enforcement mechanisms must have real teeth. CSE enforcement techniques must be effective, and it must be known that they work. Publicity seems to be able to produce compliance rates beyond the actual work of the program or agency.

Conclusions

The PRWORA has certainly had a major impact on America's poor, but the scope of that impact is far from clear. While welfare rolls across the nation have dropped dramatically, we know far too little about what has happened to those who have left welfare. The information that is available suggests that those who have left the rolls for work are marginally better off, but, in general, they need improved assistance. The data suggest that most ex-recipients are not working forty hours a week, and most are living either in poverty or just above the poverty line. Many who need and qualify for means-tested benefits such as food stamps and Medicaid are not receiving them. It is not clear from the evidence why ex-recipients are not working more hours or why they are not receiving much-needed assistance. One obvious problem is that quality child care is often not available, and even when it is, it is often too expensive or not flexible enough to allow many ex-recipients to work full-time. Many recipients who have left cash welfare may also mistakenly believe that they no longer qualify for benefits such as food stamps and Medicaid.

To make leaving the rolls for work really pay, much needs to be changed. Many states need to reduce taxes on low-income families, raise income disregards, and change their benefit reduction rates. Services such as child care need to be substantially improved in almost all the states. To make work possible and profitable, states must provide flexible, high-quality child care at affordable prices. In many cases child care will have to be free or almost free. States must also make certain that ex-recipients understand that they may continue to qualify for important benefits such as food stamps and Medicaid.

The federal government can also play an important role in making work pay better. The EITC can be amended to improve assistance to low-income families and to make more families aware of the program. New rules recently adopted by the Clinton administration give the states substantial flexibility and funding to help ex-recipients, and those diverted from welfare genuinely improve their financial condition through employment. The states now have the option of using TANF funds to subsidize working families, and this assistance will not count against the family's time-limited assistance. This is the type of policy required to help many poor families enjoy a decent level of financial security through employment.

A substantial shortcoming of PRWORA may be its very short time limits. Because the law requires most recipients to leave welfare rather quickly and holds the states to increasingly strict employment goals, states have focused on "Work First" policies. This approach de-emphasizes education and job training, even the most promising strategy of on-the-job education and training. Given how poorly most ex-recipients are doing in the job market, this may be a serious mistake. Additionally, to meet short deadlines and reduce their rolls rapidly, many states are relying on heavy-handed sanctions. The evidence shows that many sanctioned families, including the children in those families, are in dire straits. States like Oregon have shown how sanctions can be used much more thoughtfully.

On the positive side, child support collections are improving quite substantially, but it will take years of vigorous effort to bring compliance rates up to acceptable levels. Whether energetic enforcement will lead to better parenting and more thoughtful decisions about parenthood is still an open question. Teen pregnancy rates have been headed in the right direction throughout the 1990s, and PRWORA may accelerate or at least maintain this trend.

In Chapter 9 we will examine welfare reform in more depth and reflect on the policy changes that will be required to better realize the goal of improving the life of poor and low-income families through supported work.

9

Refining American Social Welfare Policy

One of the most important insights gained by studying PRWORA and its implementation is that there is a significant difference between revamping the welfare system and reducing poverty. PRWORA has fundamentally changed the American approach to ameliorating poverty, both philosophically and in terms of policy design. The philosophical change is more important than the specific policies that have been passed in an attempt to operationalize the new approach. The paradigm that PRWORA is based on, supported work, is in harmony with the America public's dedication to freedom, equal opportunity, and self-reliance (Bobo and Smith, 1994). The approach of substituting employment for welfare is likely to be long-term. It is highly unlikely that America will return to a welfare philosophy that allows large numbers of able-bodied adults who are detached from the workforce to receive cash assistance for extended periods.

The policies that have been passed to implement the new philosophy (i.e., PRWORA, its amendments, and supplemental legislation) are quite ambitious. These policies are designed to totally revamp the nation's welfare system in a relatively short period of time. Both the Democratic and Republican parties have shown a genuine interest in making the new reforms work. In a number of instances a bipartisan coalition in Congress has amended or supplemented PRWORA in an effort to improve its chances of success. President Clinton has sponsored and encouraged many of the amendments and supplemental policies. Still, given how fundamental the changes in welfare policy have been and the short deadlines allowed by these policies, it is not surprisingly that the results have been mixed. Some of the policies are working quite well, others moderately well, and others may be failures. Collectively, the new policies are reducing the welfare rolls and may be moving welfare policy in the right direction, but thus far there is no evidence that the reforms have reduced poverty. In fact, many families are certainly worse off. To really help the poor escape poverty through work, and to reduce the number of Americans who are likely to find themselves facing poverty, considerable policy innovation is still needed.

There are three complementary ways to evaluate the progress that the nation is making under the PRWORA approach. The first is to examine the best and worse characteristics and outcomes of PRWORA and its supporting legislation. This analysis provides insights into the policy changes required to make the reform approach work better. The second is to consider how the reform approach can be maintained and even improved when the economy slumps. The third is to reflect on how social policy needs to evolve over time to play a more effective role in strengthening American families.

The Pros and Cons of PRWORA

We begin by examining the best and worst features and impacts of PRWORA with the intent of identifying policy changes that need to be made to allow the supported work approach to be more successful.

On the positive side PRWORA significantly improves the approach to welfare by:

Emphasizing Supported Work over Welfare

Helping the poor become employed significantly enhances the chance that they will escape poverty, that their children will be in a positive environment, and that the next generation of poor will be considerably smaller. Over the last fifty years, almost all cash welfare recipients have lived in poverty, regardless of the state in which they have resided. While cash welfare programs will continue to leave almost all recipients in poverty, employment, especially full-time, supported employment, greatly improves the chances that families can escape poverty. Additionally, the American public can be expected to be much more sympathetic and supportive of assisting families that are members of the workforce.

Placing the Obligation of Support on Both Parents

Because of badly designed laws and poor enforcement, literally millions of parents, mostly fathers, have abandoned their families and their obligations to their children. PRWORA makes meaningful strides toward ending this abusive behavior. Holding both parents responsible for their children will not only improve the financial situation of millions of families, it will also force men to take fatherhood or the potential of fatherhood more seriously. Hopefully, this will lower the out-of-wedlock birth rate.

Emphasis on Reducing Teen Pregnancy

Teen pregnancy is the superhighway to poverty. When teens have babies out-of-wedlock, the chances that the family will be poor and that their children will have a host of serious problems is very high. Therefore, reducing the teen out-of-wedlock birth rate is essential to reducing the size of the next poverty generation. PRWORA's exclusive emphasis on abstinence is not a realistic policy, but many states are experimenting with a wide range of more sophisticated policies.

Support for Innovation

The discretion given to states in designing innovative ways to help the poor has to be applauded. The states are testing many innovative welfare experiments. The nation should learn much from these trials.

The Stress Placed on Individual Responsibility

Welfare reform is much more likely to be successful if the poor are required to adopt the attitude that they are full partners in overcoming their problems. By being made to understand that government cannot solve their problems but can help them do so, reform is much more viable.

The Emphasis on People Helping People

PRWORA, and its supporting legislation, substantially increase the number of people and organizations that have accepted the challenge of helping the poor escape poverty. The Welfare-to-Work Partnership, a private sector initiative stimulated by PRWORA, has greatly expanded the number of corporations actively involved in helping the poor to make the transaction to independence through employment. Faith-based organizations are being allowed to contract to help the poor through counseling, education, and job training. Community support groups have been recruited all over the nation to help the poor with everything from child care to transportation to job training. Hundreds of community groups have joined together to make teen antipregnancy programs work better. The federal and many state governments have accepted responsibility for finding good jobs in their agencies for ex-welfare recipients. The cumulative impact of all these efforts is very positive.

Despite these very positive features of PRWORA, there are some provisions in need of amendment or enhancement. The most obvious problems that need attention include the following:

Work Does Not Pay

The single most significant problem with PRWORA is that almost all of those ex-recipients who have joined the workforce tend to be living in poverty or very close to the poverty line. Ex-recipients who are employed are usually better off then they were on welfare, but they are still poor or near-poor. One major reason is that few ex-recipients work full-time. Whether this problem is caused by a shortage of full-time jobs, a lack of critical support services, or a lack of will is not clear. New rules issued by the Clinton administration in April, 1999, however, substantially improve the ability of the states to use TANF funds to subsidize services and underwrite private-sector jobs for families that are employed but earning low wages. Additionally, as discussed in Chapter 7, both the state and the federal governments have numerous additional ways to amend their tax and benefit reduction rates to ensure that families can work and that when they do, they earn a livable wage.

Lack of Employment by Many Who Leave Welfare

Data are still limited, but the information collected by the states thus far shows that many ex-welfare recipients who have left the rolls are not working. The numbers are not certain, but as many as 30 to 50 percent of all ex-recipients are not reporting any employment. Many of these families are probably relying on relatives, friends, and private charities. When families in need follow this path, it is not really a solution. A well-designed reform system needs to place able-bodied adults in jobs and then make every reasonable effort to help them have a real chance to prosper through viable employment.

Too Little Emphasis on Human Capital Development

Almost all the states have dramatically reduced their welfare rolls by simply requiring welfare recipients to leave the rolls as soon as possible for any job they can find. The "Work First" approach used by almost all the states may be justified by studies that show that education and job programs generally play only a modest role in helping welfare recipients to obtain a better job or earn a higher wage. However, considerable research reviewed in Chapter 7 shows that a more viable approach is to combine work with education and training. Putting people to work and then offering them on-the-job education and training enhances both the quality of the jobs they qualify for and their earnings.

Support Services Are Weak

One of the most substantial challenges faced by states trying to implement PRWORA is in providing the support services that millions of ex-recipients need to enter the workforce. The states have found it very difficult to provide all their qualified recipients with child care, health care, transportation, and many other services. At this time, the most pressing need seems to be high quality, affordable child care at flexible hours. To make PRWORA work better, support services will have to be significantly improved.

The Twenty Percent Exemption May Leave Many Families in Need

Some heads of families are not employable. Because of age, health, or the role they play in caring for others, they will never be able to join the workforce. It is prudent, therefore, to exempt those recipients from work requirements. PRWORA allows states to exempt up to 20 percent of their recipients from time-limited assistance. While the basic idea is sound, this provision may be abused. States may use this provision to ignore families that are the most difficult to assist. A clear distinction needs to be made between difficult cases and impossible cases. Families that have significant but not insurmountable barriers (e.g., low education and/or job skills, substance abuse problems, domestic violence, etc.) should be given the assistance they need to make the transition to work. There are many reasons for helping these adults, but an important one is that families that remain on welfare almost always live in poverty. This means that children in these families grow up in poverty, often without the pre-school help they need. The only real hope that most of these families have to escape poverty and really improve their lives is through employment. Of course, that small group of poor adults who cannot work should be given a level of assistance that allows them to escape poverty.

PRWORA's Deadlines Are Too Short

The intent of reform was to transform the welfare system very quickly. The evidence showing how poorly most ex-recipients are doing suggest that states are under so much pressure to meet deadlines that they are focusing more on reducing the rolls than on helping recipients succeed in the workforce. The "sink or swim" mentality is resulting in considerably casualties.

The nation's healthy economy has probably played a larger role in making PRWORA "work" than members of Congress or President Clinton ever expected. With a rapidly expanding job base, states have been able to force recipients to quickly leave the rolls for available jobs, but most of these jobs are low pay, mostly part-time, with no benefits and little chance of advancement. When the economy suffers a slump (and it will), millions of poorly trained and poorly educated ex-recipients may end up back on cash welfare. A more thoughtful and long-term approach will require the states to help people find jobs and then while they are employed, provide them with opportunities to improve their education and job skills. This approach is slower and more expensive, but the long-term outcome should be much better.

Sanctions Are Often Not Being Used Thoughtfully

Sanctions, carefully applied, can play an important role in convincing welfare recipients that they must accept responsibility for their successful transition to employment. However, the evidence reviewed in Chapter 7 reveals that many states are using sanctions in a careless and harsh fashion. This approach to sanctions does not generally produce compliance; it simply results in many families being dropped from the rolls. When these sanctions are permanent, and especially when the whole family loses benefits, both the adults and children end up in real jeopardy. The short deadlines allowed by PRWORA may be the primary reason that so many states have not used sanctions more thoughtfully. Several states, including Oregon, have adopted well-designed policies that apply full-family sanctions only after careful review and the development of a plan to protect the children in the family. The Oregon model should be adopted by all the states.

Can PRWORA's Momentum Be Sustained and Even Improved When the Economy Slumps?

Perhaps the real test of the commitment to substituting work for cash welfare will be the nation's reaction to an inevitable slump in the economy and job market. The American economy, like any capitalist economy, has always gone through periods of expansion and retraction. What happens when the United States goes into a period when inflation rises, resulting in tighter money and higher rates of unemployment?

As noted above, since the economy has been so strong since PRWORA was passed, states have found it easy to simply require millions of families to leave cash welfare for available jobs. But when the unemployment rate increases, jobs will become more scarce, forcing many ex-recipients out of the market and limiting opportunities for those on welfare. Both the federal government and the states will have many options to deal with this problem. The federal government could simply amend PRWORA to allow states to exempt a larger percentage of their caseloads from work requirements. This would be a fairly easy solution, but it is basically an abandonment of the philosophy of helping the able-bodied poor make the transition to independence through employment.

A solution more compatible with the spirit of reform would be increased reliance on a combination of options designed to subsidize employment. Private employers could be given advantageous tax credits for each employee hired, trained, and retained for twelve to twenty-four months. In a really bad economy, these credits might have to be more favorable than those currently available under the Work Opportunity Tax Credit (WOTC) and the Welfare to Work Tax Credit (WWTC) programs described in Chapters 6 and 7. Additionally, state and federal funds might underwrite on-the-job education and skill training. The expense of this approach would be justified if the result were a significantly larger percentage of all ex-recipients being able to escape poverty through decent jobs.

Another option would be increased reliance on Community Service Jobs (CSJ). As noted above, two of the most serious problems with PRWORA are that ex-recipients are finding that work does not pay and that many ex-recipients are not in the workforce. Community Service Jobs offer a viable way to address both of these problems. PRWORA gives states the latitude to use CSJs, but most states have not made significant use of this option. CSJs are complicated to set up and administer, but this approach offers some very positive benefits.

The benefits include the following: First, the research reviewed in Chapter 7 shows that most ex-recipients are not able to work their way out of poverty because they do not work full-time, and they have very low skill levels. CSJs can address both of these problems (Poglinco, Brash, and Granger, 1998). CSJs can provide full-time employment and be designed to provide education and skills training on-the-job. A full-time job would acclimate ex-recipients to a forty-hour work week and provide a better weekly wage. It is important that the CSJs provide a real service to the community. The public will not be supportive of CSJs that are make-work, and recipients can only gain real skills by doing work valuable to the community. CSJs should also be transitional, but the length of time that recipients could be employed in a CSJ should vary depending upon the characteristics and problems of the parent and the availability of opportunities in the private sector.

A second advantage of CSJs is that the success of this approach would depend substantially upon the states significantly expanding the availability of quality child care and after-school care. The value of an excellent system of programs for children extends far beyond their role in allowing parents to enter the workforce. A major study being conducted in Wisconsin shows the importance both of providing services and supplements to help ex-recipients become established in the workforce and the impact of programs for children (Bos, et al., 1999). Known as New Hope, this project shows that well-designed services and supplements can help ex-recipients and other low-income families increase their work effort and earning and improve their chances of escaping poverty through work. These changes were significant but moderate, probably because this project does not involve any type of education or training for recipients.

But one of the most important impacts of New Hope has been on the children of the recipients who have been placed in programs designed to free up their parent(s) for work. The New Hope project substantially increased the exposure of children in the project to formal child care, after-school care, and other organized activities. All of the children receiving care benefited, and their parents reported increased parental warmth and better monitoring of their children's activities (Bos, et al., 1999, Table 8). The designers of the New Hope project had expected better employment, improved material resources, and enhanced emotional well-being to result in better relationships between parents and children. This turned out to be true, especially for parents who could make a decent wage without having to work more than forty hours a week.

The study included surveys of the teachers of the children whose parents were enrolled in New Hope. Compared to a control group, boys in these families scored much better on academic performance, classroom skills such as the ability to work independently, and social competence. The boys also had fewer behavior problems. Additionally, boys whose parents were in New Hope reported higher educational expectations and higher occupational aspirations and expectations than controls, indicating that the program enhanced their ambitions for future study and careers (Bos, et al., 1999, Table 10). The daughters of parents in the program did not make educational gains, and it is not clear why. While the girls exhibited few behavioral problems, they continued to score low on achievement tests (Bos, et al., 1999, Table 10).

The impact of New Hope on both parents and children, then, was positive. The boys make very important gains, and the relationship between parents and children improved for both sexes. This study and others suggest that welfare reform could be substantially improved by full-time CSJs and by a greatly expanded base of quality programs for children in poor and low-income families. Policies of this type not only can lift more of the poor out of poverty through viable employment, but they can also play a major role in reducing the size of the next generation of Americans who are unprepared to compete in the American economy.

How Should American Social Policy Evolve If Poverty Can Be Reduced?

If the United States is successful over the next decade or two in permanently reducing poverty and poverty rolls, what options would this open up for the design and evolution of social policy? Imagine, for example, that the number of recipients on cash welfare could be reduced to 3 or 4 million, less than 2 percent of the population (see Table 5.4). This would be a huge reduction from the record enrollment levels of the early 1990s when the number of cash welfare recipients was over 14 million, or about 5.5 percent of the population. Given the changes that have taken place over the last few years, a reduction of this size is realistic.

If welfare policy is refined, not only enrollments, but actual poverty would be very significantly lowered. A lower poverty rate would reduce social welfare spending to some extent, while increasing tax revenues. How much social welfare expenditures would be lowered is impossible to calculate because reducing poverty may require significant expenditures on support services, community service jobs, training, and subsidies. Still, overall welfare expenditures should decline. As ex-recipients become established in the job market, expenditures on programs such as TANF, food stamps, and Medicaid should descend. At the same time, refined welfare programs should be able to help many ex-recipients earn incomes high enough to contribute to the tax base. Effective social welfare programs should also be able to further lower the teen out-of-wedlock birth rate, improve child support levels, lower the size of the next poverty generation through per-school and after school programs, and even reduce the size and costs of serious social problems such as crime.

The sum total of all these changes should provide the United States with the option of reducing the emphasis on welfare policy in favor of a more fully conceptualized family policy. Family policies, quite simply, are programs designed to strengthen all families. If Americans really want to eliminate poverty, antipoverty policy cannot be focused on the poor. To really eliminate poverty, America needs a comprehensive and thoughtful family policy. Family policy is in its infancy in the United States, but common in European and Scandinavian nations (Garfinkel, Hochschild and McLanahan, 1996; Garfinkel and McLanahan, 1994; Kamerman, 1991; Kamerman and Kahn, 1988; Kamerman, 1988). In the European and Scandinavian nations all citizens are guaranteed health care, high quality day care, and pre-school programs are much more universal, maternity and family leave policies are universal and financially supportive of parenthood, children's allowances are universal, programs to help all families obtain decent shelter are numerous, and the quality of education programs for low-income students is very high (Ravitch, 1996). The result is that poverty rates are much lower in these nations than in America, and this is especially true for children, female-headed families and the elderly (Smeeding, et al., 1993; Smeeding, 1992b; Wong, Garfinkel, and McLanahan 1993). There are also fewer social problems such as violent crime, and educational achievement levels are higher for students in low-income families (Ravitch, 1996).

American social policy needs to evolve in this direction. The most significant change in American families in the twentieth century has been the growth of single-parent families and the movement of women into the job market. Today the majority of all American families are headed by a single parent or two working parents. But, American social policy has not kept pace with the changes in family demographics. The result is that millions of families have little or no health insurance, millions of children do not receive quality child care and pre-school education, millions of children do not have proper after-school care, and millions of parents struggle (often unsuccessfully) to balance parenthood with employment. Quality family policy can give American families the support they need to be viable, productive, competitive members of American society and the global economy. The result would be a healthier, safer, more competitive America.

References

Acs, G. 1993. "The Impact of AFDC on Young Women's Childbearing Decisions." Paper. Washington, DC: The Urban Institute.

Acs, G., Coe, N., Watson, K., and Lerman, R.I. 1998. "Does Work Pay? An Analysis of the Work Incentives Under TANF." Memo. Washington, DC: The Urban Institute.

Adams, T., Duncan, G., and Rodgers, W.L. 1988. "The Persistence of Urban Poverty." In *Quiet Riots: Race and Poverty in the United States*, eds. F.R. Harris and R.W. Wilkins, 212–241. New York: Pantheon Books.

Anderson, E. 1990. *Streetwise: Race, Class, and Change in an Urban Community.* Chicago: University of Chicago Press.

Bailis, L.N., and Burbridge, L. 1991. Report on Costs of Living and Payment Standard Options: Executive Summary. Committee for SB 153. State of New Hampshire.

Bane, M.J., and Ellwood, D.T. 1994. *Welfare Realities: From Rhetoric to Reform.* Cambridge, MA: Harvard University Press.

———. 1983. "The Dynamics of Dependence: The Routes to Self-Sufficiency." Report prepared for the U.S. Department of Health and Human Services. Cambridge, MA: Urban Systems Research and Engineering, Inc.

Bane, M.J., and Jargowsky, P.A. 1988. "Urban Poverty Areas: Basic Questions Concerning Prevalence, Growth, and Dynamics." Center for Health and Human Resources Policy Discussion Paper Series, Harvard University.

Barber, B. 1984. *Strong Democracy*. Berkley: University of California Press.

Bartik, T.J. 1996. *Who Benefits from State and Local Economic Development Policies?* Kalamazoo, MI: W.E. Upjohn Institute on Employment Research.

Bassi, L. 1987, June. "Family Structure and Poverty Among Women and Children: What Accounts for Change?" Mimeo. Washington, DC: Georgetown University.

Bergman, B. 1989. "Occupational Segregation, Wages and Profits When Employers Discriminate by Race and Sex." *Eastern Economic Journal* 1 (April): 103–110.

Bernstein, J., and Garfinkel, I. 1997. "Welfare Reform: Fixing the System Inside and Out." In *The National Government and Social Welfare: What Should Be the Federal Role?* eds. J.E. Hansan and R. Morris. Westport, CT: Auburn House.

Blank, R. 1997. "Why Has Economic Growth Been Such an Ineffective Tool Against Poverty in Recent Years?" In *Poverty and Inequality: The Political Economy of Redistribution*, ed. J. Neil, 188–210. Kalamazoo, MI: W.E. Upjohn Institute for Employment Research.

———. 1994. "The Employment Strategy: Public Policies to Increase Work and Earnings." In *Confronting Poverty: Prescriptions for Change*, eds. S. Danziger, G. Sandefur, and D. Weinberg, 168–204, Cambridge, MA: Harvard University Press.

Blank, R., and Ruggles, P. 1996. "When Do Women Use AFDC and Food Stamps? The Dynamics of Eligibility Versus Participation." *Journal of Human Resources* 31(1): 57–89.

Bloom, D. 1997. "After AFDC: Welfare–to-Work Choices and Challenges for States." New York: Manpower Demonstration Research Corporation. Available at www.dhhs.gov/programs.

Bloom, H.S., Orr, L., Cave, G., Bell, S., and Doolittle, F. 1993. "The National JTPA Study." Report to the U.S. Department of Labor. Bethesda, MD: Abt Associates.

Blum, B.B., and Berrey, E.C. 1999. "Welfare Research Perspectives: Past, Present and Future." National Center for Children in Poverty. New York: Columbia University.

Bobo, L., and Smith, R. 1994. "Antipoverty Policy, Affirmative Action, and Racial Attitudes." In *Confronting Poverty: Prescriptions for Change*, eds. S. Danziger, G. Sandefur, and D. Weinberg, 365–395. Cambridge, MA: Harvard University Press.

Bos, H., et al. 1999. "New Hope for People with Low Incomes: Two-Year Results of a Program to Reduce Poverty and Reform Welfare." Memo. New York: Manpower Demonstration Corporation.

Bound, J., and Freeman, R. 1992. "What Went Wrong? The Erosion of Relative Earnings and Employment Among Young Black Men in the 1980s." *Quarterly Journal of Economics* 107(1): 201–232.

Bound, J., and Holzer, H. 1993. "Industrial Structure, Skill Levels, and the Labor Market for White and Black Males." *Review of Economics and Statistics* 75(3): 387–396.

Bound, J., and Johnson, G. 1992. "Changes in the Structure of Wages in the 1980s: An Evaluation of Alternative Explanations." *American Economic Review* 82(3): 371–392.

Brandon, P. 1995. "Vulnerability to Future Dependence Among Former AFDC Mothers." Discussion paper no. 1055–95. Madison: Institute for Research on Poverty, University of Wisconsin.

Brown, L., and Pollitt, E. 1996. "Malnutrition, Poverty and Intellectual Development." *Scientific American* 274(2): 38–43.

Bryner, G. 1998. *Politics and Public Morality: The Great American Welfare Reform Debate.* New York: W.W. Norton.

Bureau of the Census. 1999. "Educational Attainment in the United States: March 1998 (Update)." *Current Population Reports,* Series P20–513.

———. 1998a. "Poverty in the United States: 1997." *Current Population Reports,* Series P60–201.

———. 1998b. "Marital Status and Living Arrangements: March 1998." *Current Population Reports,* Series P20–514.

———. 1998c. "Measuring 50 Years of Economic Change: 1947–1997." *Current Population Reports,* Series P60–203.

———. 1998d. "Money Income in the United States, 1997." *Current Population Reports,* Series P60–200.

———. 1998e. www.census.gov. Historical Tables—Population.

———. 1994a. *Statistical Abstract of the United States: 1994,* 114th edition. Washington, DC: U.S. Government Printing Office.

———. 1994b. "Marital Status and Living Arrangements: March 1993." *Current Population Reports,* Series P-20–478.

Bureau of Economic Analysis, 1998. Frequently requested NIPA Data: Tables.

Burke, V. 1998. Cash and noncash benefits for persons with limited income: Eligibility rules, recipient and expenditure data, fiscal years 1994–96 (98–226 EPW). Washington, DC: Congressional Research Service.

Burtless, G. 1995. "Employment Prospects of Welfare Recipients." In *The Work Alternative: Welfare Reform and the Realities of the Job Market,* eds. D.S. Nightingale and R.H. Haverman. Washington, DC: Urban Institute Press.

Burtless, G., Corbett, T., and Primus, W. 1998. "Improving the Measurement of American Poverty." *Focus* 19(2):12–21.

Cain, G. 1987. "Negative Income Tax Experiments and the Issue of Marital Stability and Family Composition." In *Lessons from the Income Experiments,* ed. A. Munnell. Boston: Federal Reserve Bank.

Cancian, M., Haverman, R., Kaplan, T., Meyer, D., and Wolfe, B. 1999. "Work, Earnings and Well-Being After Welfare: What Do We Know?" Paper presented at the Welfare Reform and the Macro-Economy Conference, Washington, DC, November 19–20, 1998.

Cancian, M., Haverman, R., Kaplan, T., and Wolfe, B. 1998a, May. Memo. "Who Left Wisconsin's Welfare Rolls After 1995, and Who Stayed?"

———. 1998b., August. Memo. "Post-Exit Earnings and Benefit Receipt Among Those Who Left AFDC in Wisconsin."

———. 1998c, October. Memo. "Post-Exit Earnings and Benefit Receipt Among Those Who Left AFDC in Wisconsin."

Cancian, M., and Meyer, D.R. 1998. "Work After Welfare: Women's Work Effort, Occupation, and Economic Well-Being." Unpublished manuscript.

Casey Foundation. 1995. *Kids Count Data Book.* Baltimore, MD: Annie E. Casey Foundation.

Cheng, T. 1995. "The Chances of Recipients Leaving AFDC: A Longitudinal Study." *Social Work Research* 19(2): 67–96.

Children's Defense Fund. 1999a. "TANF Funds Are Not the Child Care Solution." Testimony before the U.S. House Ways and Means Committee. February 10, 1999. Available at www.childrensdefense.org/tanf/childcaretanf.html.

———. 1999b. *CDF Reports*. Volume 20, Number 3, March, 2.

Citizen's Board of Inquiry into Hunger and Malnutrition in the United States. 1968. *Hunger, USA*. Boston: Beacon.

Citro, C.F., and Michael, R.T., eds. 1995. *Measuring Poverty: A New Approach*. New York: National Academy Press.

Colville, L., et al. 1997. "A Study of AFDC Case Closures Due to JOBS Sanctions." Michigan Family Independence Program. Available at www.mfia. state.mi.us/sanctions.

Cook, J.T., and Martin, K.S. 1995. "Differences in Nutrient Adequacy Among Poor and Nonpoor Children." Medford, MA: Tufts University School of Nutrition, Center on Hunger, Poverty, and Nutrition Policy.

Corbett, T. 1995. "Welfare Reform in Wisconsin: The Rhetoric and the Reality." In *The Politics of Welfare Reform*, eds. Donald F. Norris and Lyke Thompson, 216–237. Thousand Oaks, CA: Sage Publications.

Council of Economic Advisors. 1995. "Living Conditions of American Families." Table 1E.

Cutler, D., and Katz, L.F. 1992. "Rising Inequality? Changes in the Distribution of Income and Consumption in the 1980s." *American Economic Review* 82(3): 546–551.

———. 1991. "Macroeconomic Performance and the Disadvantaged." *Brookings Papers on Economic Activity* 2: 1–61.

Danziger, S., Kakubson, G., Schwartz, S., and Smolensky, E. 1982. "Work and Welfare as Determinants of Female Poverty and Household Headship." *Quarterly Journal of Economics* 98(2): 519–534.

Danziger, S., and Weinberg, D. 1994. "The Historical Record: Trends in Family Income, Inequality, and Poverty." In *Confronting Poverty: Prescriptions for Change*, eds. D. Danziger, G. Sandefur, and D. Weinberg, 18–50. Cambridge, MA: Harvard University Press.

Darity, W.A., and Myers, S.L. 1983. "Changes in Black Family Structure: Implications for Welfare Dependency." *American Economic Review* 73(May): 59–64.

Dechter, A., and Smock, P. 1994. "The Fading Breadwinner Role and the Implications for Young Couples." Discussion paper no. 1051–94. Institute for Research on Poverty, Madison, WI.

Department of Health and Human Services. 1999. Percentage of the Population on Welfare. Available at www.acf.dhhs.gov.

Derr, M.K. 1998. "The Impact of Sanctioning on Utah's TANF Families." Paper presented at Association of Public Policy and Management Annual Research Conference, October, Los Angeles.

Donovan, P. 1998. "Falling Teen Pregnancy, Birthrates: What's Behind the Declines?" *The Guttmacher Report*, vol. 1, no. 5. Available at www.agi-usa.org/pubs/journals/gr010506.html.

Downes, B.T. 1968. "Social and Political Characteristics of Riot Cities: A Comparative Study." *Social Science Quarterly* 49(December): 509–520.

Duncan, G.J., and Brooks-Gunn, J. 1998. "Making Welfare Reform Work for

Our Children." [National Center for Children in Poverty] *News and Issues* 8(1): 2–3.

Duncan, G.J., and Hoffman, S.D. 1988. "Welfare Dependence Within and Across Generations." *Science* 239: 467–471.

Duncan, G.J., et al. 1999. "Does Poverty Affect the Life Chances of Children?" *American Sociological Review.* Forthcoming.

Eggebeen, D.J., and Lichter, D.T. 1991. "Race, Family Structure, and Changing Poverty Among America's Children." *American Sociological Review* 56(2): 801–817.

Ellwood, D.T. 1989. "Conclusions." In *Welfare Policy for the 1990s*, eds. P.H. Cottingham and D.T. Ellwood, 269–290. Cambridge, MA: Harvard University Press.

Ellwood, D., and Bane, M.J. 1985. "The Impact of AFDC on Family Structure and Living Arrangements." *Research in Labor Economics* 7(2): 137–149.

Ellwood, D.T., and Crane, J. 1990. "Family Change Among Black Americans." *Journal of Economic Perspectives* 4(4): 65–84.

Ellwood, D.T., and Rodda, D.T. 1991. "The Hazards of Work and Marriage: The Influence of Male Employment on Marriage Rates." Working paper, John F. Kennedy School of Government, Harvard University, Cambridge, MA.

Enchautegui, M.E. 1992. "Geographic Differentials in the Socioeconomic Status of Puerto Ricans: Human Capital Variations and Labor Market Characteristics." *International Migration Review* 26: 1267–1290.

Fagan, J. 1992. "Drug Selling and Ilicit Income in Distressed Neighborhoods: The Economic Lives of Street-Level Drug Users and Sellers." In *Drugs, Crime, and Social Isolation: Barriers to Urban Opportunity*, eds. A.V. Harrell and G.E. Peterson, 292–312. Washington, DC: Urban Institute Press.

Feagan, J.R. 1975. *Subordinating the Poor: Welfare and American Beliefs*. Englewood Cliffs, NJ: Prentice Hall.

Federal Transit Administration. 1997. "Access to Jobs: Best Practices in Welfare-to-Work Transportation." Available at http://www.fta.dot.gov.ntl.index.html.

Federman, M., et al. 1996. "What Does It Mean to Be Poor in America?" *Monthly Labor Review* May: 13–21.

Fein, D.J., and Karweit, J.A. 1999. "The Early Economic Impacts of Delaware's A Better Chance Welfare Reform Program." Washington, DC: Abt Associates, Inc.

Ferber, J., and Storch, R. 1998. "Full-Family Sanctions: Not Worth the Risk." Denver, CO: Gateway Legal Services. Available at www.dhhs.gov/family.

Fisher, G.M. 1992. "The Development and History of the Poverty Thresholds." *Social Security Bulletin* 55(4): 3–14.

———. 1997. "Disseminating the Administrative Version and Explaining the Administrative and Statistical Versions of the Federal Poverty Measure." *Clinical Sociology Review* 15(4): 164–168.

———. 1998. "Setting American Standards of Poverty; A Look Back." *Focus* 19(2): 49–50.

———. 1999. "Income (IN-) Adequacy? The Official Poverty Line, Possible Changes, and Some Historical Lessons." *Community Action Digest* 1(1): 37–42.

Fitzgerald, J. 1995. "Local Labor Markets and the Local Area Effects on Welfare Duration." *Journal of Policy Analysis and Management* 14(1): 43–67.

Foster, M. 1993. "Comparing Poverty in 13 OECD Countries: Traditional and Synthetic Approaches." *Studies in Social Policy #10*. Paris.

Freedman, S., Friedlander, D., Winston, L., and Schweder, A. 1996. "The GAIN Evaluation: Five-Year Impacts on Employment, Earnings, and AFDC Receipt," Working paper 96.1. New York: Manpower Demonstration Research Corporation.

Freeman, R.B., and Katz, L.F. (eds.). 1995. *Differences and Changes in Wage Structures*. Chicago: University of Chicago Press.

Friedlander, D., and Burtless, G. 1995. *Five Years After: The Long-Term Effects of Welfare-to-Work Programs*. New York: Russell Sage Foundation.

Fuchs, V. 1989. "Women's Quest for Economic Equality." *Journal of Economic Perspectives* 3(Winter): 25–41.

Garfinkel, I., Hochschild, J.L., and McLanahan, S.S. (eds.). 1996. *Social Policies for Children*. Washington, DC: The Brookings Institution.

Garkinkel, I., and McLanahan, S.S. 1994. "Single-Mother Families, Economic Security, and Government Policy." In *Confronting Poverty: Prescriptions for Change*, eds. S. Danziger, G. Sandefur, and D. Weinberg, 205–225. Cambridge, MA: Harvard University Press.

———. 1986. *Single Mothers and Their Children: A New American Dilemma*. New York: Russell Sage Foundation.

General Accounting Office. 1997. "Welfare Reform: States' Early Experiences with Benefit Termination." Available at www.gao.gov.

———. 1994a. *Families on Welfare: Sharp Rise in Never-Married Women Reflects Societal Trend*. Report HEHS-94–92. Washington, DC: U.S. Government Accounting Office (GAO).

———. 1994b. *Families on Welfare: Teen Mothers Least Likely to Become Self-Sufficient*. Report HEHS-94–115. Washington, DC: GAO.

———. 1994c. *Families on Welfare: Focus on Teen Mothers Could Enhance Welfare Reform Efforts*. Report HEHS-94–112. Washington, DC: GAO.

Gottschalk, P., and Danziger, S. 1986, August. "Poverty and the Underclass." Testimony before the Select Committee on Hunger, U.S. Congress.

Gottschalk, P., McLanahan, S, and Sandefur, G. 1994. "The Dynamics and Intergenerational Transmission of Poverty and Welfare Participation." In *Confronting Poverty: Prescriptions for Change*, eds. S. Danziger, G. Sandefur, and D. Weinberg, 85–108. Cambridge, MA: Harvard University Press.

Gottschalk, P., and Moffit, R. 1994. "The Growth of Earnings Instability in the U.S. Labor Market." *Brookings Papers on Economic Activity* 2(1): 217–272.

Gramlich, E., and Laren, D. 1991. "Geographical Mobility and Persistent Poverty." Paper presented at the Conference on Urban Labor Markets and Labor Mobility, Airlie House, VA, March 7–8.

Green Book. 1998. Background Material and Data on Programs Within the Jurisdiction of the Committee on Ways and Means. Committee on Ways and Means. U.S. House of Representatives, 106th Congress, 2nd Session. Washington, DC: U.S. Government Printing Office.

Greenberg, M.H. 1998. "Child Care Policy Two Years Later." Center for Law and Social Policy. Available at www.clasp.org.

Gritz, R.M., and MaCurdy, T. 1991. "Patterns of Welfare Utilization and Multiple Program Participation among Young Women." Report to the U.S. Department of Health and Human Services under Grant 88–ASPE 198A.

Groeneveld, L., Hanna, T., and Tuma, N. 1983. "Marital Stability." Final Report of the Seattle/Denver Income Maintenance Experiment, Vol. 1: *Design and Results.* Washington, DC: U.S. Government Printing Office.

Gueron, J.M., and E. Pauly. 1991. *From Welfare to Work.* New York: Russell Sage Foundation.

The Alan Guttmacher Institute. 1999. http://www.Guttmacher.org.

Hagenaars, A.K., DeVos, F., and Zaidi, A. 1994. "Patterns of Poverty in Europe." Paper presented to the 23rd General Conference of the IARIW, St. Andrews, Canada, August.

Hahn, L.H., and Feagin, J.R. 1970. "Rank-and-File Versus Congressional Perceptions of Ghetto Riots." *Social Science Quarterly* 51(September): 361–373.

Harris, K.M. 1996. "Life After Welfare: Women, Work and Repeat Dependency." *American Sociological Review* 61(1): 407–426.

———. 1993. "Work and Welfare Among Single Mothers in Poverty." *American Journal of Sociology* 99(3): 317–352.

Hauan, S.M. 1995. "Hispanics and Working Poverty in U.S. Cities." Ph.D. dissertation, Pennsylvania State University, University Park, PA.

Haverman, R. 1987. *Poverty Policy and Poverty Research: The Great Society and the Social Sciences.* Madison: University of Wisconsin Press.

Heritage Foundation. 1995. "The Impact of the Family Cap on Out-of-Wedlock Births and Abortions." Available at http://www.heritage.org.

Hoffman, S.D., Duncan, G.J., and Mincy, R.B. 1991. "Marriage and Welfare Use Among Young Women: Do Labor Market, Welfare and Neighborhood Factors Account for Declining Rates of Marriage Among Black and White Women?" Paper presented at the annual meetings of the American Economic Association, New Orleans, December.

Holcomb, P.A., Pavetti, L., Ratcliffe, C., and S. Riediger. 1998. "Building an Employment Focused Welfare System: Work First and Other Work Oriented Strategies in Five States." Memo. Washington, DC: Urban Institute.

Holcomb, P.A., and Ratcliffe, C. 1998. "Consequences for Noncompliance in Indiana." Paper presented at the Association of Public Policy and Management Annual Research Conference. Washington ,DC: Urban Institute.

Holzer, H.J. 1991. "The Spatial Mismatch Hypothesis: What Has the Evidence Shown?" *Urban Studies* 28(4): 104–122.

Hoynes, H.W. 1996. "Local Labor Markets and Welfare Spells: Do Demand Conditions Matter?" Institute for Research on Poverty, Discussion paper no. 1104–96. Madison, Wisconsin.

Hoynes, H.W., and MaCurdy, T. 1994. "Has the Decline in Benefits Shortened Welfare Spells?" *American Economic Review* 84(2): 43–48.

Hughes, M.A. 1989. "Misspeaking Truth to Power: A Geographical Perspective on the Urban Fallacy." *Economic Geography* 65(1): 185–207.

Israel, F.I. (ed.). 1966. *State of the Union Messages of the Presidents 1790–1966*, vol. 3. New York: Chelsea House.

Jarrett, R.L. 1990, May. "A Comparative Examination of Socialization Patterns Among Low-Income African Americans, Chicanos, Puerto Ricans, and

Whites: A Review of the Ethnographic Literature," Mimeo. New York: Social Science Research Council.

Jenks, C. 1992. *Rethinking Social Policy: Race, Poverty and the Underclass.* New York: Harper-Perennial.

Jenks, C., and Mayer, S. 1990. "Residential Segregation, Job Proximity, and Black Job Opportunities." In *Inner-City Poverty in the United States*, eds. L.E. Lynn, Jr. and M.G. McGeary, 319–337. Washington, DC: National Academy Press.

Johnson, A., and Meckstroth, A. 1998. "Ancillary Services to Support Welfare to Work." Mathematica Policy Research. Available at http://aspe.hhs.gov/govhsp.isp/ancillary/transp.htm.

Johnson, J.H., and Oliver, M.L. 1991. "Economic Restructuring and Black Male Joblessness in U.S. Metropolitan Areas." *Urban Geography* 12(6): 542–562.

Juhn, C., Murphy, K.M., and Pierce, B. 1993. "Wage Inequality and the Rise in Returns to Skill." *Journal of Political Economy* 101(3): 410–442.

Kamerman, S.B. 1991. "Child Care Policies and Programs: An International Overview." *Journal of Social Issues* 47(2): 179–196.

———. 1988. *Mothers Alone: Strategies for a Time of Change.* Dover, MA: Auburn House.

Kamerman, S.B., and Kahn, A J. 1988. "What Europe Does for Single-Parent Families." *Public Interest* 2(Fall): 70–86.

Kaplan, J. 1999. "The Use of Sanctions Under TANF." Welfare Information Network. Available at www.welfareinfo.org/sanctionissue.

Kasarda, J.D. 1992. "The Severely Distressed in Economically Transforming Cities." In *Drugs, Crime, and Social Isolation: Barriers to Urban Opportunity*, eds. A.V. Harrell and G.E. Peterson. Washington, DC: Urban Institute Press.

———. 1990. "Structural Factors Affecting the Location and Timing of Urban Underclass Growth." *Urban Geography* 11(1): 234–264.

———. 1989. "Urban Industrial Transition and the Underclass." *Annals of the American Academy of Political and Social Science* 501(January): 26–47.

———. 1988. "Jobs, Migration, and Emerging Urban Mismatches." In *Urban Change and Poverty*, eds. M.G. McGeary and L.L. Lynn, Jr. Washington, DC: National Academy Press.

Katz, M.B. 1986. *In the Shadow of the Poorhouse: A Social History of Welfare in America.* New York: Basic Books.

Kaus, M. 1995. *The End of Equality.* New York: Basic Books.

Korenman, S., and Miller, J. 1997. "Effects of Long-Term Poverty on Physical Health of Children in the National Longitudinal Survey of Youth." In *Consequences of Growing Up Poor*, eds. G.J. Duncan and J. Brook-Gunn. New York: Russell Sage Foundation.

Kotz, N. 1979. *Hunger in America: The Federal Response.* New York: Field Foundation.

———. 1971. *Let Them Eat Promises: The Politics of Hunger in America.* New York: Doubleday.

Landale, N.S., and Lichter, D.T. 1997. "Geography and the Etiology of Poverty Among Latino Children." *Social Science Quarterly* 78(2):874–894.

Lemann, N. 1991. *The Promised Land: The Great Black Migration and How It Changed America.* New York: Alfred A. Knopf.

Lerman, R.I. 1989. "Employment Opportunities of Young Men and Family Formation." *American Economic Review* 79(May): 62–66.

Leuchtenburg, W.E. 1963. *Franklin D. Roosevelt and the New Deal 1932–1940*. New York: Harper & Row.

Lichter, D.T., and Landale, N.S. 1995. "Parental Work, Family Structure, and Poverty Among Latino Children." *Journal of Marriage and Family* 57(4): 346–354.

Lichter, D., McLaughlin, D., Kephart, D., and Landry, D. 1992. "Race and the Retreat from Marriage: A Shortage of Marriageable Men?" *American Sociological Review* 56(2):15–32.

Loprest, P. 1999. "Families Who Left Welfare: Who Are They and How Are They Doing?" Discussion paper, Assessing the New Federalism, An Urban Institute Program to Assess Changing Social Policies. Washington, DC.

Lowi, T. 1972. "Four Systems of Policy, Politics, and Choice." *Public Administration Review* 11(2):298–310.

Magnet, M. 1993. *The Dream and the Nightmare: The Sixties' Legacy to the Underclass*. New York: William Morrow.

Mare, R., and Winship, C. 1991. "Socioeconomic Change and the Decline of Marriage for Blacks and Whites." In *The Urban Underclass*, eds. C. Jenks and P. Peterson. Washington, DC: Brookings Institute.

Massey, D.S. 1990. "American Apartheid: Segregation and the Making of the Underclass." *American Journal of Sociology* 96(2): 329–357.

Mead, L.M. 1992. *The New Politics of Poverty: The Nonworking Poor in America*. New York: Basic Books.

———. 1986. *Beyond Entitlement: The Social Obligations of Citizenship*. New York: Free Press.

Meyer, D.R., and M. Cancian, 1988. "Economic Well-Being Following an Exit from AFDC." *Journal of Marriage and the Family* 60: 479–492.

Moffit, R. 1992. "Incentive Effects of the U.S. Welfare System: A Review." *Journal of Economic Literature* 30 (March): 1–61.

Mogull, R.G. 1991. "Annual Estimates of California's Poor: 1959 Through 1990." *American Journal of Economics and Sociology* 50(3): 299–312.

Monthly Vital Statistics Report. 1998. vol. 26, no. 1. Available at www.cdc.gov/nchswww/data/mv46 1s2.pdf.

Moynihan, D.P. 1992. "How the Great Society Destroyed the American Family." *Public Interest* 108 (Summer): 53–64.

———. 1970. *Maximum Feasible Misunderstanding: Community Action in the War on Poverty*. New York: Free Press.

Murphy, K.M., and Welch, A. 1993. "Industrial Change and the Rising Importance of Skill." In *Uneven Tides: Rising Inequality in America*, eds. S. Danziger and P. Gottschalk, 81–107. New York: Russell Sage Foundation.

Murray, C. 1984. *Losing Ground: American Social Policy 1950–1980*. New York: Basic Books.

Myers, T. 1999. "Child Support Enforcement: State Legislation in Response to the 1996 Federal Reform Act." Available at www.ncsl.org.

———. 1998. "States Get Creative with Child Support Enforcement." Available at www.ncsl.org.

Nathan, R.P. 1986. "The Underclass: Will It Always Be With Us?" Paper presented to a symposium at the New School for Social Research, New York, November.

National Governor's Association, National Council of State Legislatures, and American Public Welfare Association. 1998. "Tracking Recipients After They Leave Welfare." Available at http://www.nga.org/welfare.

OECD. 1976. *Public Expenditures on Income Maintenance Programmes.* Paris: OECD.

Office of Child Support Enforcement. 1998. *21st Annual Report to Congress.* Washington, DC: U.S. Department of Health and Human Services.

O'Hare, W.P., and Curry-White, B. 1992, January. "The Rural Underclass: Examination of Multiple-Problem Populations in Urban and Rural Settings." Mimeo. Washington, DC: Population Reference Bureau.

Olson, K., and Pavetti, L. 1996. "Personal and Family Challenges to the Successful Transition from Welfare to Work." Memo. Washington, DC: Urban Institute.

Orshansky, M. 1988. "Commentary: The Poverty Measure," *Social Security Bulletin* 51(10): 22.

———. 1965. "Counting the Poor: Another Look at the Poverty Profile." *Social Security Bulletin* 28(1): 3–29.

Pawasarat, J., and Quinn, L.M. 1993. Wisconsin Welfare Employment Experiments: An Evaluation of the WEJT and CWEP Programs. Milwaukee, WI: University of Wisconsin-Milwaukee Employment and Training Institute.

Patterson, J. 1986. *America's Struggle Against Poverty, 1900–1985.* Cambridge, MA: Harvard University Press. Revised Edition.

Pauly, E., and DiMeo, C. 1996. *Adult Education for People on AFDC: A Synthesis of Research.* Washington, DC: U.S. Department of Health and Human Services and U.S. Department of Education.

Pavetti, L. 1999, January. "State Use of Sanctions." Memo. Prepared for AEI/Brookings Seminar on Welfare Reform. Washington, DC: Mathematica Policy Research.

———. 1998. "What Will the States Do When Jobs Are Not Plentiful? Policy and Implementation Challenges." Mathematica Policy Research, Inc. Presented at the Welfare Reform and the Macro-Economy Conference, Washington, DC, November 19–20.

———. 1993. "The Dynamics of Welfare and Work: Exploring the Process by Which Women Work Their Way Off Welfare." Ph.D. dissertation, Harvard University.

Pavetti, L., and Acs, G. 1997. "Moving Up, Moving Out or Going Nowhere? A Study of the Employment Patterns of Young Women and the Implications for Welfare Mothers." Unpublished manuscript.

Pavetti, L., Kristen, O., Nightingale, D., Duke, A., and Isaacs, J. 1997. "Welfare to Work Options for Families Facing Personal and Family Challenges: Rationale and Program Strategies." Memo. Washington, DC: The Urban Institute.

Pavetti, L., et al. 1996, December. "Designing Welfare-to-Work Programs for Families Facing Personal or Family Challenges: Lessons from the Field." Memo. Washington, DC: The Urban Institute.

Payne, J.L. 1998. *Overcoming Welfare: Expecting More From the Poor and Ourselves.* New York: Basic Books.

Piven, F.F., and Cloward, R.A. 1971. *Regulating the Poor: The Functions of Public Welfare*. New York: Vintage Books.

Plotnick, R.D. 1989. "Welfare and Out-of-Wedlock Childbearing: Evidence from the 1980s." Discussion paper no. 876–89. Madison, WI: Institute for Research on Poverty.

Poglinco, J.B., Brash, J., and Granger, R. 1998. *An Early Look at Community Service Jobs in the New Hope Demonstration*. New York: Manpower Demonstration Research Corporation.

Rangarajan, A. 1998. "Keeping Welfare Recipients Employed: A Guide for States Designing Job Retention Services." Off Welfare and into Work: A Report Series of the Postemployment Services Demonstration. Memo. Washington, DC: Mathematica Policy Research, Inc.

Rangarajan, A., Schochet, P., and Chu, D. 1998. "Employment Experiences of Welfare Recipients Who Find Jobs: Is Targeting Possible?" Memo. Washington, DC: Mathematica Policy Research, Inc.

Ravitch, D. 1996. "Somebody's Children: Educational Opportunity for All American Children." In *Social Policies for Children*, eds. I. Garfinkel, J. Hochschild, and S. McLanahan, 83–112. Washington, DC: The Brookings Institution.

Rector, R. 1998. "The Myth of Widespread American Poverty." Heritage Foundation Backgrounder No. 1221. Washington, DC: Heritage Foundation.

Reischauer, R.D. 1989. "The Size and Characteristics of the Underclass." Paper presented at the Annual Meeting of the Association for Public Policy Analysis and Management, Bethesda, MD, October.

Ricketts, E.R., and Sawhill, I.V. 1988. "Defining and Measuring the Underclass." *Journal of Policy Analysis and Management* 7(2): 316–325.

Rodgers, H.R. 1996. *Poor Women, Poor Children: American Poverty in the 1990s*, 3rd edition. Armonk, NY: M.E. Sharpe, Inc.

———. 1979. *Poverty Amid Plenty: A Political and Economic Analysis*. Reading, MA: Addison-Wesley.

Roosevelt, Franklin D. 1938. "Annual Message to the Congress, January 4, 1935." *The Public Papers and Addresses of Franklin D. Roosevelt*, vol. 4 . New York: Random House.

Ruggles, P. 1990. *Drawing the Line: Alternative Poverty Measures and Their Implications for Public Policy*. Washington, DC: Urban Institute Press.

Rutgers University. 1999. "A Report on the Impact of New Jersey's Family Development Program: Results from a Pre-Post Analysis of AFDC Case Heads from 1990 to 1996." Available at www.Nowldef.org.

Sandefur, G., and Wells, T. 1997. Using Siblings to Investigate the Effects of Family Structure on Educational Attainment. Discussion paper no. 1144–97. Madison, WI: Institute for Research on Poverty.

Schneider, A., and Ingram, H. 1993. "Social Construction of Target Populations: Implications for Politics and Policy." *American Political Science Review* 87(2): 334–347.

Scrivener, S., Hamilton, G., Farrell, M., Freedman, S., Friedlander, D., Mitchell, M., Nudelman, J., and Schwartz, C. 1998. "National Evaluation of Welfare-to-Work Strategies: Implementation, Participation Patterns, Costs, and Two-Year Impacts of the Portland (Oregon) Welfare-to-Work Program." Executive Summary taken from http://aspe.os.dhhs.gov/hsp/isp/portland/xsportld.htm.

Sen, A. 1992. *Inequality Reexamined.* Cambridge: Harvard University Press.

Shapiro, R.Y, Patterson, K.D., Russell, J., and Young, J.T. 1987. "The Polls: Public Assistance." *Public Opinion Quarterly* 51 (Spring): 120–130.

Sherman, A. 1997. *Poverty Matters: The Cost of Child Poverty in America.* Washington, DC: Children's Defense Fund.

Sherman, A., et al. 1998. *Welfare to What: Early Findings on Family Hardship and Well-Being.* Washington, DC: Children's Defense Fund, National Coalition for the Homeless, www.childrensdefense.org/family.

Sherradan, M. 1991. *Assets and the Poor: A New American Welfare Policy.* Armonk, NY: M.E. Sharpe.

————. 1990. "Stakeholding: A New Direction in Social Policy." Available at http://www.dlcppi.org.

Shore, R. 1997. *Rethinking the Brain: New Insights into Early Development.* New York: Families and Work Institute.

Skoro, C.L., and Johnson, D.A. 1991. "Establishing an Updated Standard of Need for AFDC Recipients." *Social Work Research and Abstracts* 27(3): 22–27.

Smeeding, T. 1992a. "U.S. Poverty and Income Security in a Cross-National Perspective: The War on Poverty: What Worked?" *Challenge* 35 (January–February): 16–23.

————. 1992b. "Why the U.S. Antipoverty System Doesn't Work Very Well." *Challenge 35* (January–February): 30–35.

Smeeding, T., et al. 1993. "Noncash Income, Living Standards and Inequality: Evidence from the Luxembourg Income Study." *Review of Income and Wealth* September: 229–256.

Smeeding, T., Rainwater, L, and O'Higgins, M., eds. 1990. *Poverty, Inequality and Income Distribution in Comparative Perspective: The Luxembourg Income Study.* London: Harvester Wheatsheaf and Washington, DC: Urban Institute Press.

Strawn, J. 1999. "Welfare-to-Work Programs: The Critical Role of Skills." Center for Law and Social Policy. Available at www.clasp.org/pubs/jobseducation/skillspapere.htm.

Testa, M. 1991. "Male Joblessness, Nonmarital Parenthood, and Marriage." Paper presented at the Urban Poverty and Family Life Conference, University of Chicago, October 10–12.

Tin, J. 1996. "Who Gets Assistance?" *Current Population Reports* (Household Economic Studies, P70–58). U.S. Bureau of the Census.

Tobin, J. 1994. "Poverty in Relation to Macroeconomic Trends, Cycles, and Policies." In *Confronting Poverty: Prescriptions for Change*, eds. S.H. Danziger, G.D. Sandefur, and D.H. Weinberg, 147–167. Cambridge, MA: Harvard University Press.

Townsend, P. 1979. *Poverty in the United Kingdom.* Harmendsworth: Penguin Books.

U.S. Department of Agriculture. 1995, September. Household Food Security in the United States in 1995: Summary Report of the Food Security Measurement Project. Table 5–1. Washington, DC: Author.

U.S. Department of Health and Human Services. 1998, August. Temporary Assistance to Needy Families (TANF) Program, First Annual Report to Congress. Washington, DC: Author.

U.S. Department of Housing and Urban Development, American Housing Survey for the United States in 1995. Current Housing Reports No. H150/95RV. Tables 2.9 and 4.9. Washington, DC: Author.

Venti, S.F. 1984. "The Effects of Income Maintenance on Work, Schooling, and Nonmarket Activities of Youth." Table 1. *Review of Economics and Statistics* 66(1): 16–25.

West, C. 1993. *Race Matters*. Boston: Beacon Press.

Wilensky, H. 1975. *The Welfare State and Equality*. Berkeley: University of California Press.

Wilson, J.Q. 1973. *Political Organizations*. New York: Basic Book.

Wilson, W.J. 1980. *The Declining Significance of Race: Blacks and Changing American Institutions*, 2nd Edition. Chicago: The University of Chicago Press.

———. 1987. *The Truly Disadvantaged: The Inner City, the Underclass, and Public Policy*. Chicago: The University of Chicago Press.

Wilson, W.J., and Mead, L.M. 1987. "The Obligation to Work and the Availability of Jobs: A Dialogue Between L.M. Mead and W.J. Wilson." *Focus* 10(2): 11–19.

Wilson, W.J., and Neckerman, K.M. 1986. "Poverty and Family Structure: The Widening Gap Between Evidence and Public Policy Issues." In *Fighting Poverty: What Works and What Doesn't*, eds. S.H. Danziger and D.H. Weinberg, 232–283. Cambridge, MA: Harvard University Press.

Wiseman, M. 1996. "State Strategies for Welfare Reform: The Wisconsin Story." *Journal of Policy and Management* 15(4): 515–546. Available at www.whitehouse.gov/WH/Work/.

Wong, Y.I., Garfinkel, I., and McLanahan, S. 1993. "Understanding Cross-National Variation in Occupational Mobility." *American Sociological Review* 55(2): 560–573.

The World Bank. 1990. *World Development Report on Poverty*. New York: Oxford University Press.

Yates, J. 1998. "Delivering Human Services Through 'Co-Location' and 'One-Stop Shopping.'" Welfare Information Network. Available at www.welfareinfo.org.

Index

About the Author

Harrell R. Rodgers, Jr., is professor of political science at the University of Houston. He has published widely on poverty and social welfare programs in the United States, western Europe, and developing nations.